DELIBERATIVE DEMOCRACY

DELIBERATIVE DEMOCRACY

Understanding the Indian Experience

Edited by

TERESA JOSEPH
SIBY K. JOSEPH

MANOHAR
2018

First published 2018

ISBN 978-93-5098-183-2

Published by
Ajay Kumar Jain *for*
Manohar Publishers & Distributors
4753/23 Ansari Road, Daryaganj
New Delhi 110 002

Typeset by
Kohli Print
Delhi 110 051

Printed at
Shri Ganpati Enterprises
Delhi 110 052

Contents

Acknowledgements

We would like to thank all the authors who have contributed articles to this volume. We also wish to acknowledge the support and co-operation extended by the management and our colleagues at Alphonsa College, Pala, Kerala and the Institute of Gandhian Studies, Wardha, Maharashtra, to make this book a reality. We are particularly indebted to Dr. K.M. Seethi, Professor, School of International Relations and Politics, Mahatma Gandhi University, Kottayam; Dr. John S. Moolakkattu, Professor and Director, Department of International Relations, Central University of Kerala, Kasargod and Editor, *Gandhi Marg*, New Delhi; Ms. Rosmy Kattoor, Assistant Professor, Department of English, Alphonsa College; and Ms. Denimol Joseph, Project Fellow, Centre for Gandhian Studies, Alphonsa College. We also take this opportunity to thank our families and friends who have always been a source of inspiration and encouragement in all our endeavours.

TERESA JOSEPH AND SIBY K. JOSEPH

Introduction

TERESA JOSEPH AND SIBY K. JOSEPH

Political theorists have long contended that democracy should not be based merely on voting but also on informed public debate. However, it was only during the recent decades that initiatives aimed at realizing these theoretical discussions gained momentum. 'Deliberative democracy' considers the participation of citizens in deliberations and decision-making as the central element in democratic processes. In deliberative democracy the public deliberation of free and equal citizens forms the basis of legitimate decision-making. It can be seen as a part of the agenda of deepening democracy, the crux of the argument being that people should have a role and equal opportunities to participate directly in the deliberations or making of decisions that affect them.

Right from the local to the international level, various efforts are being taken to include the voice of the people in the decision-making process. This often entails the inclusion of alternative channels outside the conventional institutions of representative democracy. The recent resurgence in theorizations of deliberative democracy therefore tends to place particular emphasis on its feasibility. Deliberative democrats have begun to focus on non-state sites as fruitful locations for deliberation and the concept of public sphere has become central to models of deliberative democracy. The nature of deliberative democracy is to a large extent dependent on the nature of civil society as well as the public sphere.

Although there is some agreement on the general notion of deliberative democracy, there are diverse perspectives on it which call for different levels of democratic processes. While a number of scholars have contributed to the development of the concept, the ideas of Jürgen Habermas in particular, have contributed much to the increased focus on deliberative democracy and public sphere.

It was largely under his influence that the notion, that it is the transformation rather than merely the aggregation of preferences that is the essence of democracy, gained significance. Habermas puts forward a theory of deliberative democracy which is inclusive with political deliberation not being restricted to the political elite. On the contrary, both the public as well as private spheres participate in the political process through rational discussion. As such, democracy consists of both an informal track of public communication in civil society, and a formal track of deliberative decision-making by traditional political institutions. These institutions respond to the public discussions of the informal track. Informal communication in the public sphere helps to identify new problems and bring them to public attention, while also suggesting ways to address them. Through formal political processes and institutions, different proposals are deliberated, evaluated and authoritative decisions are taken after due consideration. Thus, the two track model helps to combine mass participation, with political decisions that are arrived at through formal deliberations.

The basic contention of deliberative democracy is that in order for political choice to be legitimate, it must be the result of deliberation among free, equal, and rational agents. However, there are several challenges to realizing this deliberative concept of democracy, including how to achieve the two basic norms of political equality and inclusion, particularly in societies with deep social cleavages, the control or even manipulation of public discussions by organized social and political power, and so on. The positions of governments often dominate public discourse and decision-making, and exclude alternative viewpoints. Similarly, the values and interests of particular social groups often play a disproportionate role in various parts of the deliberative system. Public spheres are often dominated by a particular perspective or ideology, sidelining alternate viewpoints. Ultimately the moot question remains as to whether deliberative democracy will be able to bring about actual transformation in society, where power, social divisions, and property relations continue to reign supreme. The actual extent of democracy in any society may depend on various such factors including the economic and social structure of society, the nature of the public sphere and civil society, the features of the political system, the extent of freedom of expression, etc. Nevertheless dialogue and deliberation have an indispensable role to play in any democratic system.

Attempts at deliberative democracy have varied across societies and there are numerous challenges to realizing this concept of democracy. The contemporary realities of Indian politics present a wide spectrum for analysing such issues. In terms of procedural democracy and the working of democratic institutions, India's record is considered to be noteworthy. However, questions relating to deliberative democracy have come to the fore, particularly in recent years, with questions of inclusion and equality posing major challenges. Social hierarchies of class, caste, gender, literacy, etc., pose challenges for both the process as well as the outcome of deliberations. While there is often a semblance of dialogue, the moot question is whether there is in fact actual deliberation taking place.

At certain structural levels initiatives have been taken to include the voice of the people in the decision-making process, particularly in the context of the move towards decentralized governance. Decentralization was expected to bring the process of decision-making closer to the people. Representative democracy moved towards a more participatory form of democracy with the 73rd and 74th Constitutional amendments, which created a people's assembly or Gram Sabha for deliberation by citizens. With the possibility of deliberation and people's participation in policy decision-making being much higher in local spaces, this initiative enhanced expectations of panchayats emerging as fruitful spaces of deliberative democracy. Yet, inequalities of power, *inter alia* tend to undermine the quality of deliberations as well as the outcome of decisions, with issues of presence rather than deliberation *per se* becoming major concerns.

Similarly, globalization, transformations in the field of communication and technology, particularly the mass media, and differences in material conditions, have all contributed to a changing public sphere, bringing into question the feasibility of critical debates in the public sphere, and raising questions about whether Indian democracy is indeed becoming less deliberative. However, new counter movements have emerged that aim at expanding political spaces and raising new discourses on democracy. The case of India reveals the challenges of deliberative democracy in divided, unequal societies, the need for a level playing field for effective deliberation and institutions to facilitate structured deliberation.

The present volume provides diverse perspectives on the concept of deliberative democracy, focusing on the case of India. The articles in the volume address various dimensions of the issue, ranging from a theoretical conceptualization of deliberative democracy to its role in constitution-making, Gandhian contributions to deliberative democracy, civil society interventions and the role of the media in deliberative processes in India, the participation of new social movements, Dalit and ecological movements, as well as the intricacies of deliberation and decentralization, and issues of development, marginalization and mobilization.

The introductory article to this volume, by John S. Moolakkattu examines the discourse on deliberative democracy and discusses the different approaches to the concept, raising a number of lingering questions that are relevant points of debate. In the context of Habermas' 'two track' model of deliberative democracy, Teresa Joseph and A.M. Thomas reflect on the question of deliberation in the process of constitution-making, focusing on the case of India and the United States, as well as providing an overview of the constitution-making/re-writing processes of the late twentieth and early twenty first centuries in various other countries.

Examining the engagements with deliberative democracy and alternative politics in India, Siby K. Joseph focuses on the Gandhian tradition. He discusses how *satyagraha* has provided adequate space for contestation as well as reconciliation, offering a conducive and creative forum for deliberation as well as action, besides opening new vistas for alternative politics, and examines the succeeding waves in the search for alternative politics and deliberative democracy in India. Addressing the phenomenon of civil society intervention in the Indian polity, K.M. Sajad Ibrahim reflects on the emergence of civil society organizations and the diverse factors that have contributed to making their presence felt in Indian democracy, drawing particular attention to questions of corruption, human rights violations, the crisis of credibility among political parties, globalization and the partial withdrawal of the state. M.V. Bijulal explores the deliberative process in the Aam Aadmi Party's (AAP) decision-making, particularly with regard to its slum rehabilitation policy, drawing attention to several governmental measures of the party, which evolved as the result of a dialogical process between communities of 'urban marginalities' and the political network of functionaries of the party at the lower level.

Decentralization and deliberative democracy forms the focus of two articles of this volume. Given the fact that decentralization was expected to bring the process of decision-making closer to the people, John S. Moolakkattu and Jos Chathukulam survey the various mainstream and Indian perspectives on decentralization, participation and democracy, exploring the question of reconciling the demands of deliberative democracy with participatory democracy. At the same time, Jeevan Kumar specifically attempts to locate the Gram Sabha as an institution of the Panchayat Raj system in India, in the discourse on deliberative democracy, capturing the essence of the normative expectations of deliberative democracy and the ground reality vis-à-vis Gram Sabhas in the country.

Sabu Thomas and J. Prabhash focus on Information and Communication Technology (ICT) and the role of mass media in deliberative democracy. Interrogating the impact of the digital age on democracy, Sabu Thomas examines how ICT interventions have made modern democracy more deliberative and have accommodated hitherto sidelined actors in the process, documenting the transition from a public sphere based on national institutions of territorially-bound societies to a public sphere centred on the media system including the Internet. J. Prabhash's discussion on the 'mediated' public sphere and deliberative democracy examines how globalization and revolutionary changes in the field of information and communication technology and the mass media have affected the nature of the public sphere and its consequences for deliberative democracy in India.

Reflecting from the margins, K.M. Sheeba, Elizabeth Abraham and George K. Alex address questions of development, Dalit counterpublics and ecological governance in the context of deliberative democracy. K.M. Sheeba's narrative on development, state and mobilization examines how with the Indian state linking itself to the hierarchies of global economic and political power, strong counter movements have emerged, raising a new discourse on democracy, inventing political practices and expanding the arena of politics much beyond representational institutions. Focusing on Dalit counterpublics, Elizabeth Abraham, documents the rise of Dalit human rights organizations, and reveals how these organizations have played an important role in setting a new discourse, influencing the secular democratic space of the Indian public sphere, enabling a wider discursive space, and facilitating the dissemination of the issue to a wider public, transgressing national boundaries. Exploring questions of neoliberal ecological governance in the context of people's struggle for nature in India, George K. Alex reflects on how movements for ecological justice and the debates on ecology provide new avenues of discourses to challenge and recreate deliberative spaces and democratic dialogues, generating notions of plurality, which is the space and subject matter of alternative politics and deliberative democracy.

In essence, this volume explores the dynamics of deliberative democracy, highlighting the Indian experience. It is hoped that the articles in this volume will enrich readers, providing new insights into the theoretical as well as practical concerns and complexities in the field of deliberative democracy, and contribute to the ongoing debates in this area of study. It will facilitate an understanding of the broad contours and evolving nature of democracy in India and how the Indian experience can inform larger debates on deliberative democracy.

CHAPTER 1

Deliberative Democracy: A Conceptual Overview

JOHN S. MOOLAKKATTU

Deliberative democracy has in recent times attracted much interest in the West and the idea is increasingly finding resonance in developing countries where the earlier focus was more on participatory forms of democracy. This chapter provides an overview of the discourse on deliberative democracy, which Gutmann and Thompson (2004) describe as a second order theory capable of sorting out conflicts among first order theories through a process of mutual elimination and outwitting. They feel that conflicts should be dealt with through justifiable processes rather than through bickering, and one such process is deliberation. Dryzek (2010) states that deliberative democracy originally began as a theory of democratic legitimacy. The distinction made between the Schumpeterian conception of democracy and participatory democracy also contributed to its early crystallization. The latter was counterpoised to the idea that 'democracy is just a system in which rulers are selected by competitive elections' (Przeworski 1999: 23). This model of aggregative democracy is also the main rival of deliberative democracy. In it, differences are to be resolved through practices like the majority vote in parliament. The deliberative idea has triumphed over participatory democracy in the West. Citizens are seen as willing to engage in 'communicatively rational' discourse, devoid of manipulation. Group deliberation is expected to overcome the problem of bounded rationality that ordinary citizens experience when they act as individuals and help reduce the cost of acquiring information through information pooling

(Niemeyer 2011). In a deliberative setting, participants should adhere to the most logical argument even if it is not their own and encourage others also to evolve a consensus around it.

What does deliberative democracy mean? Gutmann and Thompson (2004: 7) defined it as a 'form of government in which free and equal citizens (and their representatives), justify decisions in a process in which they give one another reasons that are mutually acceptable and generally accessible, with the aim of reaching conclusions that are binding in the present on all citizens but open to challenge in the future'. Deliberation is one way of resolving moral disagreement in public affairs in a legitimate manner. It also encourages civic mindedness in an era of individualized living. In addition, it serves as a means to correct mistakes committed or decisions that may have been taken based on misunderstanding or incomplete understanding.

Elite deliberation is clearly a theory that prizes deliberation by representatives of the people, not by the people themselves. If deliberation takes place in the parliament, it is a case of elite deliberation. Some make a distinction between micro and macro deliberation. 'While micro-understandings of deliberative democracy focus on deliberation in relatively small groups, macro-understandings draw our attention to the discursive aspects of democracy, the argumentation and contestation that takes place within the broader public sphere' (Ercan and Hendricks 2013: 424).

Deliberative democracy does not stop with aggregation of views, but seeks to achieve a change in such views as a result of free deliberation. In such cases, the very act of forming an opinion is also the result of listening to arguments and information provided by others (Habermas 1989). Agreement can be eventually reached based on this shared knowledge (Perczynski 2001). Deliberative democracy believes that legitimacy of decisions made is enhanced when they are based on the principle that those who are affected by public decisions should have not only enough space to influence them, but also enabling conditions and skills to discuss them before such decisions are actually taken (Cohen 1989). Depending on the depth of the process, deliberation involves the advancement of reasons for the position that one puts forward, paying keen attention to the opinions of others and allowing change in one's own preferences as a result of reasoned arguments and new information, setting aside in its wake, crass self-interest and embracing the common good. It sets a standard towards which democracies should aspire in order to deepen the process (Mansbridge et al. 2010). Further, 'the core intrinsic value of deliberative decision-making is that it expresses respect for citizens as persons capable of giving and responding appropriately to reasons' (RostbØll, 2009: 31).

Gutmann and Thompson (2004) point out that deliberative democracy is better than aggregative forms in managing disagreement even if no agreement is reached due to the superior quality of the process involved in it. According to them:

> In the face of disagreement, deliberative democracy tells citizens and their representatives to continue to reason together. If the disagreement is resolvable on reciprocal terms, deliberation is more likely than aggregation to produce agreement. If it is not so resolvable, deliberation is more likely than aggregation to produce justifiable agreement in the future, and to promote mutual respect when no agreement is possible. By engaging in deliberation, citizens acknowledge the possibility that they may change their preferences. The preferences that they assert now may not be the preferences they find they wish to express later. The very nature of the deliberative process of justification sends a signal that its participants are willing to enter into a dialogue in which the reasons given, and the reasons responded to, have the capacity to change minds. (Gutmann and Thompson 2004: 20)

To deliberate implies a number of related meanings such as to weigh, to ponder, to consider, and to reflect. The supporters of deliberative democracy believe that a more robust and active public engagement is indispensable to democracy and democratic deepening, and deliberation is one key means of addressing the current democratic deficit. They say that various forms such as mini-publics, citizens' juries, consensus conferences, planning cells, etc., can serve as useful deliberative sites. People's planning in Kerala was designated by some as a case of empowered deliberative democracy (e.g., Fung and Wright 2001). Deliberation should take place in public open spaces unlike Rousseuvian democracy where individuals reflect on what is right for society and come to vote. This is not to say that all deliberative democrats subscribe to this view. Scholars like Goodin

(2000) say that deliberation can take place in the form of internal reflection or individual deliberation which is useful before and after group deliberation. Historically, different sites have been identified as ideal deliberative forums such as citizen deliberation (Aristotle and Pericles), parliament (Burke) and institutions (*Federalist Papers*).

PARTICIPATORY AND DELIBERATIVE DEMOCRACY

Participatory and deliberative democracy have different origins. The first has a predominantly Third World orientation and is often, though not exclusively linked with development studies. The latter is a contribution from the developed world, particularly North America and Western Europe. Participatory democracy favours citizen participation and its increase while deliberative democracy emphasized the quality of politics and the public sphere. Participatory democracy is centred around the direct action of citizens while deliberative democracy is based on argumentative exchanges and public debates which precede decisions. Participation is sometimes associated with the property of quantity while deliberation is intimately linked with quality. This suggests some incompatibility between the two with an enhancement in quantity leading to a decline in quality and vice versa. It is therefore a challenge to have both deliberation and participation. Deliberation presumes a rational and well informed set of actors while participation is based on the capability of ordinary citizens whose knowledge and logical abilities may not be so developed. More balanced accounts of fusing the two see deliberation as representing a more qualitative form of participation which cruder forms should aspire to achieve. While the original deliberators had focussed on rationality and a strand of elitism not favouring inclusion, newer variants of deliberative democracy embrace social inclusion, plurality and activism along with deliberation. More people are now inclined to see participation and deliberation as complementary normative principles rather than incompatible. In this view 'deliberation is a kind of participation' (Hauptmann 2001: 408) or an extension of 'participation in politics'

(Gutmann and Thompson 1996: 13) or a higher or fuller form of participatory democracy. One could call it fuller because participatory democracy seeks to work in tandem with aggregative democracy and it is by bringing in reasoned arguments and 'preference transformation' that it can become deeper.

Commentators have highlighted a few problematic areas in the equation between participatory democracy and deliberative democracy. For example, attempts to improve the quality of deliberation may take place only at the cost of public participation given the tendency to make the exercise confined to the more informed and intelligent rather than the wider public. Conversely, more of participation in the form of more people either attending a meeting or participating in a referendum need not improve the quality of deliberation in the form of reasoned discussion, although other goals such as influencing the legislative decisions may be achieved. In a complex modern society with a large population, achieving both deliberation and participation may not be easy as people without adequate information and interest in public affairs are unlikely to be involved in the deliberative forums. Hence, as the scope of participation increases, the space for enhancing the quality of deliberation declines (Cohen and Fung 2004).

THREE GENERATIONS

The first-generation deliberative democrats like Jürgen Habermas (1984, 1989, 1992, 1996) and John Rawls (1993) laid a normative framework for deliberative democracy and the role of reason in enabling communication, leading to preference change and consensus formation. According to Habermas (1984: 24), 'the unforced force of the better argument' shall prevail. There will be no limitation of space or time as far as deliberation is concerned. Same is the case with the topics over which deliberation takes place, as well as the reasons and information advanced. There will be equal opportunity for participation, which will not be constrained by power differentials of the participants. Coercion of all kinds would have no place in such processes (Habermas 1996: 228, 230). He also talked about an 'ideal speech situation' where the force of the better argument alone would prevail. But these thinkers seemed to have operated at the ideal realm and the model that they presented was seemingly oblivious of the complexities of contemporary societies.

The second-generation deliberative democrats, particularly James Bohman (1996) and Gutmann and Thompson (1996), in considering the institutionalization of deliberative democracy, took complexity seriously, and reformed the theory of deliberative democracy in the process. They have fused the first-generation deliberative democracy of Habermas and Rawls with practical requirements. For the second-generation deliberative democrats, the predominant view is that preferences will adapt to public reason and new information, but not in a uniform manner. Consequently, consensus will not be reached and forms of communication other than the exchange of reason can, will and should be included. This is a response by deliberative democrats to the criticisms by Iris Marion Young (2000) and Lynn Sanders (1997) that relying solely on public reason as the only form of communication for deliberation can actually exclude subordinate and minority groups whose faculty of public reasoning may not be so developed or may use alternative means of communication in its place. It is such considerations that lead Young (1996) to advocate 'communicative democracy', which she considers different from deliberative democracy by favouring greeting, rhetoric and storytelling over rational argument, rendering communication more compatible with a diverse range of social groups. Second-generation deliberative democracy, with its attempt to accommodate pluralism, has therefore room for these other forms of communication (Gutmann and Thompson 1996: 132-7). However, they still offered little substantive detail in terms of the types of institutions required to ensure that deliberative democracy could be actualized in complex societies. This has paved the way for a third generation.

In the 'second-generation' deliberative democracy theory, consensus is not considered realistic. Following Gutmann and Thompson (1996, 2004), the goal is a deliberative agreement in mutual justification, which may also be an 'agreement to disagree'. The 'third generation' of deliberative democracy theory has taken a step further along this path: deliberation in this context is considered successful (i.e. legitimate) even when the parties advocate only their own interests, and public reasoning takes the form of intense negotiation (Baber and Bartlett 2005; Elstub 2013; Mansbridge et al. 2010). The third generation promotes an institutional design of deliberative democracy that accepts the plural nature of public reason. This has led to concerns with self-interest and the need to have a broader understanding of communication beyond just reasonable exchange. In some ways this break up of deliberative democracy, its diversity, has made it a more universal theory. Deliberative democracy is now a less specific, distinct model of democracy. It has much more in common now than it did before (in its first generation, for example) with other models such as liberal democracy (Elstub 2015).

In contrast to 'aggregative' models, deliberation promotes the legitimacy of collective decisions, encourages public-spirited perspectives on public issues, promotes mutually-respectful processes of decision-making, and exposes all decisions to critical scrutiny. There are a number of big questions in deliberative democracy such as whether deliberation should be seen instrumentally or in expressive terms, whether the focus should be on the procedure of deliberative democracy or on its substance, whether consensus should be a goal or more pluralist/agonist forms are desirable particularly in heterogeneous societies, the question between representation and participation, whether the target of democratization should be the government or civil society and whether deliberation should be confined to the domestic realm or go beyond the level of the state (Gutmann and Thompson 2004).

Democratic deliberation could be studied and justified following three approaches. The first is the Preference-Based Model grounded in economics and social choice theory according to which deliberation corrects information problems that prevent transformation and stabilization of individual preferences, and aggregation of individual into collective preference and transformation from 'self-regarding' to 'other-regarding', individual self-interest to the common good. The second is the Rational Proceduralist Model which is grounded in normative political theory (arguments around justice (e.g. Rawls) and legitimacy (Habermas) by which moral claims are to be couched in rationalist debate, language and reasons knowable to all (the 'reason-giving requirement') enabling the better argument to win, leading to assent and legitimacy of collective decisions. Finally, we have the Integrative Model that seeks to integrate heterogeneous views and publics; deliberation integrates a public as public, producing a public where none existed (McAfe 2004).

SOME LINGERING QUESTIONS

A number of questions remain. Can we scale up deliberative democracy to a macro level say on key national level public policies? Can there be real deliberation in the midst of socio-economic inequalities? Is there not a bias in favour of the well-educated and articulate middle class and discrimination against the poor, ethnic minorities and women in deliberative democracy? Some (e.g. Gutmann and Thompson) say deliberative democracy has the potential 'to expose inequalities to public criticism and create less unjust conditions in the future'. But 'oppressions are systematically reproduced in major economic, political and cultural institutions' and cannot be overcome through deliberative democracy. Is a deliberative system more conducive to the inclusion of self-interest? What does this mean for the role of interest groups in a deliberative system? To what extent is the idea of a deliberative system rendered unachievable if citizens do not have the necessary psychological attributes for effective deliberation? When power interferes with reason, Estlund (2002) argues, it is legitimate for the less powerful to use power of their own to create a power balance. Does the unwillingness of people to deliberate in public settings make a deliberative system impossible and is deliberation among the public compatible with political representation? Are people really willing to deliberate, criticize others or prefer a quiet life? These lingering questions are points of serious debate in deliberative democracy.

There are elitist criticisms like that of Richard Posner who argues that there is no use consulting the public about substantive policy. Deliberative democracy also tends to neglect the fact that many actors in political life are motivated more by passions and interests than reasons (Przeworski 1998; Sanyal 2015). Partisanship is also a factor in places like Kerala if we look at the way deliberation in village assemblies (Gram Sabhas) is structured. The focus is too heavily on micro-deliberative forums at the expense of considering some of the broader challenges facing mass democracies (Dryzek 2010). Most often people lack the skills and knowledge—impracticality of large-scale deliberation. Critics of deliberation say that the reason-giving clause actually works to the advantage of the more privileged sections (Sanders 1997), a viewpoint that is contested by deliberative enthusiasts who say that argument is a weapon that both the poor and the weak can effectively employ (Gutmann and Thompson 1996). Deliberative democracy did not ostensibly recognize the centrality of conflict to politics by arguing that, with the right mechanisms, people can reach agreement, or even consensus. People have different views about how society should be organized and it is wrong to suggest that people can put aside these major differences and reach agreement. As it has been developed in political theory, agonistic pluralism is a critical reaction to the dominant liberal orientation towards consensus, neutrality and rational argumentation by stressing the need to acknowledge the inevitable partiality, conflict and passionate nature of politics and the public sphere. The task of politics is to transform the existing antagonisms, or 'the political', into a situation of agonism, in which the 'other' is no longer an enemy (to be destroyed) but a legitimate adversary, a political opponent to be engaged with. Politics can only arrive at a 'conflictual consensus' at best (Mouffe 1999: 103).

Deliberative processes aim to reach consensus, which once established, some argue, will stand in the way of further rational public discourse, leading to the very undermining of deliberative democracy itself, due to the tendency of participants to conform to the consensus rather than subject it to further rational scrutiny (Friberg-Fernros and Schaffer 2014). Agonist and difference democrats have argued that consensus as an ideal of democratic interchange is both impossible and dangerous (Markell 1997). Consensus is unattainable or unlikely due to the facts of value pluralism in modern societies and the incommensurability of normative and epistemic frameworks (Valadez 2001). Moreover, consensus is politically perilous, because it violates this plurality and might serve to oppress or exclude certain interests, ideas and identities (Young 2001). For instance, Chantal Mouffe (1995) warns that seeking to eradicate all political antagonism while aiming for a universal rational consensus is 'the real threat to democracy'. Taking on this challenge, theorists have sought to make the ideal of democratic deliberation more feasible under real circumstances, in societies characterized by social inequality and cultural diversity (Elstub 2010). Consequently, deliberative theory 'has moved away from a consensus-centred teleology' (Chambers 2003: 321) to develop alternative notions of legitimate outcomes of deliberation. Even Habermas (1996) concedes that reaching a rational consensus is not possible in all social contexts.

Jane Mansbridge et al. (2010) suggest four forms of legitimate communicative agreement short of strong consensus. The deliberative goal of enhanced epistemic and ethical reasoning runs counter to the limits of citizen learning. Second, opportunity costs are involved in deliberation. Rational argument leaves little space for storytelling. Third,

> the activist is suspicious of exhortations to deliberate because he believes that in the real world of politics, where structural inequalities influence both procedures and out-comes, democratic processes that appear to conform to norms of deliberation are usually biased toward more powerful agents. The activist thus recommends that those who care about promoting greater justice should engage primarily in critical oppositional activity, rather than attempt to come to agreement with those who support or benefit from existing power structures. (Young 2001: 671)

Fourth, critics contend that 'the demands for reason, consensus, and the common good may marginalize or exclude members of disadvantaged groups' (Mansbridge et al. 2006: 5).

Can the Gram Sabha be considered a deliberative forum? Some recent accounts tend to suggest so, although what takes place in such forums is not deliberation based on reasoned argument. Those who see it as a site for development-related deliberation, however, seem to acknowledge its limitations as a deliberative forum by suggesting that more than reason, it is passion or emotion that rules the roost in the Sabha given the power differentials within which the Sabha is held. Emotions fulfil a role in generating power for the subaltern public in deliberative settings (Sanyal 2015). Its positive functions enforce accountability and justice and also engage in naming, shaming and challenging officials, both elected and appointed on some occasions. The author tends to look at such emotions as not structural. In fact, they are the result of the type of relations the post-colonial state created with the citizenry which made them look upon themselves as mere beneficiaries rather than full citizens with entitlements. Again, it is often seen that most people who come to the Sabha seldom speak. Mahatma Gandhi, often seen as the foremost champion of local democracy, was unconvinced about the power of the citizens to deliberate although their power to remove an under-performing government through a process of recall was never contested. He thought that the Gram Panchayat of five persons was good enough a body to engage in deliberation dispassionately keeping the common good in view (John 2009).

CONCLUSION

The foregoing discussion suggests that a one size fits all approach to deliberative democracy is not desirable. It is perhaps not realistic enough to believe that rational argument will always prevail. For some people, to be defeated by rational argument would bring in a sort of cognitive dissonance, and they would rather stick to their position to achieve congruence. On highly contentious issues, deliberative processes may not always be the best way forward. Deliberative sites should focus less on consensus formation and more on dialogues centred on articulation of different voices. They could serve as sites for Freirean model conscientization (Moolakkattu 2006). It is better to talk about multiple sites of deliberation (churches, universities, trade unions, etc.) leading to the idea of a deliberative system rather than focus only on specific sites. Existing institutions of democracy in India need more deliberation, and inputs from different sites could inform them.

Some argue that deliberative theorists have yet to respond to the challenge that divided societies pose to their theories. There is another potential side to it in the sense that endemic political conflict can spur the movement for deliberative democracy. All treat divided societies as the current test-case for projects of deliberative democracy, acknowledging that clashing cultural or ethnic or religious identities are hard-fought political contests with limited evidence of inter-group listening or learning (O'Flynn 2006). Dryzek (2010) is most ambitious in searching for 'transnational discursive democracy' that can move beyond the global regulatory apparatus sponsored by neoliberal international cooperation. For Dryzek the deliberative project has to keep moving the frontiers of feasible democracy beyond the regulatory reach of the formal institutions of the state and even transnational governance.

Recently, there has been discussion about the cultural embeddedness of public deliberation enabling even the West to learn from endogenous democratic practices of non-Western societies (Sass and Dryzek 2014). For example, in some societies of East Asia influenced by Confucian values, characterized by a high degree of social hierarchy and social harmony, people are reluctant to publicly display disagreement. In such societies, actual processes of deliberation may look different from what Western deliberation theorists have envisaged (Min 2009). Also, in many Muslim countries men and women are required to deliberate separately, and this would create different deliberation dynamics. Finally, deliberation also requires a certain degree of toleration of opposing views. In many Gram Sabhas in the northern parts of Kerala, political competition is so stiff that reasoning in a bounded manner alone is allowed. Such an encumbered form of public engagement is unlikely to open the space for deliberation. Finally, deliberation should contribute to the development of a critical faculty among the participants to prevent a synchronization of the force of better argument and the force of the more powerful in such forums.

REFERENCES

Baber, Walter F. and Robert V. Bartlett (2005): *Deliberative Environmental Politics: Democracy and Ecological Rationality*, Cambridge, MA: The MIT Press.

Chambers, Simone (2003): 'Deliberative Democratic Theory', *Annual Review of Political Science*, 6: 307-26.

Cohen, Joshua (1989): 'Deliberation and Democratic Legitimacy', in Alan Hamlin and Philip Pettit (eds.), *The Good Polity*, Oxford: Basil Blackwell.

Cohen, Joshua and Archon Fung (2004): 'Radical Democracy', *Swiss Journal of Political Science*, 10(4): 23-34.

Dryzek, John S. (2009): 'Democratisation as Deliberative Capacity Building', *Comparative Political Studies*, 42(11), November: 1379-1402.

Dryzek, John S. with Simon Niemeyer (2010): *Foundations and Frontiers of Deliberative Democracy*, Oxford: Oxford University Press.

Elstub, Stephen (2010): 'The Third Generation of Deliberative Democracy', *Political Studies Review*, 8(3): 291-307.

—— (2015): 'A Genealogy of Deliberative Democracy', *Democratic Theory*, 2(1): 100-17.

Ercan, Selen A. and Carolyn M. Hendriks (2013): 'The Democratic Challenges and Potential of Localism: Insights from Deliberative Democracy', *Policy Studies*, 34(4): 422-40.

Estlund, David (2002): *Democracy*, London: Wiley.

Friberg-Fernros, Henrik and Johan Karlsson Schaffer (2014): 'The Consensus Paradox: Does Deliberative Agreement Impede Rational Discourse?' *Political Studies*, 62(S1): 99-116.

Fung, Archon and Erik Olin Wright (2001): 'Deepening Democracy: Innovations in Empowered Participatory Governance', *Politics and Society*, 29(1): 5-41.

Goodin, Robert E. (2000): 'Democratic Deliberation Within', *Philosophy and Public Affairs*, 29(1): 81-109.

Gutmann, Amy and Dennis Thompson (1996): *Democracy and Disagreement*, Cambridge, MA: Belknap Press.

—— (2004): *Why Deliberative Democracy?*, Princeton: Princeton University Press.

Habermas, Jürgen (1984): *The Theory of Communicative Action*, vol. I, Boston: Beacon Press.

—— (1989): *The Theory of Communicative Action*, vol. II, Boston: Beacon Press.

—— (1992): 'Further Reflections on the Public Sphere', in Craig J. Calhoun (ed.), *Habermas and the Public Sphere,* Cambridge, MA: The MIT Press.

—— (1996): 'Three Normative Models of Democracy', in Seyla Benhabib (ed.), *Democracy and Difference: Contesting the Boundaries of the Political,* Princeton: Princeton University Press.

Hauptmann, Emily (2001): 'Can Less Be More?: Leftist Deliberative Democrats' Critique of Participatory Democracy', *Polity,* 33(3): 397-421.

John, M.S. (2007): 'Gandhi and the Contemporary Discourse on Decentralisation', in T.M. Joseph (ed.), *Local Governance in India: Ideas, Challenges and Strategies,* New Delhi: Concept: 20-31.

Mansbridge, Jane, Janette Hartz-Karp, Matthew Amengual, and John Gastil (2006): 'Norms of Deliberation: An Inductive Study', *Journal of Public Deliberation* 2(1), www.services.bepress.com.

Mansbridge, Jane, James Bohman, Simone Chambers, David Estlund, Andreas Føllesdal, Archon Fung, Cristina Lafont, Bernard Manin and José Luis Martí (2010): 'The Place of Self-Interest and the Role of Power in Deliberative Democracy', *Journal of Political Philosophy,* 18(1): 64-100.

Markell, Patchen (1997): 'Contesting Consensus: Rereading Habermas on the Public Sphere', *Constellations,* 3(3): 377-400.

McAfe, Noëlle (2004): 'Three Models of Democratic Deliberation', *The Journal of Speculative Philosophy,* 18(1): 44-59.

Min, Seong-Jae (2009): 'Deliberation, East Meets West: Exploring the Cultural Dimension of Citizen Deliberation', *Acta Politica,* 44(4): 439-58.

—— (2014): 'On the Westernness of Deliberation Research', *Journal of Public Deliberation,* 10(2), available at: http://www.publicdeliberation.net

Moolakkattu, John Stephen (2006): 'Deliberative Democracy and the Gram Sabha', *Gandhi Marg,* 27 (3 & 4): 349-64.

Mouffe, Chantal (1995): 'Politics, Democratic Action and Solidarity', *Inquiry* 38 (1&2): 99-108.

—— (1999): 'Deliberative Democracy or Agonistic Pluralism?', *Social Research,* 66(3): 745-58.

Niemeyer, Simon (2011): 'The Emancipatory Effect of Deliberation: Empirical Lessons from Mini-Publics', *Politics and Society* 39(1): 103-40.

O'Flynn, Ian (2006): *Deliberative Democracy and Divided Societies,* Edinburgh: Edinburgh University Press.

Parkinson, John (2006): *Deliberating in the Real World: Problems of Legitimacy in Deliberative Democracy,* Oxford: Oxford University Press.

Perczynski, Piotr (2001): 'Associo-deliberative Democracy and Qualitative Participation', *Critical Review of International Social and Political Philosophy,* 4(1): 71-84.

Przeworski, Adam (1999): 'Minimalist Conception of Democracy: A Defence', in Ian Shapiro and Casiano Hacker-Cordon (eds.), *Democracy's Value,* Cambridge: Cambridge University Press: 23-55.

Rawls, John (1993): *Political Liberalism,* New York: Columbia University Press.

RostbØll, Christian F. (2009): 'Dissent, Criticism, and Transformative Political Action in Deliberative Democracy', *Critical Review of International Social and Political Philosophy,* 12(1): 19-36.

Sanders, Lynn (1997): 'Against Deliberation', *Political Theory,* 25 (3): 347-76.

Sass Jensen and John S. Dryzek (2014): 'Deliberative Cultures', *Political Theory,* 42(1): 3-25.

Valadez, Jorge (2001): *Deliberative Democracy, Political Legitimacy, and Self Determination in Multicultural Societies,* Boulder: Westview.

Young, Iris Marion (1996): 'Communication and the Other: Beyond Deliberative Democracy', in Seyla Benhabib (ed.), *Democracy and Difference: Contesting the Boundaries of the Political,* Princeton: Princeton University Press: 120-35.

—— (1999): 'Justice, Inclusion and Deliberative Democracy', in Stephen Macedo (ed.), *Deliberative Politics: Essays on Democracy and Disagreement,* Oxford: Oxford University Press.

—— (2000): *Inclusion and Democracy,* Oxford: Oxford University Press.

—— (2001): 'Activist Challenges to Deliberative Democracy', *Political Theory,* 29(5): 670-90.

CHAPTER 2

Deliberative Democracy and Constitution-making

TERESA JOSEPH AND A.M. THOMAS

Discourses on deliberative democracy have over recent decades seen an increasing shift from its justification to an emphasis on questions of institutional design. Similarly, various initiatives are being taken from the local to the global level to realize the theoretical position that democracy should be based not merely on voting but more importantly on the incorporation of public debate. There has been an increasing realization that the success of deliberative democracy particularly in fractured societies can be ensured only if its institutional designs including the constitution, are created with utmost caution.. The importance of deliberative democracy in constitution-making and vice versa is clearly of significance. The focus of this paper is on the question of deliberation in the constitution-making processes, emphasizing questions of inclusion, political equality and the deliberative setting, which are the basic norms of deliberative democracy, rather than on normative issues surrounding the concept, which are addressed elsewhere in this volume. The paper explores the levels of deliberation in the constitution-making processes of the world's largest democracies, India and the United States, as well as the constitution-making/re-writing processes of the late twentieth and early twenty-first centuries in several other countries, so as to place the issue in perspective, drawing lessons for deliberative democracy and constitution-making.

The writings of Jürgen Habermas have contributed significantly to the development and focus on deliberative democracy. He addresses the problem of how discursive formation of opinion can be institutionalized, contending that political choice, to be legitimate, must be the outcome of deliberation among free, equal, and rational agents. He speaks of a model of deliberative democracy in which citizens rule themselves through participation in legally institutionalized decision-making processes, and where only outcomes which are approved by everyone in an open debate are considered legitimate (Eriksen and Weigard 2003: 113). In Habermas' inclusive theory, political deliberation is not restricted to political elites. Deliberative democracy as envisaged by him is set within a constitutional order that protects personal and political liberties, and brings together two 'tracks' in the process of collective decision-making. There is an informal track of free public communication and a formal track of decision-making through deliberation by conventional political institutions. The formal track responds to the informal discussions of the first track. Yet, these two tracks of deliberative politics play distinct roles. Informal communication in the public sphere provides an unregulated space for identifying problems, communicating them to the public, and suggesting ways to address them. In this process, the communicative structures of the public sphere constitute a wide network of sensors that react to the pressure of social problems and stimulate influential opinions. Formal political processes and institutions provide institutionally regulated ways to assess ideas and deliberate proposals, evaluate alternative solutions, and make authoritative decisions. Thus in the second institutional track authoritative decisions are taken by translating the opinions formed in the informal sphere into legal regulations. This two-track model suggests a way to combine mass participation with deliberation in formal politics. While discourse in the public sphere is open-ended, decision-making procedures are subject to various conditions of deliberative-democratic legitimacy (Habermas 1996: 300-6).

INCLUSION, POLITICAL EQUALITY AND THE DELIBERATIVE SETTING

Two of the basic norms of deliberative democracy are inclusion and equality. A wide range of interests, opinions, and perspectives need to be included if the 'best arguments' are to be discussed. Deliberative theorists are in agreement that ordinary citizens should have the opportunity to take part in political deliberation, but they disagree over how many citizens should actually do so. On the one hand, there is the normative position that ideally all citizens should be involved in the deliberation. Opinion-formation at the grassroots level would take place in a reflective way. These reflected opinions are then communicated to political leaders through a variety of channels like personal encounters, public meetings, the media, and the internet. As Habermas (1996: 299) argues, all those affected by a political decision should be included in the deliberation. In this way, citizens should be a strong countervailing force against the two traditional influences in politics: money and administrative power. On the other hand, some theorists such as Fishkin (2009) consider it unrealistic that virtually all citizens participate in political deliberation. They argue that one has to think of a more realistic way to involve the grassroots level in deliberation of political issues. They advocate the so-called mini-publics, or groups of randomly selected citizens (Steiner 2012: 32-3). But the question of who deliberates is also an important issue. Bias and distortion can arise in the selection of representatives. The goals of optimizing representation and optimizing deliberation may not always work *in tandem*. Some would point to an ambiguity in the idea of a democracy that is supposed to be both representative and deliberative. However, as Elster (1998a: 13) argues, if deliberation is the key to political decision-making, what matters is the full representation of diverse views rather than of individuals.

The norm of political equality ensures that all participants are not only free to speak but also have the same opportunity to do so and that all affected individuals are included on equal terms in the decision-making process. This also means that they have equal opportunities to express their interests and concerns, question each other, respond to criticisms raised, and critique the arguments and proposals of others. This necessitates that the participants have equal respect for each other. Participants must be equal in the sense that none of them should be in a position to coerce others into accepting specific proposals or outcomes (Banks 2008: 1049).

Combining political equality with deliberation therefore requires that the deliberation takes place on a face-to-face basis.

In other words, as Addis (2009: 71) contends, certain conditions exist for a well-functioning deliberative system. All those who are expected to obey the laws and institutions of society have the right to participate fully and equally in the development of those institutions and laws. They are to deliberate by advancing and defending propositions with reasons that are accessible to others, who are also free and equal participants. Decisions are not simply based on the counting of votes but also on the sharing of views. Moreover, deliberative democracy assumes that each party comes to the dialogue with the intention of reaching consensus or fair terms of cooperation. In the deliberative process decisions will lead to further dialogue and revision, as participants consider the preferences and perspectives of others and in the process transform their own positions and preferences. Furthermore, as Banks (2008: 1049) points out, since decisions are made based on reason and dialogic examination, those who participate are more likely to transform their views than those who do not participate. Inclusion and equality facilitate interest transformation taking place on a much larger scale.

Today, theories of deliberative democracy have increasingly moved beyond questions of justification towards problems of institutional design. The deliberative setting can be seen as a set of institutional conditions that promote deliberation. The ideal deliberative setting according to Cohen (1999: 398) can be specified as one in which people are free, equal, and politically reasonable, and have conflicting, reasonable philosophies of life. Under these conditions, considerations that one takes to be true or compelling cannot be simply put forth, as such considerations may be rejected by others who are also reasonable and hold conflicting views. On the other hand, reasons that are compelling to others who are regarded as equals with conflicting reasonable commitments need to be found. Considerations that do not meet these tests will be rejected in the ideal deliberative setting. With regard to institutional design, Bohman (1998: 415) points out that many of the features of democracy have been reinterpreted so as to promote the deliberative ideal.

Deliberation clearly has some of the good effects that theorists attribute to it: instilling community-mindedness, drawing citizens out of their parochial interests, and increasing the quantity and variety of data that form the basis of collective decisions (Stokes 1998: 136). Deliberation is sometimes advocated on the grounds that it allows a person or a group to present before others 'how things look' from perspectives, situations, and vantage points that the others may have never considered. Deliberation can facilitate compromise, improve consensus, and disseminate principles in public life. As long as the participants are, or can be motivated not to appear selfish or self-interested, then public discussions rather than mechanical voting procedures would encourage public-spirited justifications and proposals, which could work to the benefit of all (Fearson 1998: 52-5). Deliberative decision-making encourages decision-makers to interact with others by cooperating with them and together building on ideas. As such, participants should continue to be open to each other's influence right up to the point of final decision-making (Levy 2010: 815). The attraction of deliberative democracy in general is also its potential to reclaim the democratic ideal that the government should reflect the 'will of the people' formed through public reasoning of citizens. However, good deliberation in all kinds of forums and networks is not sufficient for deliberative democracy, which must be strongly supplemented with corresponding representative institutions. Hence, deliberative democracy has to be instituted by a constitution of some sort which itself needs to be framed through a deliberative process ensuring inclusion and equality.

DELIBERATIVE DEMOCRACY AND CONSTITUTION-MAKING

The constitution, being the ultimate law of a nation and the foundation of public life, necessitates the participation of civil society in the process of its making. But, in the context of deliberative democracy, it is not only the question of 'how' a constitution is made, but also 'what it says' that is of importance. Constituent assemblies may involve deliberative democracy in two ways. While deliberation among citizens or democratically elected representatives may be part of the process of adopting the constitution, promoting deliberative democracy may also be one of the goals of the framers (Elster 1998b: 97). With regard to the 'how' part, the constitution-making procedure must be fair for the outcome to be fair and useful for future generations. When differences are resolved, constitution making becomes part of peace-making especially in divided societies. It becomes a forum for reconciling party-based divisions, negotiating conflict and redressing grievances (Hart 2003).

According to Habermas (2001: 774), 'a constitution that is democratic—not just in its content but also according to its source of legitimation—is a tradition-building project with a clearly marked beginning in time'. Deliberative democracy, as put forth by Habermas, can be deemed useful in the constitution-making process because it guarantees participation by both decision-makers and members of the public without decision makers necessarily dominating the process. If participation is fair, then the outcome of the constitution is also seen to be fair. Genuine public participation necessitates social inclusion, equality, personal security, and freedom of speech and assembly. A vibrant civil society, civic education, and smooth channels of communication between all levels of society promote this process. But only a considerable commitment of time and resources will make genuine public participation possible. The significance of Habermas' theory of deliberative democracy is that it provides principles that may be useful for the procedure of constitution-making (Hart 2003).

The application of Habermas' deliberative democracy would mean that political parties would allow people to speak out what they think and this may not necessarily be what the dominant parties hold. To a significant extent this would help to achieve transparency. It would ensure that there are no hidden motives in the process of constitution-making and that political parties shun self-interest and allow public debate to take place. As Hart (2003: 5) contends, participatory constitution-making has become one of the criteria of a legitimate process. However, the participation should not involve indoctrination and propaganda to influence public debate, but the public should be given constitutional education that is largely free from bias. This implies no individual or group of individuals will take unfair advantage of the process for selfish benefits (Gwaravanda 2012: 127-9). Habermas (2001: 771-5) suggests that the normative bases of constitutional democracy should be seen as the result of a deliberative decision-making process that the founders undertook to create a voluntary, self-determining association of free and equal citizens. Thus the founding constitutional act can be seen as a decisive point in a nation's history, because with this act the ground for a new kind of practice is established.

The actual processes by which constitutions all over the world have been adopted vary widely. Not all involved deliberation, nor were all adopted by democratic procedures. Throughout history, cases of constitutions imposed from above, as well as those which came into existence as a result of deliberation and democratic participation can be seen. A look at the history of constitution-making reveals that the processes involved may have been undemocratic and non-deliberative, undemocratic but deliberative, democratic and non-deliberative, or democratic and deliberative.

A constitution may be imposed from above or from outside without any element of deliberation or democratic participation. The Prussian Constitution that was adopted in 1850 was not a creation of the revolutionary forces involved in the events of the day but that of a king who made one to suit his purposes by the systematic exclusion of democratic influence. However, by creating one, Prussia became a constitutional state if not a democratic one (Weichlein 2011: 284). Again, the Japanese Constitution of 1947, which replaced the Meiji Constitution of 1889, was one imposed by the United States occupation administration. By all accounts it was democratic, but created for the 'democracy deficient' Japanese by a group of individuals led by General Douglas MacArthur. The Japanese people had no role in its creation, but it endures to this day because of its democratic nature.

Documents adopted by democratic and non-deliberative processes include the French Constitution of 1799 which was based almost entirely on the old system of government of the Roman Republic; the Constitution of 1802 that made Napoleon Bonaparte

First Consul for life; and the Constitution of 1804 by which he became Emperor of France; as well as the Constitution of 1852, written by and for his nephew Louis Napoleon. Although their adoptions went together with referendums, plebiscites or plebiscitary elections, there was no deliberation in the constitution-making process. A more recent example is the making of the French Constitution of 1958, written by and for Charles de Gaulle. Initially, he sought a free hand in preparing the new constitution and presenting it for ratification by referendum. When this idea met with resistance, he created a Consultative Constitutional Committee that discussed his draft and made non-binding recommendations to him, virtually all of which he ignored. The Constitution was later ratified in a referendum by a majority of the French voters, adding an element of democracy without deliberation. There is another sense in which a constituent assembly might be democratic and yet not deliberative, namely if the delegates are sent with bound mandates and obey them rigorously. There is a tendency for constituent assemblies to claim the power to determine their own powers. They tend to resist, therefore, if the upstream powers that convene the assembly and select the delegates try to constrain their freedom of action (Elster 1998b: 98-9).

Constituent assemblies can also be deliberative as well as democratic. Their democratic nature can be gauged either with regard to the mode of election of delegates or the internal decision-making procedures. Democracy in the mode of electing delegates depends not only on the extent of the suffrage, but also on the choice of the electoral system. Before the rise of political parties and the invention of proportional representation, there was no assurance that an assembly would be representative of its electorate. The Frankfurt National Assembly of 1848 which was convened inter alia to create a constitution for the German states, for instance, although elected (in principle) by universal manhood suffrage, included no women or peasants, only a few small shopkeepers, virtually no manual workers, and no industrial workers at all. The Weimar National Assembly of 1919, by contrast, was elected by proportional representation. An assembly can be considered more democratic if delegates are chosen in a one-step rather than a two-step election. The United States Constitution and the Bonn Constitution of 1949, for instance, were written by bodies elected by the state legislatures.

The making of the Constitution of India, the world's largest democracy, is of special interest in this context. While examining the levels of deliberation in relation to constitution-making, it can be seen that in this case the individuals involved in the writing of the constitution were rather elitist or representatives of the privileged. The absence of deliberation in the public sphere is evident. However, the proclaimed objective here was the creation of a political system for the common man—in short the creation of a democratic constitution. Paradoxically, a constitution which embodies universal adult suffrage in the world's largest democracy was drafted by a Constituent Assembly consisting of members who were elected by restricted franchise. As the prospect of Independence loomed large after the end of the Second World War, efforts were made to create a constitution for independent India. As early as 1928, B.R. Ambedkar (2002: 32), appearing before the Simon Commission, insisted on incorporating universal adult franchise in the Constitution of India. As he saw it, elections were a weapon in the hands of the most oppressed sections of society and voting rights would give them political and legal equality. His views were shared equally by others including Jawaharlal Nehru. Universal adult franchise and equal rights for women were advocated by the Motilal Nehru Report on a Draft Constitution for free India. The Indian National Congress in a resolution at its Karachi session of 1931 highlighted the idea of political equality, expressed in the notion of universal adult franchise, as crucial to the future of *Purna Swaraj* or Total Independence. The party argued that it would be a significant move towards a more participatory and inclusive electoral process. On the issue of a Constituent Assembly, which it had demanded as early as in 1934, it wanted a body which was elected on the basis of universal adult suffrage or as near it as possible, to write a constitution. This idea was confirmed at later sessions of the Congress. Writing in the 12 November 1939 issue of *Harijan,* Mahatma Gandhi agreed that a Constituent Assembly was the best way to deal with the problems of communalism in India.

In September 1945 the Labour Government in Britain announced that it approved of the creation of a Constituent Assembly for India. As a prelude to the creation of a constitution, it ordered elections for the provincial legislatures in India. In the Cabinet Mission Plan that was announced on 16 May 1946, it was decided that the provincial legislatures should act as the electoral bodies for the Constituent Assembly. The formula was that the provinces be represented in the Constituent Assembly in the approximate ratio of one for one million of the population. The Cabinet Mission Plan was sensitive to the idea that the Constitution had to be created by representatives elected on the basis of universal adult franchise, but was aware that the ensuing process would lead to an unacceptable delay in the formulation of the new Constitution (Lerner 2011: 113). Hence a compromise had to be made by holding elections based on the then existing situation. The Congress party also was aware of the problems involved. However, its position in the provincial legislatures was comfortable and there was nothing to lose under the proposed scheme. Of the 1585 seats in the provincial assemblies it had won 925 or 58 per cent of all seats. Moreover, it had also won 85 per cent of the non-Muslim seats. The Muslim League decided to boycott the Constituent Assembly as the Congress refused to concede to 'its demand for sectional meetings drafting group constitutions' (Bandyopadhyay 2004: 453). In the July 1946 elections to the Constituent Assembly, the Congress party won 203 out of the 212 seats in the general category. However, in the separate categories for the Muslims and the Sikhs, it only won four and one respectively.

A rough estimate is that in pre-Independence India only 13 per cent of Indians enjoyed the right to vote. The prevailing notion of representation was that those who had been voted to be members of the Constituent Assembly acted on behalf of all the people of India. Whosoever was chosen was elected by an arrangement that was characterized by restricted franchise and divided electorates. Altogether the Constituent Assembly consisted of 389 members—296 members from British India and 93 from the princely states. However, consequent to the partition under the Mountbatten Plan of 3 June 1947, a separate Constituent Assembly was created for

Pakistan and representatives of certain provinces ceased to be members of the Assembly (Sherwani 1989). During the deliberations of the Constituent Assembly, the question of representation remained an irritant. As late as November 1948 Damodar Swarup Seth raised the issue that the Constituent Assembly was not representative enough to consider the draft constitution and insisted that a new Constituent Assembly be elected on the basis of universal adult franchise (Chaube 2000: 108). However, a large section of members of the Constituent Assembly attempted to legitimize its existence by affirming that it represented all the people of India.

An analysis of the composition of the Constituent Assembly will show that it was dominated by the upper castes and Brahminic elites within the Congress. The party itself was not notably democratic in its own workings and was controlled by middle-class and professional interests (Corbridge and Harriss 2003: 23). Ideologically also there was a considerable void in the Assembly. Many socialist leaders who could not join the Constituent Assembly went to the extent of suggesting dissolution of the Assembly and its re-election by universal adult suffrage. However, this lacuna was ameliorated by the presence of a large number of Congress leaders who subscribed to socialist principles. From a practical sense also, legal experts took over the process within the Assembly and the drafting of the Constitution was dominated by two dozen lawyers. The Assembly spent 114 out of the total session of 165 days discussing the draft constitution. Members debated and discussed the clauses of the draft constitution threadbare, much of which was done in committees. A perusal of the Constituent Assembly Debates will show that the discussions were often of high quality and the procedures thoroughly democratic though it was not unusual for passions to run high. H.R. Khanna (2008: 14) states that the deliberations 'provide a fascinating study and throw a flood of light on national thinking on the political plane'. The debates when printed ran into 12 bulky volumes (*Constituent Assembly Debates*).

Interestingly, the debate in the Constituent Assembly was accompanied informally by an unofficial debate in a forum of the Congress party known as the Congress Assembly party which was dominated by an oligarchy. Many participants of this elitist group were also members of the Constituent Assembly. Every provision of the Constitution was debated in detail in the Congress Assembly party and very often its outcome was decided before it was passed on to the floor of the Constituent Assembly. Members representing the princely states could also attend the Assembly party meetings (if they were members of the All India States People's Conference) or if they had been elected and not nominated. The discussions in the forum were frank, candid and at times heated. On certain occasions, Rajendra Prasad, the Chairman of the Constituent Assembly, postponed debate on the floor of the Constituent Assembly, so that a solution to the problem could be found out in private. Unanimity, consensus and persuasion dominated these private interactions. The oligarchy within Congress was also influential in promoting consensus. In case of sustained opposition or differences of opinion, the issue used to be voted at the party forum. In case of support for a particular issue from a large majority, it was adopted as a party decision and a whip was issued. On less important issues the whip was made use of as a matter of routine. However, on issues where members were almost equally divided, no whip was issued and the matter was to be settled in the Constituent Assembly by vote. A whip was invariably avoided on matters of great importance involving conscience, like the language issue. Emphasis was often placed on achieving a consensus on issues. Usually the question remained within the Assembly Party meeting, until some agreement through consensus was arrived at. Once, the Congress Assembly Party made a decision on a particular aspect of the Constitution, passage through the Constituent Assembly was almost a foregone conclusion. Maya Tudor (2013: 161) observes that 'before independence, even before the precise structural contours of the sovereign successor state were known, this Congress Assembly Party was at work debating and drafting constitutional provisions'.

Above all these criticisms, is the one which points out that the Constitution of India was not ratified by the people as it was done in the case of the United States. Critics state that one could understand the concerns of the nationalist leaders regarding the immediate formation of a Constituent Assembly at the time of impending independence despite the fact that franchise was restricted. They point out that by the time the Constitution was adopted and came into effect in 1950, the principle of universal adult franchise could have been implemented and the legitimacy of the Constitution could have been established by getting it ratified by a majority of the citizens of the country.

As in the case of the Constitution of India, the making of the Constitution of the United States was devoid of full-fledged democratic ideals and was not based on a mandate that was fully representative. Yet, many regard the Constitution of the United States as the world's most celebrated one. In fact, many constitutions that were made in other countries in later years and decades followed the American model. Many others borrowed cardinal features of the U.S. Constitution in part if not in entirety. However, when it comes to a discussion on the degree of deliberation involved in the making of the U.S. Constitution several criticisms are raised. Many would describe its making as 'the undemocratic birth of a democratic constitution'. This issue has to be seen in a historical context. Colonial America was not as egalitarian as is commonly regarded. Not all people had the right to vote since the basic principle governing such a privilege was that a voter needed to have a stake in society. Democracy as a concept did not have the status one accords it today for it had associations with anarchy and mob rule. The general feeling, elitist to the core, was that the right to vote should be restricted to property owners or those who paid taxes. These were the qualities of responsible citizens who commensurately earned the right to vote. In each of the 13 American colonies, with certain variations, qualifications were prescribed for voters. For instance in 1763 a voter in Delaware was expected to own 50 acres of land or property worth £40, whereas in Rhode Island it was land valued at £40 or worth an annual rent of £2. In Connecticut the qualification was possession of land worth an annual rent of £2 or livestock worth £40 (Crews 2007). Some colonies also required religious tests for voters, effectively excluding Catholics and Jews. Consequently, while 80 per cent of the white male population could vote in rural America, in urban areas it was as low as 40 to 50 per cent. All this was a reflection of the dominant English notions with regard to race, religion, gender, industriousness and prudence. Consequently, African Americans, Native Americans, non-Protestant sects and women were excluded from the arena of democracy. There may have been a few exceptions, but it was a far cry from the idea of universal adult suffrage.

When the Constitutional Convention at Philadelphia was convened in 1787, it naturally meant that the delegates would be representatives of only the above mentioned privileged sections and not the largely disenfranchised population. The delegates were all white, adult males; property owners with the right to franchise; who also represented such people. As pointed out, it was an elitist view of the times that only property-owners would take the right of citizenship seriously since they had a literal stake in the young nation. It is precisely for these reasons that in later years constitutional scholars have looked into the class character of the delegates to the Philadelphia Convention. An analysis of the delegates would clearly show that they were wealthy men: owners of large plantations, slave holders, land speculators, bankers, merchants, lawyers and holders of government bonds. Moreover, they were men with an education level far greater than that of an average American, conversant with the classics and works of Western philosophy and political science (McDonald 1985). The deliberations of the Constitution were held in great secrecy. The *Philadelphia Independent Gazetteer* described it as a 'Dark Conclave.' The delegates had agreed among themselves to keep the proceedings private and were forbidden to make public the content of the debates. This 'behind the curtains' deliberation indeed aroused public suspicion, but apologists of this secrecy say that it made compromise easier by shielding the delegates from outside pressure. Any account made available much later, of what transpired there has been the effort to make a detailed and precise note-taking by James Madison, one of the prominent delegates who took upon himself this responsibility (Madison 1966). From Madison's account it can be seen that there were passionate and intense discussions at the Convention. Of the 55 delegates, 47 spoke during the formal sessions. The members often energetically disagreed with each other on important issues. On the question of what powers the national government should be granted there was relatively little discussion. But on the question of who would control the national government, the debate was long and heated. On the questions of representation in the national government between large and small states, slavery and differing economic interests of the regions, the deliberations were complicated.

Once the Constitution was approved and signed, it was sent to the states to be ratified by constitutional conventions created specifically for the purpose. Alexander Hamilton thought that ratification by the people would give the new Constitution greater moral power and prestige. The ratification process was supposed to be accompanied by a rigorous debate. However, only a few people participated in the ratification. The voters could not vote for or against the Constitution, their choice was confined to selecting delegates to the state ratifying conventions. Further, out of a total population of 40,00,000, only an estimated 16,00,000 voted.

One should nevertheless not discount the debate that took place in the public sphere between the signing of the Constitution and its ratification. As the Constitution was presented for popular endorsement, a bitter verbal war ensued. Pamphleteering and other forms of deliberation came to the fore. The newspapers of the time were submerged by anonymous readers writing under pseudonyms, either praising or condemning it. Of the former, the most brilliant were written under the name 'Publius'. Their authorship was later attributed to Alexander Hamilton, James Madison and John Jay and compiled to form *The Federalist.* To this day, they are regarded as the best exposition of the Constitution. On the opposing side one would find works like *Letters of the Federal Farmer* by Richard Henry Lee.

In *The Federalist* No.10, Madison refers to representatives refining and enlarging public views. This refined opinion could be considered deliberative. As he saw it, public views are refined and enlarged by passing them through the medium of a chosen body of citizens (*The Federalist* 1937: 53-62). Fishkin (2009: 15-17) states that the framers of the Constitution relied on the metaphor of the 'filter'. They were sensitive to large meetings of citizens who though virtuous could behave differently under existing social conditions. The solution was to create conditions where the formulation and expression of deliberative public opinion would be possible. Representative institutions were expected to refine public opinion through deliberation. However, American democracy has transformed itself over the decades. Referenda and other instruments of mass democracy that reflect raw public opinion have been given more emphasis than refined or more deliberative views.

From a contemporary analysis it would seem that both the making of the Constitution and some of its provisions were undemocratic. Leaving voting qualifications to states disenfranchised many Americans for almost one and a half centuries. The Upper House of Congress, the Senate had its members elected by the state legislatures until the Seventeenth Amendment in 1913. The framers had deliberately avoided direct election to keep a check on the multitudes. Above all the Constitution interposed an electoral college between the voters and the Presidency. However, apologists state that despite the original reflection of some distrust of popular rule, a balanced, institutional framework within which democracy could evolve was created. In the past, most critics of the U.S. Constitution laid emphasis on the economic motives of the Founding Fathers and the rebuttal of such views rather than the absence of deliberative democracy in constitution-making. It is perhaps only in recent times, with the increase in the scholarship on deliberative democracy that these questions are being raised.

Constitution making processes and the extent of deliberation in the late twentieth and early twenty-first centuries could also be examined in this context. During the 1990s, as the post-Cold War world was being ushered in, several countries in the former Communist as well as the Third World created new constitutions for themselves. Post-Communist constitutions jettisoned traces of their former ideologies and adopted the major precepts of liberal democracy in their new constitutions. In most cases, constitutions were reflections of their dominant political cultures. However, most of them turned out to be elite documents because they were not drafted by constituent assemblies but by parliamentary commissions and ratified, in certain cases, by referendums. Opinions of important groups were excluded from constitution-making (Partlett 2012). Contrary to these has been the Romanian experiment of 2013. The Romanian Parliament began a procedure to revise the constitution and consequently established a deliberative body called the Constitutional Forum. It was meant to be an autonomous and consultative structure for the purpose of organizing debates and consultations with members of society regarding the revision of the Constitution (Gherghina 2014). Parliament also set up a committee with the task to discuss proposals that emerged from the deliberative practices of the Forum. Deliberations were aimed at producing proposals that were later submitted to the parliamentary committee for approval. In short, the objective of the Forum was to act as a deliberative body that gathered proposals from citizens and civil society organizations and to prepare a report which would serve as the basis of the work of the Parliamentary Committee (Preuss 2006-7). Following public debate and consultations with the Venice Commission, the Council of Europe's advisory body on constitutional matters, the constitutional revision draft was submitted to the Constitutional Court which found 26 draft amendment proposals in conflict with the existing constitution. In the meantime developments in Romanian politics stalled the move for revision. While the Constitutional Forum as a civic, inclusive precursor to the parliamentary revision process is procedurally speaking promising, critics think that it might remain largely inconsequential. Further, its work remains relatively limited and without due consequence, and in which important voices are ultimately not taken into account (Blokker 2013: 187-204, 2014).

The making of South Africa's Constitution is one that involved public participation and deliberation. As the transformation from apartheid to democratic rule occurred, there were discussions on the future constitution for the country. At this point there was not much participation of civil society. Following elections to the Constituent Assembly in April 1994, steps were taken to ensure a broad participatory process in the drafting of the Constitution by emphasizing principles of inclusivity, accessibility and transparency. A widespread campaign to educate the public about constitutional issues and fundamental rights was also initiated. The campaign made use of the media, advertisements, a biweekly Assembly newspaper and the internet. Radio programmes in eight languages reaching an audience of 10 million people per week were broadcast. Further, about a thousand workshops were held throughout the country over a year. About 600 civil society organizations and 117,000 people participated in the deliberations. About 14,000 people presented submissions and over two million people signed petitions on different issues. All these made it possible for the public to make their views known to the Constituent Assembly which processed them meticulously. After the publication of the draft constitution, the public was again invited to submit their views. However, the final negotiation process was held *in camera* in the Constituent Assembly and was subject to criticism for being an arena for deals between political parties. The Constituent Assembly finally approved the Constitution with an 85 per cent majority. A widespread public dialogue that consisted of face-to-face town meetings to nationally televised debates between elite experts complemented closed sessions of hard bargaining and rhetorical appeals by leaders including Nelson Mandela in the final stage of the South African constitutional debate (Chambers 2010: 85). Polls held later showed that a majority of South Africans were satisfied with the way the entire exercise was conducted (Segal and Cort 2011).

As regards the Constitution of Afghanistan written in the first decade of this century, it was created by a 35-member team that included Afghans and foreign legal experts who spent a year working on it. An important question confronting the framers was whether to open the constitutional process to debate and deliberation in Afghan society. One argument was that the legitimacy of the Constitution would be ensured if there was an opportunity for debate, discussion and incorporation of diverse views. On the other hand, detractors stated that this exercise would destabilize the process by highlighting controversial issues and therefore it was better to keep the debate out of the public sphere. A compromise solution was ultimately found by conducting a public consultation process. At a nationwide series of public meetings, nearly half a million Afghans were asked what they thought should be included in the Constitution. But rather than eliciting views on concrete issues, the discussion was limited to abstract and vague principles. Civil society groups assisted the process by holding consultations and training sessions. The wide range of responses received was then sent to the Constitutional Drafting Commission. However, complications arising from Afghanistan's complex factional tribal politics prevented these opinions from seeing the light of day. The draft was drawn up in relative secrecy and, after several delays the final version was issued in November 2003. A constitutional grand council known as the *Loya Jirga*, consisting of a diverse group of representatives who were appointed by provincial authorities and transitional government officials, began to debate the draft of the document in mid-December. There were heated debates on several issues, walkouts, threats to boycott as well as refusals to vote on amendments. After three weeks of sessions the delegates were asked to stand for one minute to denote their accession to the document. Interestingly, no formal count or recording of dissenting votes was done. On 4 January 2004 the Constitution was finally adopted (Thier 2006-7: 558-79).

The Iraqi case is another example of post-Cold War constitution-making. Here one would find an externally coerced regime change and the imposition not only of rulers but also of a constitution aimed at transforming an autocratic system to a democratic one. The United States, following the military defeat of the Saddam Hussain regime, established an interim constitution. This was followed in 2005 by a constitution drafted by Iraqi political forces under the auspices of the Americans (Preuss 2006-7). The constitution-making effort was done in the midst of an anarchic and precarious security environment fraught by deep societal divisions. In January 2005 elections to a National Assembly were held. The National Assembly created a Constitutional Committee which was initially composed of 55 Assembly members and was later augmented by the inclusion of 15 more representing the Sunni Muslims who had boycotted the elections. The drafting of the Constitution took three months and a referendum was held in October 2005. Between the beginning of the drafting and the referendum, a Leadership Council consisting of senior Iraqi politicians held negotiations among themselves, thereby rescinding the efforts of the Constitutional Committee. During the drafting phase consultations were made with outside experts. Some public conferences were also held with Shiite clerics and students who had an overwhelming influence in Iraqi politics. A committee was constituted to hold a national debate where a few civil society organizations and women's groups held discussions. Unfortunately there was no procedure to incorporate the opinions and viewpoints of the public in the deliberations and drafting of the constitution. Moreover, the media only reported a general coverage of the issues. Jawad (2013: 22) states that 'Iraqis went to vote on a permanent constitution they had not seen, read, studied, debated, or drafted. Even stranger is the fact that they voted on an incomplete draft.'

The Zimbabwean experience with deliberative democracy in constitution-making could also be examined here. Zimbabwe was governed from 1980 on the basis of a constitution that was based on the negotiations that took place at Lancaster House in London between conflicting parties before that period. From then onwards Zimbabwe had experienced the autocratic rule of Robert Mugabe. An effort to have a new constitution drafted by a constitutional convention was defeated in a referendum in 2000. Political unrest and economic problems brought into the political scene an opposition to the government led by the Movement for Democratic Change, and the government was forced to come to the negotiating table. Thabo Mbeki, the former South African President mediated in the issue and the Global Political Agreement (GPA) was entered into in 2008 by the three main political parties in Zimbabwe. The parties agreed on creating a new constitution in 18 months which was to be approved in a referendum. The process of constitution-making was led by the Constitutional Parliamentary Committee (COPAC). A First All Stakeholders Conference agreed on 17 thematic areas of the constitution and established as many sub-committees of COPAC. This was followed by a public outreach programme during which Zimbabweans were consulted on what they wanted to see incorporated in the new constitution. During this stage, 4,821 meetings involving approximately 1.2 million people were held throughout the country. In addition, 51 written submissions and 2,397 electronic submissions, including those from the Zimbabwean diaspora were submitted. The experiences of similar processes elsewhere were also analysed. The United Nations Development Programme at the request of the government provided international experts to assist with a data analysis tool that was used to analyse the field data from the public outreach programme for drafting purposes. Further, an experienced Strategic Adviser provided strategic support and technical expertise to COPAC to assist with the translation of the data into a constitutional framework, as well as facilitation of identification of constitutional issues and principles used to guide the drafting process. The final draft constitution was subsequently adopted by all the major political parties. On 16 March 2013 it was submitted before a national referendum and was approved by an overwhelming majority of the people who voted. Ephraim Gwaravanda (2012: 123-9), writing in the context of the Zimbabwean constitution-making process raised the hope that Habermas' theory of deliberative democracy could be used to overcome partisanship in the constitution-making process. He points out that it is particularly useful because it emphasizes rational discourse and tries to remove prejudices and egoistic tendencies in constitution-making.

Certain Western liberal democracies also have in recent times made efforts to incorporate a greater degree of deliberative democracy in reforming their constitutions. The efforts of Iceland are worth mentioning here. The process of constitutional rewriting in Iceland between 2010 and 2013 was unprecedented in the sense that it involved a great deal of deliberative democracy in constitution making. Citizens were involved in the effort partly through the method of crowd-sourcing. To this end, the *Althingi* or parliament of Iceland appointed a Constitutional Committee of seven to arrange the initial formalities and organize a national assembly comprising 950 individuals drawn at random from the national registry. In November 2010 a National Forum attended by these 950 people was held. This group put forth the basic values and viewpoints which it thought should be the basis of the Constitution. The ideas of this group later formed the basis of the work of a consultative Constitutional Assembly of 25 representatives selected from a pool of 522 citizens from all walks of life, a majority of them without any particular political or special interest affiliations. Interestingly, political parties were excluded from the preparation and drafting phases of the new constitution. These 25 constitutional drafters used social media to open up the process to the rest of the citizens and invite responses on twelve successive drafts. The entire exercise was lauded internationally as being innovative and participatory. However, it also raised several questions. First, was it possible in a constitutional democracy to sidestep elected representatives in the national parliament by championing 'the people?' Certainly the involvement of citizens in the initial stages of constitution-making and the importance of their opinions mattered greatly, particularly because it strengthened the democratic foundations and legitimacy of the constitution. However, one has to bear in mind the issues of popular involvement on the one hand and actual constitution-making on the other. The 950 people were chosen for their non-involvement in politics but they also happened to be inexperienced in legislative work. If their efforts had been augmented in the *Althingi,* it would have qualitatively improved the constitution (Thorarensen 2014). In 2012 a national referendum was held where 67 per cent approved of the changes. It then went to parliament to be ratified where it kept lingering. In the meantime parliamentary elections in 2013 brought the opponents of reform back to power. Since they were not interested in pursuing the matter, things came to a standstill.

CONCLUSION

Today, scholars in general tend to agree that public participation and deliberation are important elements of the democratic process of constitution-making. Participatory constitution-making is increasingly being accepted as a democratic norm, permitting citizens to be involved in the making of their constitutions and their future. However, although it seems to be an emerging trend, examples such as the cases of constitution-making in Iceland and South Africa reveal the ground realities in realizing this ideal. As seen in the case of India, deliberative democracy and constitution-making in plural societies, particularly severely divided societies is most often very complex and difficult, the most important basic conditions/ prerequisites for both being inclusion and political equality. Deliberation clearly depends to a large extent on the nature of the public sphere and civil society as well as political institutions.

Over recent years scholars have been trying to address specific issues such as whether a parliament or a constituent assembly is better equipped for the task of constitution-making, whether transparency or an element of secrecy in negotiations are more likely to produce consensus, and whether deadlines should be prescribed for the conclusion of different stages of the process. No less important are the consequences of a high degree of popular participation in constitution-making. There will be no clear resolution to the tension between forms of representation, making it an instance of conflicting values of democratic design. Another problem is getting the size of a deliberative assembly right. A larger body may appear to be more representative. But with increasing size genuine deliberation becomes more difficult. Above all, in a democracy, deliberation ends in aggregation. Governments are expected to govern on the basis of voting, not on deliberation. Ultimately, some people will have to give in to an opinion that is different from theirs or to a decision that is against their interest. They are forced to do so, by the sheer force of numbers, rather than from the validity of reasons (see for example, Brandt et al. 2011: 18; Fishkin 2009: 106; Levy 2010: 827 and Przeworski 1998: 141-2).

Critics argue that deliberative democracy is generally incapable of processing deep differences. However, as Addis (2009: 82) points out, the deliberative approach acknowledges the importance of these differences and the fact that they are constituted partly through narratives and discourses. Consequently these differences could be transformed through sustained institutional dialogue among the various groups. As such, only deliberative democracy has the capacity to process deep differences. As dialogues and discourses may have been institutionally entrenched, deliberation makes it possible for various groups to continue to create and transform their individual and collective identities and interests.

Scholars of deliberative democracy also remind us of the need to understand the larger goal of deliberation, that it is necessary to go beyond an analysis of individual institutions and processes to understand their interaction in a system as a whole. Most democracies are intricate structures in which a wide variety of institutions, associations and sites of contestation accomplish political work. This necessitates the need for what may be called a systemic approach to deliberative democracy. The actual extent of democracy in any society may depend on various factors, including the economic and social structure of society, and the nature of the public sphere and civil society (Mansbridge et al. 2012). If deliberative democracy is to work in severely fractured societies, it requires taking institutional designs seriously, however difficult that may be. Every society has its own distinct experience and definite points of cleavage. Hence institutions will have to respond to those needs and histories (Addis 2009: 73). While no institution can guarantee that its members will assume a wide and flexible view of their own as well as others' interests, as Levy (2010: 810) argues, deliberative democratic bodies have to at least leave open this possibility by placing decision makers in the position to learn from and cooperate with each other.

An observation of post-Cold War constitutions in general reveals one thing in particular, that if politicians are entrusted with drafting or ratifying constitutions, they could place their own interests above public interest. On the other hand, it also reveals that a constitution drafted by persons who are not well versed in such technical matters runs other risks. Often a constitution that does not have the support of existing institutions or political parties, and an establishment with entrenched interests in the present order, may not be ratified. However, these experiments have lessons for deliberative democracy and constitution-making. They reveal that a workable model for constitutional reform with a high level of civic participation, with a reform process that relies exclusively on civil society during the drafting phase can function well. Above all they indicate how consultations with the public can be achieved concerning the substance and aims of constitutions.

The various cases examined reflect to a certain extent the conditions necessary for and the challenges and constraints of deliberative democracy in the process of constitution-making. Questions of inclusion and political equality which form the crux of the issue continue to be matters of concern. The two-track model of a combination of mass participation through the informal public sphere; with political decision-making through deliberation in formal politics, seems to be a preferred model with several efforts having been taken to make it a reality. However, as evidenced, such a model of deliberative democracy is not without challenges and needs to be made more feasible in constitution-making, particularly in the context of the ground realities of constitution-making in fractured societies.

REFERENCES

Addis, Adeno (2009): 'Deliberative Democracy in Severely Fractured Societies', *Indiana Journal of Global Legal Studies*, 16(1), Winter: 59-83.

Ambedkar, B.R. (2002): *The Essential Writings of B.R. Ambedkar*, New Delhi: Oxford University Press.

Bandyopadhyay, Sekhar (2004): *From Plassey to Partition: A History of Modern India*, New Delhi: Orient Longman.

Banks, Angela M. (2008): 'Expanding Participation in Constitution Making: Challenges and Opportunities', *William and Mary Law Review*, 49(4): 1043-68.

Blokker, Paul (2013): 'Constitution-Making in Romania: From Reiterative Crises to Constitutional Moment?', *Romanian Journal of Comparative Law*, 3(2): 187-204.

—— (2014): 'Illiberal Constitutional Tendencies and Legal Resentment in Hungary and Romania', Paper prepared for the IXth World Congress: Constitutional Challenges: Global and Local, The International Association of Constitutional Law and The Department of Public and International Law, University of Oslo, 16-20 June 2014, www.jus.uio.no.

Bohman, James (1998): 'The Coming of Age of Deliberative Democracy', *The Journal of Political Philosophy*, 6(1): 400-25.

Brandt, Michele, Jill Cottrell, Yash Ghai and Anthony Regan (2011): *Constitution-Making and Reform: Options for the Process*, Geneva: Interpeace.

Chambers, Simone (2010): 'Open Versus Closed Constitutional Negotiation', in David Kahane et al. (eds.), *Deliberative Democracy in Practice*, Vancouver: UBC Press: 77-91.

Chaube, Shibani Kinkar (2000): *Constituent Assembly of India: Springboard of Revolution*, New Delhi: Manohar.

Cohen, Joshua (1999): 'Reflections on Habermas on Democracy', *Ratio Juris* 12(4), December: 385-416.

Constituent Assembly Debates: Official Report (1949), New Delhi: Lok Sabha Secretariat.

Corbridge, Stuart and John Harriss (2003): *Reinventing India: Liberalization, Hindu Nationalism and Popular Democracy*, New Delhi: Oxford University Press.

Crews, Ed (2007): 'Voting in Early America', *Colonial Williamsburg Journal*, Spring, www.history.org.

Elster, Jon (1998a): 'Introduction', in Jon Elster (ed.), *Deliberative Democracy*, Cambridge: Cambridge University Press: 1-18.

—— (1998b): 'Deliberation and Constitution Making', in Jon Elster (ed.), *Deliberative Democracy*, Cambridge: Cambridge University Press: 97-122.

Eriksen, Erik O. and Jarle Weigard (2003): *Understanding Habermas: Communicating Action and Deliberative Democracy*, London: Continuum.

Fearson, James D. (1998): 'Deliberation as Discussion', in Jon Elster (ed.), *Deliberative Democracy*, Cambridge: Cambridge University Press: 44-68.

Fillmore-Patrick, Hannah (2013): *The Iceland Experiment (2009-2013): A Participatory Approach to Constitutional Reform*, Sarajevo: Democratization Policy Council (DPC): August.

Fishkin, James S. (2009): *When the People Speak: Deliberative Democracy and Public Consultation*, Oxford: Oxford University Press.

Gherghina, Sergiu (2014): 'A Constitution by the People?: The Legitimacy of Deliberation in the Romanian 2013 Reform', paper prepared for the ECPR General Conference, Glasgow, 3-6 September, www.ecpr.eu.

Gwaravanda, Ephraim Taurai (2012): 'Habermas' Deliberative Democracy Theory and the Zimbabwean Constitution-Making Process', *African Journal of Political Science and International Relations*, 6(6): 123-9.

Habermas, Jürgen (1991): *The Structural Transformation of the Public Sphere: An Enquiry into a Category of Bourgeois Society*, Cambridge: Polity Press.

—— (1996): *Between Facts and Norms: Contributions to a Discourse Theory of Law and Democracy*, Cambridge, MA: The MIT Press.

—— (2001): 'Constitutional Democracy: A Paradoxical Union of Contradictory Principles?', *Political Theory*, 29(6), December: 766-81.

Hart, Vivien (2003): *Democratic Constitution-Making*, Washington DC: United States Institute of Peace, Special Report 107, July.

Jawad, Saad N. (2013): *The Iraqi Constitution: Structural Flaws and Political Implications,* LSE Middle East Centre Paper Series 1, November.

Khanna, H.R. (2008): *Making of India's Constitution,* Lucknow: Eastern Book Co.

Lerner, Hanna (2011): *Making Constitutions in Deeply Divided Societies,* Cambridge: Cambridge University Press.

Levy, Ron (2010): 'Breaking the Constitutional Deadlock: Lessons from Deliberative Experiments in Constitutional Change', *Melbourne University Law Review,* 34: 806-38.

Madison, James (1966): *Notes of Debates in the Federal Convention of 1787,* New York: Norton.

Mansbridge, Jane, et al. (2012): 'A Systemic Approach to Deliberative Democracy', www.wrap.warwick.ac.uk.

McDonald, Forrest (1985): *Novus Ordo Seclorum: The Intellectual Origins of the Constitution,* Lawrence: University Press of Kansas.

Partlett, William (2012): 'The Dangers of Popular Constitution-Making', *Social Science Research Network Report,* 3 December, www.brookings.edu.

Preuss, Ulrich K. (2006-7): 'Perspectives on Post-Conflict Constitutionalism: Reflections on Regime Change Through External Constitutionalization', *New York Law School Law Review,* 51(3): 468-94.

Przeworski, Adam (1998): 'Deliberation and Ideological Domination', in Jon Elster (ed.), *Deliberative Democracy,* Cambridge: Cambridge University Press: 140-60.

Rawls, John (1997): 'The Idea of Public Reason Revisited', *Chicago Law Review,* 64(3): 765-807.

Segal, Lauren and Sharon Cort (2011): *One Law, One Nation: The Making of the South African Constitution,* Auckland Park: Jacana.

Sherwani, Latif Ahmed (1989): *The Partition of India and Mountbatten,* New Delhi: Atlantic.

Steiner, Jurg (2012): *The Foundations of Deliberative Democracy: Empirical Research and Normative Implications,* Cambridge: Cambridge University Press.

Stokes, Susan C. (1998): 'Pathologies of Deliberation', in Jon Elster (ed.), *Deliberative Democracy,* Cambridge: Cambridge University Press: 123-39.

Sunstein, Cass R. (1998): 'Health-Health Trade-offs', in Jon Elster (ed.), *Deliberative Democracy,* Cambridge: Cambridge University Press: 232-59.

The Federalist (1937): New York: Modern Library.

Thier, J. Alexander (2006-7): 'The Making of a Constitution in Afghanistan', *New York Law School Law Review,* 51(3): 558-79.

Thorarensen, Björg (2014): 'Why the Making of a Crowd-Sourced Constitution in Iceland Failed', *Constitution Making and Constitutional Change*, www.constitutional-change.com.

Tudor, Maya (2013): *The Promise of Power: The Origins of Democracy in India and Autocracy in Pakistan*, Cambridge: Cambridge University Press.

Weichlein, Siegfried (2011): 'Nation State, Conflict Resolution, and Culture War, 1850-78', in Helmut Walser Smith (ed.), *The Oxford Handbook of Modern German History*, Oxford: Oxford University Press.

CHAPTER 3

Deliberative Democracy, Public Sphere and the Search for Alternative Politics in India: Gandhian Contributions

SIBY K. JOSEPH

Democratic polity of different shades has become the system of governance in most parts of the globe, and liberal democracy with representative government has become its most dominant form. But democratic polity has essentially transformed itself through the ages. It started with limited franchise and ultimately culminated in universal franchise. Initially, it was identified with the idea of a minimal state which came to be reflected in the well-known saying 'that government is best that governs the least'.[1] But the rise of trade union movements in the wake of the Industrial Revolution posed a serious challenge to the concept of minimal state. The state had to grapple with the problems created by modern industrial society. What gave it further momentum was Marxist thought which sought to espouse the cause of the working class or the proletariat. The transition from minimal state to welfare state radically changed the entire character of democratic governance.

However, the existing patterns of democracy suffer from certain basic flaws and weaknesses. The entire superstructure of democracy was based on the basic principle of representation. It was assumed that popular will and aspirations could be actually represented by their representatives. It was often not understood that there could be a big disconnect between the people, particularly the poor and marginalized sections of society and their representatives. It also failed to anticipate that the so-called people's representatives could develop their own vested interests, putting aside those of their constituents. Besides, it could hardly do anything about changing the existing class structure of society, which was based on injustice and inequities. Thus, the entire theoretical proposition of liberal democracy that people were the ultimate source of power was found to be baseless. On the contrary, it turned out to be a system dominated by the elite, who had no compunction in indulging in acts of corruption and domination. Even the entire process of law-making was vitiated as more often than not, laws were made to tighten the grip of the elite on the existing socio-political order. The people hardly made any contribution to the law-making process. They were not given any genuine opportunity to voice their opinions or ventilate their grievances, failing to make any contributions in the entire process of deliberation. Since the elitist nature of democracy could not be demolished in any of the above systems, serious attempts were made to find ways and means to provide scope for popular participation in law-making as well as other processes of decision-making. A number of scholars came to the conclusion that the only way to really democratize the system of governance would be to design a new system in which the people could really articulate their views, participate in the decision-making process and even contest the decisions already taken and suggest new laws in the place of existing ones.

It was in this context that a number of attempts both at the intellectual and the practical levels emerged in the 1960s. New intellectual and anti-war movements symbolized serious attempts to go beyond organized political institutions and processes. Writers like Frantz Fanon, Regis Debray, Che Guevara and Herbert Marcuse emerged as intellectual icons among a section of left intellectuals. All these also led to a number of popular movements in which scholars like Bertrand Russell, Jean-Paul Sartre and others participated. Some kind of popular rebellion gripped the academic campuses particularly in Europe, India and the United States. However, by the beginning of the 1980s, they lost their steam. Yet the search for making democratic polity more participatory and people-oriented continued. Participatory democracy, sustainable development, etc., became the catchwords of new socio-political movements. Deliberative democracy belongs to the same genre of new movements. In parenthesis, it appears that the entire attempt was to strengthen the sinews of democratic polity by giving the people a vital role in the entire process which was long due to them. It is in this perspective that the concept of deliberative democracy needs to be understood.

Deliberative democracy is based on the premise that all stakeholders of democracy have a basic right to deliberate as well as contest the decisions taken by the government. The term 'deliberative democracy' was originally coined by Joseph M. Bessette in his work *Deliberative Democracy: The Majority Principle in Republican Government* in 1980. This idea was further elaborated and substantiated in his subsequent work *The Mild Voice of Reason: Deliberative Democracy and American National Government.* He argues that the architects of the American Constitution

> wanted both *deliberative democracy*, one which would foster rule by the informed and reasoned judgments of the citizenry and *energetic democracy* in which the national security and vital interests would be defended against external threats and in which national laws and policies would be effectively enforced throughout a territory unprecedented in size for a republican government. (Bessette 1997: 1)

According to Amy Gutmann and Dennis Thompson (2004: 7) deliberative democracy is 'a form of government in which free and equal citizens (and their representatives) justify decisions in a process in which they give one another reasons that are mutually acceptable and generally accessible, with the aim of reaching conclusions that are binding in the present on all citizens but open to challenge in the future'. They emphazise its four major dimensions, that is the dialogue between citizens and their representatives should be reciprocal, accessible, binding, dynamic or provisional. In other words, the dialogue should be carried out in such a way as to generate mutual respect, open and tentative argumentation which could even lead to changing previous decisions and laws, but the final decision arrived at through this process would be fit for implementation.

Carmen Sirianni and Lewis Friedland point out that

> deliberative democracy rests on the core notion of citizens and their representatives deliberating about public problems and solutions under circumstances that are conducive to reasoned reflection and refined public judgment; a mutual willingness to understand the values, perspectives, and interests of others; and the possibility of reframing their interests and perspectives in light of a joint search for common interests and mutually acceptable solutions.

In their view, deliberative democracy unlike liberal pluralist political theory is not based on the assumptions that citizens have a fixed ordering of preferences when they enter the public sphere. In fact, a genuine dialogue in the public sphere could go a long way in revising the given preferences through the inputs of multiple perspectives and could lead towards a better understanding of the issues involved and could even provide a forum for joint action.

Joshua Cohen analyses three advantages of the ideal deliberative procedure. They are: (1) it helps to account for some familiar judgements about collective decision-making, in particular about the ways that collective decision-making ought to be different from bargaining, contracting and other market-type interactions, both in its explicit attention to considerations of the common advantage and in the ways that that attention helps to form the aims of the participants; (2) it accounts for the common view that the notion of democratic association is tied to notions of autonomy and the common good; (3) the ideal deliberative procedure provides a distinctive structure for addressing institutional questions.

The concept of the public sphere is central to the discourses of deliberative democracy. The basic idea of the public sphere was enunciated by Jürgen Habermas in his classic work of 1962, *The Structural Transformation of the Public Sphere: An Inquiry into a Category of Bourgeois Society,* which was revisited and elaborated subsequently by a number of scholars. The term 'public sphere' was used to denote social arenas where any public issue in its various dimensions is discussed and articulated leading to the emergence of a collective body that is 'the public'. Habermas made it clear that the public sphere is constituted when private people come together as a public. They contest the bourgeois public sphere as regulated from above by public authorities and posit it with their own concept of public sphere so as to engage in a public debate on general rules which govern commodity exchange and social labour. According to Habermas (1991), commodity exchange and social labour come under the realm of private sphere whereas the sphere of public authority deals with the state or the realm of the police and the ruling class. The public sphere encompasses both these spheres and through the medium of public opinion it connects the state with the needs of the society. He looks upon the public sphere as a regulatory institution against the authority of the state. Rousiley C.M. Mala gives a clear explanation about the process and focus of the public sphere. According to her 'the focus of deliberative politics is not the final act of voting, but the way in which opinion is formed within the public sphere and how such opinion may influence the formation of the political will, which occurs within the formal decision-making arenas of the political system'.

It could therefore be safely said that with all its limitations, the concept of public sphere is meant to provide a forum where people can come together to have a dialogue on issues relating to their life which might lead to the making of better laws or changing the decisions of the authority through public contestation. It is evident that there is an intimate relationship between deliberative democracy and public sphere.

However, there are strong contrarian views on the efficacy of deliberative democracy. The nature of public discourse might exclude marginalized sections of society because they may not have the intellectual acumen to participate and influence the course and direction of ongoing debate in the public sphere. The whole concept of deliberative democracy is relevant only in the context of liberal democracy, as authoritarian regimes hardly provide an opportunity for any meaningful popular participation in the decision-making process. Besides, under the garb of deliberative democracy, self-interest and coercive bargaining might work as a hidden agenda behind rational argumentation and counter argumentation. It could be further argued that deliberative democracy by creating an adverse relation between the state and civil society might result in undermining even the legitimate authority of the state leading to chaotic or anarchical situations.

GANDHIAN TRADITION OF ALTERNATIVE POLITICS IN INDIA

It is true that the concepts of deliberative democracy and public sphere as such were not part of public discourse during the freedom struggle or in post Independent India for a long time. But a closer examination of the nature and structure of public discourse in India since the days of the freedom struggle would make clear that it had more or less covered the same ground. One may be reminded that even the Moderates in the Indian National Congress, with all their limitations, placed the problems facing the country in the public discourse so as to influence public opinion both in India and England. The militant nationalism led by Bal Gangadhar Tilak, Aurobindo Ghose and others gave further fillip to public debate by drawing popular participation particularly during the Swadeshi movement. It is well known that they used even village fairs and religious gatherings as forums for public discourses. However, it was Mahatma Gandhi who really made a distinct departure in the realm of deliberative democracy and public sphere by including the masses as important partners in the whole political process. Besides, his concept of *satyagraha* as a new weapon of national struggle presented a real opportunity to the people for wholesome deliberation in the public sphere. Gandhi was firmly of the opinion that before the actual launching of *satyagraha* the entire gamut of issues involved should be thoroughly discussed and debated among the people. This was clearly nothing but a sort of deliberative process in which the people were supposed to make their own contributions. In fact, Gandhi went much beyond the Western concept of deliberative democracy by introducing the action plan of *satyagraha* in his political thinking. *Satyagraha* does not stop at mere deliberations of issues in the public sphere but offers an effective instrument of action, if the deliberative process fails to resolve issues. It is also to be noted that Gandhian *satyagraha* is based on the premise of relative truth and not absolute truth. Thus it provides adequate space both for contestations as well as reconciliation. Ultimately, both contesting parties would end up being partners in the joint search for truth and reconciliation. From the very beginning of his social and political life Gandhi favoured deliberation and dialogue along with an action plan which he subsequently termed as *satyagraha.*

Hind Swaraj, Gandhi's seminal work written in 1909, was a reaffirmation of his faith in the efficacy of *satyagraha.* It was an embodiment of deliberative democracy and public sphere. Even the dialogic form which he adopted in it, was symbolic of a sustained and detailed deliberation between the editor and reader. It goes without saying that Gandhi himself was the editor, and the reader was a representative of extreme nationalism in India. A content analysis of *Hind Swaraj* clearly reveals that Gandhi dealt with all the major issues not only concerning India but also those of the world and put them in the public domain by publishing it in book form, both in Gujarati and English. He also sent copies of *Hind Swaraj* to a number of leading intellectuals of the world including Leo Tolstoy and sought their opinions on his major formulations. In *Hind Swaraj* he had vehemently rejected the basic notion of political representation which was and continues to be the mainstay of liberal democracy.[2] He did not stop at just presenting a critique, but also offered an alternative system of governance in which popular participation would be the most dominant feature. His schemata of Panchayat Raj was based on such an understanding. Furthermore, the entire system of representation was to undergo a radical change to make people the real wielders of power. This was not just a reformative step in the popular notion of liberal democracy, but was a radical alternative to it. While deliberative democracy was clearly a delayed attempt to make democracy a little more people oriented by giving them the opportunity to participate in public discourse, it hardly challenged the centralized power of the state or the dominance of what C. Wright Mills (1956) called the power elite. In sharp contrast, Gandhi presented a system of governance in which the fulcrum of power actually remained with the people (see Joseph 2011; Pradhan and Joseph 2013: 56-69). A close examination of his Panchayat Raj system would reveal that it was not based on mere devolution of power but was rather meant to work as a foundation of people's power. In other words, it was for the people at the grassroots level to decide what power they wanted to retain and what power they wanted delegated to the higher echelons of authority. Thus, it was a bottom-up approach and not a top-down system of governance. The fact that Gandhi stood by his bottom-up approach of political process was evident even during the Gandhi–Nehru debate in 1945. In his letter to Jawaharlal Nehru dated 5 October 1945, Gandhi made it clear that he stood by his ideas enunciated in *Hind Swaraj,* in particular the system of decentralized political governance and economy. Nehru on his part did not mince words. Rather, in his letter to Gandhi dated 9 October, he rejected outright the major ideas of the latter. He asserted that the only way India could join the comity of nations with dignity was to go through the process of industrialization and concomitant urbanization. True to his words, as the first prime minister of India, he opted and implemented the Western model of parliamentary democracy and economic development. An analysis of the discourses in the Constituent Assembly makes it clear that the basic ideas and ideals of Gandhi including his much preferred *Panchayat Raj* and *Gram Swaraj* were literally ignored (see AVARD 1962). It was in the midst of the constitution-making process in India that Gandhi was assassinated on 30 January 1948. That perhaps gave still greater freedom to Nehru and his associates to go ahead with their scheme of things. But the Gandhian stream of ideas did not entirely disappear. It resurfaced in the works of Vinoba Bhave, Jayaprakash Narayan (JP) and Ram Manohar Lohia.

Vinoba Bhave concentrated more on the Constructive Programme and voluntarism, giving up of the entire concept of militant *satyagraha* as a weapon in the hands of the people to fight against injustice and inequities. He did make some mark as the leader of the Bhoodan movement but his rejection of *satyagraha* marred the revolutionary nature of the Gandhian movement under his leadership. Some of the leaders of the Congress Socialist Party (CSP) led by JP remained vehement critics of Gandhi when he was alive (see Narayan 1936). But in post-Independent India, two of its prominent leaders, viz., JP and Ram Manohar Lohia became the real torchbearers of

Gandhian ideas. JP even opted out of the socialist movement and joined hands with Vinoba to promote the cause of the Bhoodan movement and other constructive programmes. He became a *jivan dhani* to carry forward the Gandhian idea of village reconstruction. However, by the late 1960s he was thoroughly disillusioned with the Sarvodaya movement and even led a split to promote a more militant form of Gandhian ideas which Vinoba rejected. This led to the Bihar movement which had its final goal as Total Revolution.[3] The basic idea behind Total Revolution was that social change should involve much more than a mere change of regime. It had to achieve revolutionary changes in all walks of national life including political, social, economic and other fields. In the wake of this movement and Indira Gandhi losing her election case in the Allahabad High Court, came the subsequent imposition of emergency rule in the country. The movement against Emergency took such a sharp turn that Indira Gandhi was forced to revoke the Emergency and call for national elections in the early part of 1977. All these led to the installation of the Janata government. Thus, JP contributed to alternative politics in India by leading a struggle against the then existing government and placing a political alternative before the nation. It is true that there were inherent weaknesses in the coalition government that was formed after his movement and it was far removed from his ideas and expectations during the movement. JP's real contribution lay in popularizing alternative politics through his movement and writings. In a major theoretical writing, *Reconstruction of Indian Polity*, he placed before the country his basic ideas regarding alternative politics. He referred to Indian democracy as an inverted pyramid that stands on its head. The obvious task of every citizen would be to set this picture right. That would enable the pyramid to stand on its base. It would be impossible for the millions of Indian voters to participate in the government if that were to be run only from Delhi or a few capitals of the states. In order to ensure the participation of the people in government it must be brought as near to the people as possible. For achieving this goal, JP suggested an alternative system that would ensure political and economic decentralization. To realize Swaraj from below Jayaprakash Narayan (2000) advocated the Panchayat Raj system of governance. He visualized Panchayat Raj as the basis of true participatory democracy. He clearly laid down the various conditions to be fulfilled in his system of governance. He was aware of the fact that the success of political decentralization depends largely on the extent to which the country would go ahead with economic decentralization. For the transformation of the pyramid or fulfilment of democracy, he advocated the direct participation of the people in decision-making through the institution of the Gram Sabha. The structure of democracy should be built on several tiers beginning with the basic tier of the Gram Sabha going right up to the Lok Sabha with clear-cut demarcation of powers, functions, duties and resources of each tier. Higher tiers of representatives of bodies would be constituted of lower tiers in order to ensure the exercise of power from below upwards rather than from above downwards. This document took into consideration the realities prevailing at that time and presented his ideas basically from a Gandhian frame of reference. This tract was mainly a reaffirmation of the Gandhian ideas of decentralized governance. However, the Janata government which emerged as a result of JP's movement failed to materialise his dreams of participatory democracy.

Another leader who made significant contributions in the field of alternative politics was Ram Manohar Lohia. He was also one of the founders of the CSP and a freedom fighter in his own right. Despite being a leader of CSP which had a Marxist orientation, Lohia was personally quite close to the ideas and ideals of Gandhi. In the post-Independence period, it was Lohia who carried forward the Gandhian *satyagraha* both in letter and spirit. Unlike Vinoba and JP, he insisted that *satyagraha* was the most seminal contribution of Gandhi and in its absence Gandhi would just appear to be a pacifist. He led a split in the Indian Socialist movement and founded his own Socialist Party in 1956 on the major premises of Gandhian ideas. Lohia took a very critical view of liberal and social democratic traditions which were prevalent mostly in the Western world. His primary thesis was that both the liberal and democratic socialist traditions have primarily evolved based on the ground realities of Western societies. As such they failed to take into account the realities of Indian society. In one of his major formulations he tried to delineate the major characteristics of the class structure of Indian society in general and the nature of the Indian elite in particular. He asserted that any struggle for socialist democracy would be meaningless unless the elitist nature of Indian society is really understood. In his opinion, the nature of the Indian elite and Indian class structure radically differed from its European counterparts. In that part of the world, the control over the means of production presented the dividing line between the ruling classes and the common people. However, in the Indian context, apart from the institution of private property, two other factors, viz., caste and language, go a long way to make the Indian society one of its kind. Here the real elite comprise those upper strata of society which apart from controlling private property also comes from the English knowing upper castes. Therefore, neither liberal democracy nor socialism could take an effective form unless a sustained struggle was launched against all these three symbols, that is, property, caste and the English language. That was the idea behind his two major single point movements—*jati todo* (break the caste system) and *angrezi hatao* (remove English language). According to him, it was only through such movements that the roots of democracy could be deepened in the country. He not only founded his Socialist Party on such ideological grounds but also wrote extensively on these themes. Moreover, he went around the country propagating his new thesis calling for a major debate on the nature and structure of Indian society and also real ways and means for deepening democratic and socialist principles. It was such an understanding that prompted him to put forth his concept of what he called 'preferential opportunities' which resulted in the demand for 60 per cent reservation for backward classes. Whether he was admired or ridiculed for his novel formulations, he certainly contributed a great deal to the process of deliberative democracy by provoking countrywide discourses on his new concept of preferential opportunities. The idea behind the preferential treatment was that certain sections of Indian society had been forced to lag behind for centuries and hence the Western concept of equal opportunity would result in a society based on inequality and inequity.

Therefore such sections of society would have to be given preferential treatment in terms of reservations both in legislature, employment and even in educational and cultural fields.

Besides, Lohia in his own way, took forward the Gandhian ideas of decentralized polity and economy by pleading for a four-pillared state—*chaukhamba rajya*—in which the village, district, province and central government would be integrated in an organic manner in a system of functional federalism (Grover 1996: 315-34). Like Gandhi, he believed that power should remain with the people and only with their consent should higher authorities be handed over political power. He organized innumerable *satyagrahas* particularly involving the people of backward classes. It was through his movements that many people who had remained outside the political process became stakeholders in the polity of the country. His *satygrahas* were a forum for public education, popular debate and participation that changed the complexion of politics particularly in north India. He will be remembered in history as one who brought about a revolution for the backward classes and went to the extent of calling for preferential opportunities in favour of non-elitist sections of Indian society. It was in this context that he called for *sapta kranti* or seven revolutions (Grover 1996: 269-80), to remove inequalities based on gender, race and caste, and the creation of a just society. All this occurred much before the Mandal Commission came into existence. In fact, B.N. Mandal, the Chairman of the Commission was a leader of the Socialist Party led by Lohia. He went beyond what is today's deliberative democracy in the West, as his movement became a forum not only for deliberation but also for militant action. He raised several questions including 3 *annas* vs. 15 *annas* which spoke volumes for the kind of poverty and misery the Indian people were afflicted with. The moot point in the debate was whether the average daily per capita income of an Indian was 3 *annas* or 15 *annas.* Lohia insisted on its being just 3 *annas* whereas the government led by Nehru pleaded that it was 15 *annas.* Lohia was bold enough to declare in the Lok Sabha that this poor country spent as much as Rs. 25,000 a day on the security of the prime minister.[4] Leaving aside the veracity of the statistical nature of the debate, the issue itself drew millions of people into the entire process of public discourse. All these gave him an image of being a leader who really wanted the marginalized sections to participate both in deliberations and actions on issues which were of vital interest to them (Jaffrelot 2003).

The next wave in the search for alternative politics came during the first decade of the twenty-first century in the wake of globalization and liberalization which has left millions of people on the margins and given rise to various kinds of corrupt practices. It is in this context that the anti-corruption movement led by Anna Hazare, and later joined by Arvind Kejriwal and others needs to be assessed. The new movement and its leaders particularly Anna Hazare with all his sincerity, simplicity and honesty became reminiscent of the Gandhian movement of yesteryears. But Anna Hazare's demand for Jan Lokpal was within the framework of the institution of the state in which Gandhi had refused to repose his faith. Nevertheless, it did somehow touch the Gandhian chord in the hearts of the people as they rallied around Hazare and his movement. Kejriwal's defection and his founding of the Aam Aadmi Party (AAP) dealt a setback to the India Against Corruption (IAC) movement. It virtually weakened the hands of Hazare and he was forced to be satisfied with the much diluted Lokpal Bill passed by the United Progressive Alliance (UPA) government in December 2013. Meanwhile, Kejriwal with his new political formation contested the Delhi elections and made a remarkable show in political terms by winning a sizable number of assembly seats. Arvind Kejriwal, taking over the post of chief minister, and the AAP coming to power in Delhi in January 2014, was seen as a harbinger of new and alternative politics in India. He also tried to take forward some of the Gandhian ideas like *swaraj*[5] and *satyagraha.* It is to be noted that Kejriwal's *dharna,* as the chief minister, during the second half of January 2014, demanding action against police officials who refused to carry out a raid on an alleged drug and prostitution racket was not exactly in accord with Gandhian *satyagraha.* Also some of the actions taken by his ministers are certainly not Gandhian in their character. Although he could not fulfil the tall promises made to the people during the election, he changed the texture of Indian politics during his first brief tenure of 49 days, forcing other chief ministers to follow suit in certain areas. Whether or not AAP will be able to play a major role in politics in future, the fact remains that AAP has changed the political roadmap of the country and shaken the foundations of parliamentary democracy.

On the basis of above discussion, it may be concluded that Indian leaders since the days of the national movement, particularly under the leadership of Gandhi presented a more radical form of deliberative democracy. *Satyagraha* has provided a conducive and creative forum of deliberation as well as action. At times it may have crossed the moral threshold of Gandhian *satyagraha* but there is no denying the fact that in its absence, all talk of deliberative democracy and public sphere would be nothing but hollow words. *Satyagraha* has also opened up new vistas for alternative politics. The real challenge lies in the search for alternative politics through the medium of *satyagraha* which has to go on uninterruptedly without crossing the moral threshold.

NOTES

1. Henry David Thoreau, the American author and noted philosopher, wholeheartedly accepted this as his motto in his well-known essay 'On the Duty of Civil Disobedience'.
2. Gandhi wrote in *Hind Swaraj*,

> The best men are supposed to be elected by the people. The members serve without pay and therefore it must be assumed, only for the public weal. The electors are considered to be educated and therefore we should assume that they would not generally make mistakes in their choice. Such a Parliament should not need the spur of petitions or any other pressure. Its work should be so smooth that its effects would be more apparent day by day. But as a matter of fact, it is generally acknowledged that the members are hypocritical and selfish. Each thinks of his own little interest. It is fear that is the guiding motive. What is done today may be undone tomorrow. It is not possible to recall a single instance in which finality can be predicted for its work. When the greatest questions are debated its members have been seen to stretch themselves and to doze. Sometimes the members talk away until the listeners are disgusted. Carlyle has called it the 'talking shop of the world'. Members vote for their party without a thought. Their so-called discipline binds them to it. If any member, by way of exception, gives an independent vote, he is considered a renegade. If the money and the time

wasted by Parliament were entrusted to a few good men, the English nation would be occupying today a much higher platform. Parliament is simply a costly toy of the nation. These views are by no means peculiar to me. Some great English thinkers have expressed them. One of the members of that Parliament recently said that a true Christian could not become a member of it. Another said that it was a baby. And if it has remained a baby after an existence of seven hundred years, when will it outgrow its babyhood?

3. The Bihar movement was initiated by the students of Bihar in 1974 under the leadership of Jayaprakash Narayan against the misrule and corruption indulged in by the Bihar government and subsequently it turned against the government at the centre. It was also called the Total Revolution movement or JP movement. For a philosophical discussion on Total Revolution, see Narayan (2003).
4. See http://drlohia.blogspot.in.
5. Kejriwal analysed the problems of a centralized system of governance in his book *Swaraj* (2012) and placed a definite formula to empower the people. It includes the following: (a) Give people the power to 'Recall' the elected representatives; (b) Make all government officials accountable for their acts of omission and commission; (c) Decentralize power and distribute it to people at the grassroots level, on the level of Gram Sabhas and Resident Welfare Associations (RWA) in the cities; (d) Exercise the right to voice/ enforce one's opinion in the formulation of laws and policies through Gram Sabhas and RWAs (see acmumbai.org.).

REFERENCES

Association for Voluntary Agencies in Rural Development (AVARD) (1962): *Panchayat Raj as the Basis of India's Polity*, New Delhi: AVARD

Benhabib, Selya (1992): 'Models of Public Space: Hannah Arendt, the Liberal Tradition, and Jurgen Habermas', in Craig Calhoun (ed.), *Habermas and the Public Sphere*, Cambridge MA: The MIT Press: 73-98.

Bessette, Joseph M. (1997): *The Mild Voice of Reason: Deliberative Democracy and American National Government*, Chicago: University of Chicago Press.

Cohen, Joshua, *Deliberation and Democratic Legitimacy*, www.cdd.stanford.edu

Dharampal, 'Panchayatraj and India's Polity', www.multiworldindia.org.

Fishkin, James S. and Robert C. Luskin (2005): 'Experimenting with a Democratic Ideal: Deliberative Polling and Public Opinion', *Acta Politica*, 40: 284-98.

Gandhi, M.K. (1930): *Hind Swaraj or Indian Home Rule*, Ahmedabad: Navajivan.

Grover, Verinder (ed.) (1996): *Rammanohar Lohia*, New Delhi: Deep and Deep.

Gutmann, Amy and Dennis Thompson (2004): *Why Deliberative Democracy*, Princeton: Princeton University Press.

Habermas, Jürgen (1991): *The Structural Transformation of the Public Sphere: An Inquiry into a Category of Bourgeois Society*, Cambridge MA: The MIT Press.

Jaffrelot, Christophe (2003): *India's Silent Revolution: The Rise of the Lower Castes in North India*, New York: Columbia University Press.

Joseph, Siby K. (2011): 'Swaraj and Governance', in Siby K. Joseph and Bharat Mahodaya (eds.), *Reflections on Hind Swaraj*, Wardha: Institute of Gandhian Studies and Carcassonne: Gandhi International.

Kejriwal, Arvind (2012): *Swaraj*, New Delhi: Harper India.

Mala, Rousiley C.M., 'Deliberative Democracy and Public Sphere Typology', www.ec.ubi.pt.

Mills, C. Wright (1956): *The Power Elite*, London: Oxford University Press.

Narayan, Jayaprakash (1936): *Why Socialism?* Benares: All India Congress Socialist Party.

—— (2000): *Swaraj for the People*, Varanasi: Sarva Seva Sangh.

—— (2003): *Total Revolution*, Varanasi: Sarva Seva Sangh.

Pradhan, Ram Chandra and Siby K. Joseph (2013): 'Panchayat Raj and Gandhi's Vision of Governance', *Dialogue*, 15(2), October-December: 56-69.

Sirianni, Carmen and Lewis Friedland, *Deliberative Democracy*, http://www.cpn.org.

Thoreau, Henry David (2008): *On the Duty of Civil Disobedience*, Radford, VA: Wilder.

CHAPTER 4

Indian Democracy in a Changing World: A Case of Civil Society Intervention

K.M. SAJAD IBRAHIM

With the advance of globalization, the theory and practice of democracy has undergone certain transformation, particularly in the countries of the Third World. Given their historical, socio-economic and political circumstances, this transformation was not universal in nature, nor was a complete emulation of Western democracy considered to be a practical or ideal alternative. In the case of India, for the past several years, democracy has been submerged with numerous problems and challenges including corruption scandals, human rights violations, the partial withdrawal of the state, and so on. It is in this context that several new social movements, often powerful, with strong popular support made their presence in the Indian polity.

How one evaluates civil society activism, arguably depends on what one expects of democracy. Is democracy only about providing the essentials of living a life that we recognize as distinctively human, such as having adequate income, food, shelter, education and health? Or is democracy about something more than that, such as, empowering ordinary citizens to speak back to a history which is not of their making? And do contemporary forms of civil society activism promote this end as well? There are several questions related to the recent civil society intervention in Indian democracy, including the birth of the Aam Aadmi Party. This article attempts to address the recent phenomenon of civil society intervention in Indian politics.

The most important objectives of civil society movements in India are to fight against corruption and to confront human rights violations, besides addressing issues of poverty, disease, illiteracy, homelessness and environmental degradation, which continue to stalk the lives of millions of citizens. While it is undoubtedly true that political parties are in a crisis of credibility, the political class and their institutions cannot be faulted for all the existing problems, despite the fact that even civil society groups that have joined the ranks of the political class have consistently attacked them.

TRAJECTORIES OF INDIAN DEMOCRACY

Indian democracy has been witness to more threats internally rather than externally. However, Indian political leaders tend to use external threats such as cross-border terrorism, Pakistan's involvement in terrorist strikes, etc., as being more serious. Yet, internal issues are deep rooted, posing a serious threat to India's democratic polity. Two broad issues are important in this respect. One is the magnitude of the corruption scandals which have made deep wounds in the Indian economy, while the other is the gross violation of human rights, such as the violence against minorities, communalism, atrocities against women and children, terrorist strikes, etc.

It can be argued that India has made impressive progress since Independence in 1947. Food grains production has increased manifold and the nation has been self-reliant in food for over several decades. The average life span increased from thirty-two years to about sixty years during the last fifty years. However, these accomplishments fall far short of India's potential. Illiteracy and functional illiteracy still persist, accounting for a major proportion of illiterates in the world. Preventable diseases are still soaring as immunization coverage is inadequate. A large number of the people lack basic sanitation facilities and do not have access to clean water. India's share in the world's total output of goods and services, as well as its share in international trade has decreased, while population growth has seen a multifold increase over recent decades. The truth is that while India did achieve some measurable progress, the rest of the world has moved forward more rapidly, leaving it behind.

An impartial and efficient judiciary has an important role in strengthening democracy. The legal system in India has sound institutional foundations, which incorporates basic democratic principles such as impartiality, secularism, and equality before the law. In practice, however, its functioning is, in many ways, at variance with democratic goals. An important concern is that the legal system is virtually paralysed by a backlog of thousands of 'pending cases'. Throughout India, the government has to a certain extent failed to fulfil its social commitment by failing to hold its bureaucrats and politicians accountable for unlawful activities while simultaneously failing to uphold collective promises. These dual poles give rise to what can best be described as oligopolies of violence, as citizens turn away from the government to actors perceived to be providing more effective services.

India faces an unprecedented number of corruption challenges that are as much moral as economic and political in their nature. Since July 1991 India embarked on the path of globalization and liberalization which brought about a number of changes in its social, political, economic and even administrative systems, all of which had an important bearing on the nature and dynamics of the culture of corruption in India. At the social level, globalization brought about rapid change in the value system and thought processes of the people. It gradually transformed Indian culture and created a neoliberal dream especially amongst the Indian middle class. Through privatization and disinvestment, globalization and liberalization threw up newer avenues for corruption in India, which were unheard of or inconceivable thirty years ago. Fresh cases of corruption erupt at frequent intervals, and the central government has been forced to devote much of its time to defend its stand.

The Comptroller and Auditor General (CAG) of India, in a report tabled before parliament, revealed that the Indian exchequer may have lost as much as US $39 billion because of a flawed 2G spectrum auction. Unfortunately, the telecommunications scandal is not the only one that haunts the Indian political scene. A host of other scandals—ranging from dubious and inflated contracts for the Commonwealth Games held in 2010 to corporate influence peddling for favourable news reports, to retired military personnel caught in questionable but lucrative real estate deals—are wracking the land. In fact, this web of scandals, have deeply damaged India's democracy and it could lead to a loss of public faith in the country's democratic political institutions (Ganguly 2011). Nevertheless, there is a greater degree of civic vigilance in India today, which has been made possible by the electronic media and the press. Whether it is the 2G spectrum scam or the Commonwealth Games scam, the media has brought the scandals to the attention of the public.

Other cases include the systematic looting of mineral resources in southern and eastern India by Indian corporations and foreign multinationals that has driven thousands of tribal people away from their traditional lands. Massive profits and continuous scandals involving corrupt officials are buttressed with despair amongst those living in the mining areas. Thousands of villagers are displaced annually for mining projects, with the vast majority unable to reclaim their previous living standards (Miklian 2011). Mining companies encourage the suppression of anti-mining activism by the state. Various reports point out that a number of journalists and workers from non-governmental organizations have been harassed or even killed for reporting on illegal mining activities. Local government actors often labelled those who resisted mining displacement as Maoists; as such, a large insurgency force has been active in many parts of central India (Bhattacharyya 2010).

The number of people displaced from ostensible 'development' projects over the last sixty years was estimated at 60 million, only a third of whom have been resettled. Moreover, most of the displaced were the rural poor, marginal farmers, fisher-folk; 20 per cent were Dalits and 40 per cent were tribals/Adivasis, who continue to face severe displacement threats. Resettlement, where provided, is on the peripheries of cities/towns with inadequate housing or access to civic services, livelihood, natural resources, health care and education. Acquired land is seldom replaced with alternative land of commensurate or better quality. Another side of the picture is that around 13 to 18 million families in rural India are landless; 8 million of them lack homes of their own. The Indira Awas Yojana rural housing scheme does not benefit the poorest. Less than 2 per cent of women hold land titles. Land reform measures lack implementation and the desired impact (UN 2011).

Social unrest and protests deepened in resource-rich areas of central and eastern India, where rapid economic growth has been accompanied by rapidly growing inequality. Mining and infrastructure projects threaten widespread displacement of forest-dwelling tribal communities. Central Indian states like Chhattisgarh, Andhra Pradesh, Jharkhand, Orissa and West Bengal are home to impoverished communities of indigenous peoples (Adivasis). The corporate acquisition and privatization of land, mineral and other resources primarily affect the already marginalized Adivasis. As a result there has been a resurgence of strong resistance movements including both popular protests as well as Maoist ('Naxalite') insurgencies (UN 2011).

One immediate impact of the change ushered by globalization was the steep decline in the political culture of India. Politics has become more competitive in nature, marking the end of one-party dominance and initiating the era of coalition politics and minority governments, often leading to political uncertainty and instability. The compulsion of facing the electorate more often and various other factors, have resulted in political parties often indulging in corruption. Money collected through corrupt means is allegedly used to fund elections, build patronage based support or to bribe opposition Members of Parliament at times of political crises. The compulsions of coalition politics have also forced the government to fulfil the often unjustified demands of regional political parties, contributing to the systematic looting of government treasuries and the rapid decline in ethical standards of important public offices. As far as economic matters are concerned, the deregulatory reforms have given business both a new status inside the public-policy process and unprecedented influence with the powerful Planning Commission. The post-liberalization era has been a boon for India's entrepreneurs, since the state systematically started to disinvest its public investments in 1991 (Drache 2012).

The National Rural Health Mission was launched with a view to ameliorate availability and access to quality health care facility for the rural poor. Growing privatization of health care has, however, led to gross disparities in service distribution between the rich and the poor, and rural and urban areas. The growing disregard of primary health centres and the inability to introduce 'compulsory licensing'—particularly for essential and life saving drugs—is disturbing. The only means of addressing serious illnesses is through health insurance, available to less than 15 per cent of the population.

The persistent human rights violations across the country also present manifold challenges. Major human rights violations include reports of extra-judicial killings of persons in custody, killings of protesters, and torture and rape by police and other security forces. Investigations into individual abuses and legal punishment for perpetrators do take place, but for many abuses, a lack of accountability due to weak law enforcement, lack of trained police, an overburdened judiciary, and lengthy court backlogs prolong the trials and create an atmosphere of impunity. Poor prison conditions and lengthy detentions are other significant problems.

Custodial killings and police abuse, including torture and failure to implement policies to protect vulnerable communities, continue to damage India's record of human rights. Impunity for abuses committed by the security forces also continues particularly in Jammu & Kashmir, the north-east, and areas facing Maoist insurgency. New state controls over foreign funding of non-governmental organizations (NGOs) have led to restrictions on legitimate efforts to protect human rights. However, killings by the Border Security Force on the Indo-Bangladesh border decreased dramatically (UK Border Agency 2012).

Thousands of Kashmiris have allegedly disappeared during the conflict in the region, their whereabouts unknown. A police investigation in 2011 by the Jammu & Kashmir State Human Rights Commission found 2,730 bodies dumped into unmarked graves at 38 sites. At least 574 were identified as the bodies of local Kashmiris. The government had previously stated that the graves were of unidentified militants, most of them Pakistanis whose bodies had been handed over to village authorities for burial. Many Kashmiris strongly believe that some graves include the bodies of victims of enforced disappearances (Human Rights Watch 2011).

Maoist insurgents, also known as Naxalites, who are active in ten states, claim to fight for the rights of the marginalized tribal, Dalit, and landless communities. Governance has often been defective in regions where the Maoists have found popular support. Due to corruption and illegal mining, the revenue available for public services and infrastructure in many of the areas has been severely limited. Maoist forces continue their operations by killings and extortion, and targeting government schools and hospitals for attacks and bombings. Human rights activists seeking accountability for abuses such as arbitrary arrests, torture and other ill-treatment, and killings have been threatened by both Naxalite forces as well as security agencies (Choudshary 2013).

A number of progressive legal and policy initiatives have been taken by the central government to address the challenges of human rights violations. However, the lack of implementation of these measures, due to bureaucratic inertia, lack of adequate allocation of resources, contradiction between economic policies, 'development priorities' and national and international human rights commitments, continue to act as obstacles to the realization of human rights for India's most vulnerable.

CIVIL SOCIETY INTERVENTION

Good governance and civil society participation occupies a central space in development discourses today. Civil society participation has been repeatedly highlighted as a precondition for good governance. In fact, a broad spectrum of development interventions across the world has further stressed the need for greater civil society participation. However, it is found that in the absence of synergic capacity building of both state institutions as well as civil society actors, at least in the case of India, an empowered civil society is not reciprocated automatically by the state vis-à-vis their expectations (Roy 2008).

The civil society—good governance experience in India emerged from the local forest protection committees in tribal-majority regions (Chopra 2002; D'Silva and Pai 2003) in the face of direct conflicts of interests between tribal communities and the government that permitted private corporations to exploit forest produce, while restricting those communities from accessing the same resources and often displacing them from their natural habitat. The social and political landscape of the country being divided along various lines, devising a model wherein all such interventions with popular participation can be included is not an easy task. Civil society, therefore, reflects in its response, reaction and interaction with government actors, the economic and social situation that prevails in a given context.

The neoliberal reforms prescribed by the International Monetary Fund (IMF) and the World Bank which have had adverse consequences in the Third World have also affected India where the partial withdrawal of the state has led to a more active civil society. Due to their preference to work with NGOs, the presence of international aid organizations have added further to this development. It is apparent that the partial failure of the state to address social and economic needs has had its impact not only on the levels of development, but also on the quality and character of civil society. In a sense, this failure has compelled groups and individuals to engage with civil society, but the inability to provide basic education and other forms of social services has seriously hampered the development of civil society. As a consequence, various aid agencies in India have utilized the competence and infrastructure of civil society in order to encourage social development. NGOs such as women's organizations have been incorporated in the governmental development plans. This, of course, compromises the independence of these NGOs and strictly speaking they do not qualify as NGOs after accepting governmental support. But this form of cooptation, as well as the general trend of state withdrawal, also has important consequences for future plans of social development. While the state is often seen as inefficient and corrupt, the NGOs are viewed as committed and accountable. Leaving the negative description of the state aside, the positive image of civil society in India today rests more on ideological and theoretical definitions rather than an accurate appraisal.

In a large developing country like India, there are numerous gaps left by the government in the development process—sometimes by intention, sometimes due to lack of funds, sometimes due to lack of awareness. These are the gaps that many NGOs try to fit into. Due to the inherent social, religious, ethnic and economic cleavages of Indian society, civil society is permeated by inequality and various forms of conflict. The expectations of efficiency, commitment and accountability of civil society should also be seen in this light, as various forms of inequality are likely to influence it. A more realistic perspective would be to define Indian civil society as a public arena in which various interests encounter and compete, battling not only the state, but also other groups within civil society. This arena would also be influenced by the power relations in society, reproducing various cleavages and inequalities (Singh 2012).

With over six decades of democracy as well as consistent economic growth during the last decade, India is looked upon as a model for developing democracies. Yet, India continues to suffer from democratic deficits, such as poor transparency and accountability of government institutions, lack of autonomy for local bodies, non-availability of avenues for participation of citizens in policy making and policy implementation, etc. This brings to attention the need for reinventing or reforming democracy, so that citizens have more space to participate in the decision-making process. What is required in this context is civic action to mobilize the government to undertake reforms for deepening democracy.

The numbers relating to corruptions that were exposed during 2011-12 angered the approximately 250 million strong middle class in India. India Against Corruption (IAC), along with Team Anna, emerged at the opportune moment and as soon as the call for protest was made, people came out in large numbers in big cities. In Delhi, this group represented on the one hand unemployed youth and college students, and on the other hand well to do professionals—doctors, engineers, lawyers and technocrats. Hyderabad, an emerging software hub witnessed the participation of youth, middle class, women's associations, social activists and followers of Mahatma Gandhi. Azad Ground, the heart of Mumbai, the financial nerve centre of India, swelled with support from old and young, men and women, professionals and students. Intelligentsia, social movement leaders and film actors also joined in the protests and made their presence felt in the movement.

Scams like the Commonwealth Games scam, Adarsh Housing scam, and the 2G Spectrum scandal brought about a second wave of the anti-corruption movement led by Anna Hazare. The 2011 anti-corruption movement led to a series of demonstrations and protests across India aimed at establishing strong legislation and enforcement against endemic political corruption. The movement gained momentum since 5 April 2011, when Anna Hazare started his hunger strike at Jantar Mantar in New Delhi. The chief legislative objective of the movement was to alleviate corruption in the Indian government through the Jan Lokpal Bill.

Within a short span of time, the movement was able to receive widespread support from the masses, through demonstrations, hunger strikes, marches and rallies, as well as the use of social media to organize, communicate, and raise awareness. After a series of consultations and studies, the leaders of the IAC initiative prepared a draft Jan Lokpal Bill which proposed strong, efficient and politically independent institutions, the Lokpal and the Lokayuktas for the investigation of corruption charges against public officials and politicians. The bill also provided for a time-bound redress grievance cell and speedy investigation of corruption cases. However, the government, after reaching a consensus with the opposition parties presented their own Lokpal Bill. With pressure from the Anna Hazare Team, the government made necessary modifications in the Bill relating to its accountability to political leaders including the prime minister. Finally after eight unsuccessful attempts over the last five decades, India on 18 December 2013, took the historic step of enacting the Lokpal law which brought out an anti-corruption watchdog, including within its purview, the office of the prime minister (*Times of India*, 18 December 2013).

According to the National Council for Applied Economic Research, India's middle class was almost 160 million in 2011 and was likely to rise up to 267 million in a period of five years (*Economic Times*, 6 February 2011). Many of the participants in this movement who may not have voted even once, were compelled to come out onto the streets to voice their collective dissent against corruption. The foot soldiers of the Anna Hazare movement were educated, urbane and belonged to the middle class. Even in the age of globalization, this movement was able to fire the idealism of the growing middle class of twenty-first century India. Unlike the Jayaprakash Narayan movement of the 1970s which used techniques like mass struggle, propaganda, and organization, this movement used Twitter updates, SMS campaigns, candlelight vigils and media management to garner support amongst the educated, technosavvy Indian middle classes. The earlier anti-corruption movement launched by Jayaprakash Narayan did not challenge the state system. It was a more inward-looking movement which focused on the need for reforming the individual first and then society, which reflects the collective consciousness of the individual and lastly the state system. However, the Anna Hazare movement was primarily directed at reforming the state.

Although a developing country with a strong presence of political parties, the people of India were not adequately aware about their rights. Moreover, a weak civil society existed in the country since Independence. Given this background, this movement was noteworthy in the sense that it aimed to discuss a political issue which had a relevant social value, with apolitical methods. Earlier such civil society movements mainly focused on environmental or social issues with varying degrees of success. Therefore, Anna Hazare's effort in the history of civil society movements in post-Independent India struck a departure from the traditional path and moved into a new phase. His movement symbolized a landmark in the history of civil society in the country as it attracted the attention of the people in a big way and ended with some success. This movement added a new chapter in Indian democracy, projecting the strength of direct intervention of people in public affairs, if the situation so warranted.

At the turn of the twenty-first century, civil society organizations in India came together in a number of campaigns, each of which had a very specific focus: assuring the provision of social goods to the citizens of India. It has estimated that India's growth rate will quickly outstrip the growth rate of the other projected major power, China. Yet poverty, disease, malnutrition, illiteracy, and homelessness continue to stalk the lives of millions of citizens. It is this particular contradiction that has been foregrounded by civil society campaigns since the late 1990s (Chandhoke 2007).

CONCLUSION

Most civil society movements in India were concerned with human rights violations until the Anna Hazare movement took the initiative against corruption. Its slogans being very close to the hearts of the ordinary people of India, it became a popular civil society movement in the country. It was able to make an impact on the government, which led to the enactment of legislation based on their demands. Now the question is whether a civil society movement can represent the majority opinion of the people, ignoring the role of parliament. In a democratic framework, the direct answer should be in the negative. No civil society movement can represent a substitute to parliament, because it represents only a section of the people. Moreover, in the Indian context, civil society has its own limitations, as a sizeable section of the population is illiterate and ignorant about their rights and duties. Hence, there is every possibility of the movement being misused for narrow political and social objectives. If civil society dictates terms to parliament, it could result in a dangerous situation of creating an extra-constitutional body. As such, civil society movements should be prevented from assuming the role of a legislature itself. However, it is equally important to be aware of the reasons for the emergence of such civil society movements. In this context, political parties of the country are to be blamed for the degeneration of democratic values, with people having lost their faith in political leaders/parties due to their involvement in corruption and the resultant sidelining of the development process.

In the present context, while India needs civil society intervention, this should not be allowed to emerge as the dominant agent of democracy, dictating terms to parliament, but its intervention should be able to challenge the degeneration of political parties. A compromise between civil society and political parties is likely to produce an improved democracy. When political parties develop narrow loyalties, and distance themselves from ordinary people, civil society groups try to overcome the situation by forming their own political parties. The birth of the Aam Aadmi Party needs to be viewed in this context. In fact, the people voted AAP into power in the 2015 Delhi State Assembly elections, not based on any ideology, but with the hope that this party would be able to fulfil their expectations. However, AAP as a party has had to face many internal crises like any other political party and the lack of a proper framework of a political party may affect its overall performance. The AAP experience can therefore be seen as an experiment in the Indian democratic system, and as such the question remains as to whether much can be expected from a civil society movement turned political party.

REFERENCES

Bhattacharyya, Sambit and Roland Holder (2010): 'Natural Resources, Democracy and Corruption', *European Economic Review*, 54(4), August: 608-21.

Chandhoke, Neera (2007): 'Engaging with Civil Society: The Democratic Perspective', *NGPA Working Paper Series*, 2, 13 July, www.lse.ac.uk.

Chopra, K. (2002): 'Social Capital and Development Processes: Role of Formal and Informal Institutions', *Economic and Political Weekly*, 37(28): 2911-16.

Choudshary, Saroj (2013): 'The Struggle of Mankind: Human Rights and its Future Perspective,' *International Journal of Research Pedagogy and Technology in Education and Movement Sciences* (*IJEMS*), 2(2), December, www.ijems.net.

D'Silva, Emmanuel and Sudha Pai (2003): 'Social Capital and Collective Action: Development Outcomes in Forest Protection and Watershed Development', *Economic and Political Weekly*, 38(14): 1404-15.

Debroy, Bibek (2000): *In the Dock: Absurdities of Indian Law*, New Delhi: Konark.

Drache, Daniel (2012): 'India: The Most Fragile of Democracies', *Canada Watch*, Winter, cited in www.robarts.info.yorku.ca.

Ganguly, Sumit (2011): 'Corruption Eating at India's Democracy', *East Asia Forum*, 13 May, www.eastasiaforum.org.

Human Rights Watch (2011): *India: Investigate Unmarked Graves in Jammu and Kashmir*, www.hrw.org.

Kohli, Atul (2001): *The Success of India's Democracy*, Cambridge: Cambridge University Press.

Miklian, Jason (2011): 'Revolutionary Conflict in Federations: The Indian Case', *Conflict, Security and Development*, 11(1): 25-53.

Roy, Indrajit (2008): 'Civil Society and Good Governance: (Re-)Conceptualizing the Interface', *World Development*, 36(4): 677-705.

Singh, Vijender (2012): 'An Analysis of the Concept and Role of Civil Society in Contemporary India', *Global Journal of Human Social Science*, 12(7), April: 69-77.

UK Border Agency (2012): *India: Country of Origin Information (COI) Report*, www.gov.uk.

United Nations (2011): *Human Rights in India: An Overview, Joint Stakeholders' Report*, New Delhi: WGHR.

CHAPTER 5

Rights of the Urban Poor in Delhi and Deliberative Democracy: Understanding the Aam Aadmi Party Experience

M.V. BIJULAL

The political victory of the Aam Aadmi Party (AAP) in the Delhi Assembly elections, at the time of an unprecedented political supremacy of the Bharatiya Janata Party (BJP), the incumbent ruling party of India, indicates a significant political situation. This situation is based on a long-term political process of direct civil action in Delhi. Initially, the visible process of this civil action was the interrogation of governance mechanisms through informed public initiatives and counter corruption activities. The civil actions that preceded the formation and prominence of the AAP as a political party were pioneered by urban political actors of a petite-bourgeois character.[1] One of the departures that this movement had from the past was that it encoded a democratic culture through the ways in which the leaders related to the common people. This paper is an attempt to illustrate the connection between the AAP and the contemporary civil protest continuity for the rights of the marginalized people in Delhi, where most of the prominent leaders of the AAP are active. In this context it highlights the deliberative process in the party's decision-making particularly with regard to the protection of the rights of the urban poor, focusing on its urban slum rehabilitation policy.

One of the pioneering campaigns by the people who later became important functionaries of the AAP was the campaign against the privatization of the water distribution network in Delhi. This drastic and unconsulted governance change raised threats to both the urban poor as well as a majority of the people who depended on the state for water at an affordable price. The campaign against the privatization of water was a confluence site for the interests of different urban economic and social classes. On a larger level, the campaign as well as the information and insights that it communicated on the negative economic and social impact of water privatization in Delhi, has arguably helped stall such experiments being repeated in other cities of the country. It also provided an opportunity for the marginalized people across the state to become aware of the fact that they have 'rights to have rights'. It is also important to connect the AAP to the right to information campaign, both before as well as after the passage of the Right to Information Act, particularly in the areas of the city where large numbers of common people lived. Such civil actions were the key to the wide and continuing support for the party. In a sense, it gained the support of the poor people of the city as well as those who lived in lower-middle class locations by capitalizing on the decades-long latent and visible protests for the rights to livelihood, residency and political representation.

The AAP has an interesting linguistic twist attached to its name, which itself is a departure from the usual ways in which the names of political parties symbolized their allegiance to the common people. The 'people', usually referred to in Hindi as *janata*, was an important component in the names of political parties, especially after the 1970s. The AAP used the term *aam aadmi*, which in the first instance is a counter expression of the term *khas* which broadly means special/privileged. It is also important to revisit the term *aam aadmi* in the context of the party's relation to the roles assumed by its leadership and the urban political cultural change mediated through their political actions. Delhi's political culture as located in the relationship of leaders to the common people was quite reflective of a patrimonial structure with the submission of an ordinary (*aam*) person's will to that of the local political leader, who was the locally visible agent of a highly hierarchical political party system. The role of the *aam aadmi* was to become, or continue to remain, a pawn to ensure support in elections. With nearly 300 urban villages and hundreds of unauthorized/semi-authorized colonies as well as slums, Delhi represents a hybrid populace with a majority of the slum dwellers being swept out of discussions. On the other hand, the omnipresence of a powerful minority dominates all narrations. This has also been the case with the prevalent common thinking on Delhi in other parts of the country.[2] Histories of the denial of the right to livelihood to the marginalized majority have always remained concealed. The political scene was dominated by the dependence of the *aam aadmi* or servile associations on the agents of power in every locality.[3] This relationship has kept the socially and economically marginalized people voiceless, relegating a majority of the citizens of Delhi into political invisibility. The AAP challenged the historically entrenched political domination of the Indian National Congress (INC) and later the BJP, which had displaced the INC from power in a convincing manner in the 1990s. The AAP's challenge to both the dominant political parties needs to be understood in the context of the larger social change which was manifested through urban civil action that displaced the engineering of power relationships by powerful local agents.

It is pertinent in this context, to use the 'lens of technologies of government' as Das and Walton (2015) posit. This is the larger context in which the urban poor leadership operates, based on their acquired abilities through long-term interaction with those who manage the technologies, mainly the bureaucrats. For Das and Walton the operational skills of the new urban leaders differentiates them in a substantive manner from their rural counterparts, who are broadly incapable of using the means of technical control to register their status as people of systemic knowledge. This is a prerequisite for the effective realization of the rights of the poor, which are essential for their survival, from the perspective of bio-politics.

It is quite evident that the AAP provided scope for the accommodation of people from all social and economic backgrounds. The role of women in the political process was also a major aspect of positive difference from other political parties. The governmental measures which evolved as the result of a dialogical process between communities of urban marginalities and the political network of functionaries of the AAP at the lower level can also be illustrated.[4] It is pertinent to focus on the governance strategies of the AAP government for a definite understanding of the larger anchoring of the party and the government on principles of social justice and livelihood rights. The slum rehabilitation policy of the government is a specific case in point.

As indicated earlier, the political parties which had earlier won the electoral support of the majority of the urban poor did not show any kind of interest in improving their options for livelihood or security of life. It is an unseen public fact that hundreds of people living in temporary shelters died due to extreme weather conditions or diseases. One can establish that such deaths were primarily due to the misuse of systemic power, with an alibi of procedural delays. The fact of the matter is that the legal and policy environment on building shelters for victims of slum demolitions are still dominated by inhuman sanctions. Permission from the relevant authority is denied in most cases. For instance, the Jahangirpuri H Block was demolished without any prior information or consent, or even any temporary relief measures. Consequently, around 250 persons of different age groups succumbed to early death due to the callousness of the administration.[5] According to various sources, the number of people living in the slums and unauthorized colonies would account for 60-70 per cent of the total population of Delhi.

In December 2014, the government of Delhi introduced a Bill, with a comprehensive coverage for ensuring security of tenure for people living in slum settlements. This Bill was introduced with a vision to formulate an inclusive policy for the protection and maintenance of the livelihood security of the socially and economically backward sections of people in the capital city. The activities of the Delhi Urban Shelter Improvement Board (DUSIB), which was revamped in December 2015, indicate some well-imagined policies, addressing an immediate redressal of the decades-long worries of the marginalized people of the city.[6] The DUSIB, previously known as the Delhi JJ and Slum Cluster Board, had a record of ignoring the demands of victims of slum demolitions over the last three decades. Through the 2014 Bill, the DUSIB adopted a new cut-off date for legal eligibility for any person to be recognized as a slum dweller with rights of rehabilitation. Incidentally this date was 14 February 2014, the day the AAP assumed power in Delhi. The date of cut-off for eligibility in Delhi is part of a larger politics since 1990 when the then Prime Minster V.P. Singh declared a cut-off date after his visit to one of the settlements in Kalkaji, South Delhi. The cut-off date of the AAP government was in a way a major step towards recognising the constitutional rights of persons as Indian citizens, which is quite intelligible in the context of the interpretation of Article 21 by the Indian judiciary.[7] People having any proof of identity, prior to 2015 were eligible for the right to rehabilitation and improvement of facilities. Those whose names were in the voters list between 2012 and 2014 were also eligible, if they resided in any slum cluster.

A peculiar situation relating to the ownership of the lands where slums are located in Delhi has also given rise to a specific problem in this context. A classic case is the Shakur Basti railway colony demolition in 2015, where the railways 'cleared' the land, leaving people homeless and unattended. While representing for the victims of demolition, the state government argued that although the land belongs to a central government agency, the onus of relief and resettlement is on the state government. Hence, the agency has the legal obligation to inform the state government so as to provide the latter sufficient time for addressing the requirements for relief and rehabilitation. The position of the state government was accepted by the Court while hearing the Public Interest Litigation, *Ajay Maken* vs. *Indian Railways.* The court ordered that any demolition where the state government has a systemic role in post-demolition relief and rehabilitation activities needs to be communicated to and be done after the state government is prepared to face such eventualities. This incident also led to invoking a moratorium on demolitions.

While the Shakur Basti case occurred at a site where the jurisdiction of the state government was minimal, a great change in urban governance practices occurred after the promulgation of the Bill, which prescribed the eligibility for resettlement to be proof of residence till 2015. One has to keep in mind that the benefits of such a change in policy had an immediate effect on thousands of families living in 675 slum clusters, which came directly under the authority of the state government. This model is a fundamental departure from the anti-poor orientation of the urban land policy till then. It had temporal and procedural factors as constant irritants, and denied land rights to the people who were building and maintaining the city.[8]

It is interesting to note that the incumbent state government followed a rehabilitation model which was in practice till the early 1970s and was later abandoned. This plan, the *in situ* purgation, was aimed at arranging better housing and public facilities at the site of slum clusters to the maximum possible, or to relocate the slums to within a 4 km distance from the original sites, with a major objective of guaranteeing employment and social rights. The Delhi government had five ongoing pilot projects of *in situ* upgradation in different parts of the state. Two other models were environment clearance and relocation. As any casual observation of the resettlement process in Delhi during the last four decades would suggest, the relocation of slums to distant undeveloped and uninhabitable locations was a major practice. As a result, the lands where the slums earlier stood in the city were used for beautification or other purposes. Such a trade-off in land use is, by any humane standards, lower in priority than the right to ownership of tenure and shelter of urban poor. However, avoiding constitutional responsibilities, insensitive administrations and political leaderships had been promoting the land use change which largely helped the needs of the wealthy classes in the city. This prevailed over the rights of basic life and livelihood of the urban poor.

The change in the activities of the DUSIB is to be particularly noted in this context. According to Bipin Rai, one of the nominated members of the Board (as expert on slums and shelters), it was the first time ever that nominated members became part of the everyday activities of the Board. According to Rai, by setting up new people-friendly rehabilitation benchmarks, the 2015 Bill was a public policy instrument that evolved out of dialogues at several levels. Having seen how the previous models of rehabilitation were prioritized against the fundamental and human rights of the people living in slums, it could be very well assumed that the new slum rehabilitation policy of the state of Delhi was a major change. It ensured a measurable difference in the lives of the people by incorporating important human rights principles relating to resettlement after demolitions. It is in the background of such policies, which are still absent in the Indian rural or urban scenario that the turn in governance in urban slum rehabilitation in Delhi needs to be understood.

What has taken place in Delhi is an outcome of a deliberative process in decision-making, to protect the constitutionally endowed rights of the urban poor, who are rather dispossessed. This reflects the active role of an authority, here in the form of a state initiative, together with the substantial participation of civil actors. One can see that the urgent and inalienable rights for the survival of the urban poor has been restored through a governmental initiative, a move which although possible, had till then been constantly displaced from the agenda of governments in power in Delhi. Here, as Warren (1996) argues, the authority occupies a positive role, in contrast to the commonplace arguments that locate the agency in a negative sense. It is evident that in the case of Delhi, civil discourses on the moral admissibility of urban reform, witnessed an urban, poor oriented turn. In a wider sense, as argued by Cortina (2010: 157), deliberation has emerged as 'a normative ideal and as a test of democratic legitimacy'. It is in this context that the act of determining and executing the priorities of marginal peoples through interventions at the state level in Delhi merits special attention.

NOTES

1. Civil society initiatives in critiquing and countering several serious anti-poor designs in the development processes in Delhi had been on the rise since the 1990s. People's collectives against emergency during the late 1970s and slum dwellers movements under the auspices of the former Prime Minister V.P. Singh's Jan Chetna Manch during the 1990s represent two such instances of differences that challenged the authoritarian systems of dominance in political power. Coalitions of people's movements, representatives of civil society groups including independent activists and

non-governmental organizations (NGOs) were at the forefront in questioning the demolition of slums for the beautification of the city, and the violation of the right to shelter and housing of the majority living in so-called illegal/unauthorized clusters. It should be noted that political opposition towards brutalizing ordinary citizens were at the core of civil protests in urban Delhi. A petite-bourgeois character could be assigned to such movements since they were organized and directed mostly by educated and politically unattached social/public activists with a broader agenda of social change.

2. It is interesting to see that in narratives of Delhi, from tourist guide narrations to the common talk of the so-called well-educated economic migrant, there exists an image of affluence, as well as a sense of pride of the past and present, with a significant omission of the lives of the common people. This is uncritically disseminated even through different media.
3. The managing power of the dominant party, especially in the context of the emergency related, anti-poor urban demolitions and various other atrocities on them reveal this. According to personal narrations from the people of Jahangirpuri slums clusters, which the author had collected during 2005-6, political leaders like H.K.L. Bhagat used armed groups—belonging to urban poor categories—to suppress any form of resistance from the local population. In another sense, the omnipresence of this repressive mechanism is the structural equivalent of the oppressive rural social order based on feudal political technologies and caste based dominations.
4. Such inclusive practices were evident in the first election campaign of the AAP. For the first time ever, it was the AAP campaigners who visited the four colonies of the leprosy-affected people during their first Assembly election campaign. The author would like to acknowledge Kabir Elizabeth Ramakrishnan for his inputs in this regard.
5. Telephonic interview with Mr. Mukesh, previously a resident of the Jahangirpuri H Block on 12 October 2015.
6. See www.delhishelterboard.in.
7. The right to rehabilitation of people living on the streets was instructed as a constitutional duty of the executive by the judiciary in the *Olga Tellis and Others* vs. *Bombay Municipal Corporation and Others, 1985* (see www.indiankanoon.org).
8. A different perspective on the urban poor, focusing on the purpose of their everyday work and life is articulated by Indu Prakash Singh, who uses the expression 'city makers' for the urban poor instead of other institutionally tendered identities (see www.gcssfs.org).

REFERENCES

Cortina, Adela (2010): 'Communicative Democracy: A Version of Deliberative', *Archiv fuer Rechts- und Sozialphilosphie*, 96(2): 133-50.

Das, Veena and Michael Walton (2015): 'Political Leadership and the Urban Poor: Local Histories', *Current Anthropology*, 56(11), October: 44-54.

Delhi Urban Shelter Improvement Board, www.delhishelterboard.in

Supreme Court of India, *Olga Tellis and Others* vs. *Bombay Municipal Corporation* in www.indiankanoon.org/doc/709776.

The Global Centre for the Study of Sustainable Futures and Spirituality, www.gcssfs.org/indu-prakash-singh.html.

Warren, Mark E. (1996): 'Deliberative Democracy and Authority', *The American Political Science Review*, 90(1), March: 46-60.

CHAPTER 6

Mainstream and Indian Perspectives on Decentralization, Participation and Democracy

JOHN S. MOOLAKKATTU
AND
JOS CHATHUKULAM

INTRODUCTION

Decentralization has a long history. Political thinkers from Montesquieu to Madison suggest that decentralized governance can contribute to democratic participation, better representation, accountability and policy and governmental effectiveness. It is also seen as a means to moderate potential conflict between people who are ethnically and culturally different from majority groups. Several philosophic traditions have enunciated decentralization principles. The anarchist tradition is a case in point. Women's and new social movements and those belonging to the Gandhian tradition have all been known for their advocacy of decentralization. Most of the modern Indian nationalist thinkers were also not in favour of a strong centralized post-independent state.

Decentralization is a theme discussed in relation to a wide range of related subjects like public sector reform, democracy, political reform, participation, empowerment, rural development, fiscal and economic development, accountability, and capacity building (Smoke 2003). Although it has been described as 'one of the fashions of our time' (Manor 2006: 283), there is still a lack of clarity about its exact meaning. Words like 'transfer', 'spreading out', 'dispersion', 'diffusion', 'moving', 'placing', 'shifting', 'devolution', or 'delegation' are commonly used in the vocabulary of decentralization. The reason why decentralization came to be a much talked about subject stems partly from the fact that it has been adopted by people belonging to different political persuasions across the left-right divide. Bardhan (2002: 185) tells us that this includes free-market economists who 'tend to emphasize the benefits of reducing the power of the overextended or predatory state' to social thinkers who are 'both anti-market and anti-centralized state', advocating 'assignment of control to local self-governing communities'. Thus decentralization is a 'fluid and flexible discourse that can be utilized by different ideological interests' (Mohan and Stokke 2000: 250). While the discourse on decentralization evolved in the rest of the world in the context of the reform of public administration or for making development and governance participatory and close to the people, Mahatma Gandhi's advocacy of a decentralized order provided an additional source of legitimacy for such initiatives in India and a certain degree of sentimentality in that sense. A philosophical anarchist, Gandhi had faith in the vitality of the decentralized panchayat system as an alternative to the Western parliamentary system. It represented an indigenous way of organizing government in a least coercive way. Apart from performing civic functions, Panchayats were to have a key economic function of acting as a facilitator to address the basic needs of the people as well as resolving disputes peacefully. He was criticized for his lack of sociological understanding of the Indian villages. This was one reason why Dr. B.R. Ambedkar was opposed to the Panchayat system. He thought that any political arrangement built upon the village as the basic unit is bound to be disastrous for the depressed classes since caste oppression is the greatest at that level. In other words, it is only through centralized intervention that the upper caste landlords could be kept at bay. The same logic seems to have influenced Balwant Rai Mehta to give a pre-eminent position to the District Panchayat rather than smaller spatial levels like the Village Panchayat in his report (John 2007).

New public management and good governance streams also added to the impetus on decentralization For example, Osborne and Gaebler (1993: 251) who, in their well-known work *Reinventing Government*, place it as follows: 'In today's world things simply work better if those working in public organizations—schools, public housing developments, parks, training programmes—have the authority to make many of their own decisions.' But the focus of new public management was more on improving governmental effectiveness in terms of better service delivery for which decentralization was one of the means. That is not the case with good governance, which could be seen either as subsuming new public management or is implied in new public management. Decentralization has also been propped up by international agencies, including donor organizations, which may explicitly link aid to political reforms such as decentralization in some cases. Such externally induced decentralization schemes are also not so uncommon.

Decentralization is expected to bring the process of decision-making closer to the people. In that way it contributes to democratic deepening (Gaventa 2006). Decentralization reforms can spur the generation of new spaces for the development of civil society and the expansion of the citizenship idea (Avritzer 2002). This will lead to the deepening and thickening of democracy at the local level, empowerment of local leaders and mobilization and participation of the formerly excluded classes.

DECENTRALIZATION TYPOLOGIES

Samoff (1990: 519) states that in order to make sense of the different forms of decentralization and their results in particular contexts it is necessary to understand it as 'a political initiative, as a fundamentally political process, and consequently as a site for political struggle'. For long, the classification of Rondinelli and Nellis (1986: 6-10), who identified four major types of decentralization, have come to rule the roost. They are deconcentration, delegation, devolution, and privatization. Deconcentration amounted to a form of administrative dispersion of central offices to the regions. Delegation is 'the transfer of managerial responsibility for specifically defined functions to organizations outside the regular bureaucratic structure' without losing oversight by the central authority. It is an ad hoc arrangement and the central governments do not normally interfere with the functioning of these organizations, thereby giving them some measure of autonomy. Devolution implies the formation of elected local government with the necessary statutory mandate and autonomy to operate without being unduly controlled by the central authority. Privatization, though does not imply inter-governmental transfer, means the handing over of some of the governmental functions to private and voluntary organizations. Collins and Green (1994) have reservations about the inclusion of privatization. For them decentralization effectively transfers powers, functions and finance to the regions, and not mere transfer from the public sector to the private sector as happens in privatization. Echoing the same sentiments, Balogun (2000: 155) explains:

> While private sector participation in development is now accepted as a reality and a desirable option, privatisation raises questions that are radically different from those of decentralisation. For one thing, privatisation targets allocation efficiency and does not share decentralisation's concern for equity through the redistribution of power. For another, the former focuses on the contribution of a narrow circle of economic actors (investors, entrepreneurs, and individuals with access to capital or information), whereas the primary objective of decentralisation is the dispersal of economic and political power in such a way that the mass of the people have a sense of participating in decisions affecting their life and well being. Third, once the state surrenders the ownership and management of an enterprise, it (the enterprise) ceases to be part of the 'public business' for which government ministers are individually or collectively responsible. In any case, by no stretch of the imagination can privatisation be equated with mass participation in development, or regarded as a major landmark in political decentralisation.

This leaves us with three major forms: deconcentration, delegation, and devolution (Rondinelli 1999; Parker 1995). Deconcentration does not involve any transfer of authority to lower tiers of government (Litvack et al. 1998: 4) and is therefore the weakest of all forms. Delegation transfers responsibility to local governments or to semi-autonomous organizations that are not subjected to day-to-day control by a higher tier, but are answerable to it since in the ultimate analysis, the real power vests with it. Devolution is reflective of genuine decentralization in that it provides the most direct link with democracy, ensures popular participation, and seeks to achieve empowerment of the local citizenry (John and Chathukulam 2003).

Participation and decentralization are considered to have a complementary relationship in that a good decentralization scheme requires participation of some kind to ensure that the local government is responsive to local needs. Likewise decentralization can throw up greater space for participation by bringing governments closer to the people at a level at which the costs of participation are considerably less. Hence, participation is seen both as a means to and as a goal of (successful) democratic decentralization (Litvack and Seddon 1999: 17).

The following decentralization typology (Table 6.1) captures the diverse ways by which schemes of decentralization have been understood by scholars.

According to Musgrave (1959), the utility of the public sector is to be measured in terms of its efficiency in the allocation of resources, income redistribution and macroeconomic stability. Conventional understanding in public economics was that the first of these functions is suitable for local governments and the rest by the central government. Added to that is the fact that decentralization can generate regional inequalities. Local government can achieve efficient allocation of resources by being more sensitive to and knowledgeable about the needs and preferences of the local citizenry (Oates 1972). Particularly in the West where household mobility is quite common, people tend to settle down in the jurisdiction of those local governments that can provide for public services competitively. Further, decentralization may encourage experimentation and innovation, enabling good practices worthy of replication to emerge. According to Francis and James (2003: 326) the benefits of decentralization include 'improved efficiency of public service provision, more appropriate services, better governance, and the empowerment of local citizens'.

It may be noted that issues of social justice and inclusion have been less salient in decentralization initiatives other than in India where the issue of caste and more recently gender have been matters of serious governance concerns. Most decentralization schemes are urban-based as opposed to the largely rural-based decentralization in India. Decentralization schemes are often limited to some regions or cities within a country rather than embracing the country as a

TABLE 6.1: DECENTRALIZATION TYPOLOGIES

Typology	Reference
Economic (industrial, regional economic planning), Administrative (administrative/ internal, administrative/spatial, administrative/functional), Political (legislative, corporate, millennial)	Furniss (1974)
Administrative, Political	Porter and Olsen (1976)
Vertical vs. Horizontal, Selective vs. Parallel	Mintzberg (1980)
Deconcentration, Delegation, Devolution, Privatization	Rondinelli et al. (1983)
Inter-governmental/Political, Management	Devas (1997)
Fiscal, Political, Administrative	Litvack et al. (1998)
Functional, Territorial	Bray (1999)
Political, Spatial, Market, Administrative	Cohen and Peterson (1999)
Decentralization by Default, Privatisation, Deconcentration, Fiscal Decentralisation, Devolution	Manor (1999)
Structural, Decision, Resource, Electoral, Institutional [Treisman (2002): vertical, decision-making, appointment, electoral, fiscal, personnel]	Treisman (2000)
Political Decentralization, Administrative Decentralization, Administrative Deconcentration	Benz (2002)
Fiscal, Institutional (local and inter-governmental), Political	Smoke (2003)
Big Push vs. Small Steps, Bottom Up vs. Top Down, Uniform vs. Asymmetric	Shah and Thompson (2004)
Administrative, Fiscal, Political	Falleti (2005)
Political/Administrative, Internal/External, Non-competitive/Competitive, Basis of Division (territory/function/process/ target group)	Pollitt (2005)

Source: Dubois and Fattore, 2009: 710.

whole within its framework. As in any other country, decentralization, particularly devolution, serves as a means of citizen education and democracy as well as incorporation of citizen input into the local level planning processes. There are arguments that tend to suggest that decentralization should not take place before the necessary capacity is created. This is a 'chicken and egg' type argument according to Conyers (1990) as the need for building capacity emerges only if there is strong commitment to decentralization.

The current appeal of decentralization has been rooted in its potential benefits rather than any sentimentality. The benefits include: political education; training in political leadership; political stability; political equality; accountability; responsiveness; improved decision-making and inter-organizational coordination; and the promotion of competition among local governments (Smith 1985: 18-30). Political education teaches people about political debate, the selection of representatives, and the nature of policies, plans, and budgets in a democracy. Training in political leadership is oriented towards the development of skills in policy making, political party operations, and budgeting, leading to the gradual progression of local politicians as national politicians. Political stability is secured by engagement in formal politics, which strengthens trust in government so that 'social harmony, community spirit and political stability' are achieved. Decentralization also creates a mechanism to prepare the masses for the profound social and economic changes associated with development. Political equality results from more broad-based political participation which reduces the possibility of concentration of power. Since power is diffused, it can give voice to the poor and marginalized as well. Accountability improves as local representatives are constantly in touch with the people and can be held responsible for their policies and actions. Voting in elections to local bodies becomes a mechanism to register their approval or disapproval of the representative's performance. Since local representatives know the needs of the local people better, they tend to be more responsive and make an effort to meet them in a cost-effective way. Better decision-making and inter-organizational coordination take place since responsibilities and powers are clearly defined and distributed between central and local institutions. The promotion of competition is achieved when supply and demand-side benefits derive from institutional pluralism, which in turn leads to economic efficiency (Smith 1985: 30-7). These benefits are captured by another commentator in terms of three grand values: political values; governance values; and efficiency values (Wolman 1990: 30).

Given the fact that all decentralization schemes are varied and contextual, there is no automaticity about the benefits accruing from them. Instead, decentralization may engender certain problems such as the intensification of forces of secession and ethnic identities, political instability, elite capture of power, inter-regional income disparities, and macro-economic instability caused by budget deficits, local government fiscal recklessness, and local government indebtedness (Turner and Hulme 1997: 158; Prud'homme 1995). Whether these disadvantages are inherent flaws of decentralization or whether other factors are involved is a moot point.

Although the specific form that decentralization takes varies considerably across countries, some of the problems are of a similar kind. They include fiscal controls imposed by central governments on local governments, lack of accountability and autonomy, lack of qualified staff, weak institutional capacity, a lack of strategic deployment of decentralization policies, lack of coordination and conflicts between central and local government, poor incentives for local government performance and so on (Rondinelli 1990: 49-54; Smoke and Lewis 1996: 1290; Manor 2001). These problems have led many to doubt the value of decentralization. Some have advocated centralization on the grounds of its potential benefits (Prud'homme 1995).

There is no consensus about what should be done to implement decentralization policies successfully. Some theorists, based on field experience, argue that the benefits of decentralization are contingent on factors like strong enabling legal frameworks, political will, the allocation of substantial resources to local governments, high degree of central state capacity, well-developed civil society, free press, robust multi-party system, long experience with democracy, and high adult literacy (Rondinelli et al. 1989: 77-8; Crook and Manor 1998: 83-4; Manor 2001; Heller 2001: 138-9).

The challenge for all governments is to strike a balance between centralization and decentralization tendencies that does justice to the claims made by enthusiasts on both sides. How to do so, however, is a question with which most governments continue to grapple. A strong central government is also important in ensuring equity among local districts. According to the World Bank, inter-jurisdictional equity comes from the willingness of the central state to engage in redistribution among regions.

Larry Schroeder and Paul Smoke (2002: 38-9) point out that decentralizing political and economic powers to local institutions requires 'fundamental changes in attitudes about the way that the public sector works'; changing bureaucrats' monopoly over decision-making and control of local authorities; educating local communities about how to hold their authorities accountable for their actions; educating local communities about the importance of paying taxes for the services they need; and inculcating a culture of democracy. Undertaking all these tasks simultaneously can be quite daunting. For most countries carrying out decentralization reforms, the challenge may stem either from the inability to devise a political and economic mechanism to master the complexity entailed in the implementation of such policies or from a deliberate unwillingness on the part of the higher level political elites to share political power with local institutions. In some instances, more decentralization may mean overloading local institutions, while more centralization may mean less power sharing.

The centripetal forces pull power and authority towards the centre of the system, while the centrifugal forces push power and authority towards the system's subunits. Centrifugal forces can disintegrate a system, but at the same time these forces can increase access from the local to the central level, and can thereby contribute to decentralization. The classical model of federalism, in fact, is based on the federal government and the constituent units. Local government was not in the picture and was just a matter of concern for the constituent units of federation alone since such concerns fell in the exclusive jurisdiction of such units. The US federal constitution, the oldest, does not mention local government at all. The very existence of a federal structure is a significant step toward decentralization in one sense, although it is perfectly possible for units that had some kind of autonomous existence to decide to form a federation rather than be the result of such a federal arrangement. Federal states are by definition devolved, though the powers devolved by the federal government to lower level governmental units can be quite limited. When a local government system is also incorporated into a federal system, what we see is a system of multi-level governance with the local government at the bottom. The growing understanding of the need to govern and solve problems at various territorial spheres and by multi-level governmental institutions is reflective of three processes that have come into vogue in modern times: globalization, urbanization, and the shift from government to governance.

Romeo (2003: 92) points out that politically motivated decentralization undertaken by central governments may be underpinned by motives which include: 'extending the influence of the dominant political party by creating a new layer of local political personnel or countering political threats to the centre from ethnically based opposition forces by breaking their regional base into multiple jurisdictions'.

THEORY OF DECENTRALIZATION: THE IDEA OF SUBSIDIARITY

Modern decentralization tends to use subsidiarity as the organizing principle of decentralization. The principle of subsidiarity has its origin in Catholic social thought (Henkel 2002). Pope Pius XI's encyclical letter, *Quadragesimo Anno*, of 1931, provides a definition of subsidiarity which is even now widely cited. In that document, he says:

> It is indeed true, as history clearly proves that owing to the change in social conditions, much that was formerly done by small bodies can nowadays be accomplished only by large corporations. Nonetheless, just as it is wrong to withdraw from the individual and commit to the community at large what private enterprise and industry can accomplish, so, too, it is an injustice, a grave evil and a disturbance of right order for a larger and higher organisation to arrogate to itself functions which can be performed efficiently by smaller

and lower bodies. This is a fundamental principle of social philosophy, unshaken and unchangeable, and it retains its full truth today. (cited in Henkel 2002: 364)

Subsidiarity is synonymous with sphere sovereignty and does not normally envisage a hierarchical structure in which local bodies are placed at the bottom of the governmental ladder. Instead it works like a partnership in which different rungs of government work symbiotically in order to enhance citizen participation and effective delivery of services. The deciding factor from the point of view of subsidiarity is whether a particular function can be performed at a level closest to the intended beneficiaries without affecting efficiency.

From a political perspective, decentralization is considered a key strategy for promoting good governance, greater pluralism, accountability, transparency, citizen participation and development (Crook 1994: 340). Administratively, decentralization is an important process that allows decongestion of the central government and reduces the workload to manageable proportions. The theoretical argument for fiscal decentralization can be traced back to Madison and Rousseau, in the eighteenth century (Wolman 1990), though they had different reasons for supporting decentralization. Though decentralization is not specifically mentioned in *The Federalist*, No. 39, Madison held that the people must be given the mandate to elect their leaders as a way of 'composing the distinct and independent States to which they respectively belong' (*The Federalist* 1937: 246). Rousseau also favoured small government. To him, 'rulers overburdened with business, see nothing for themselves: clerks govern'. According to Wolman (1990), small democratic (local) governments reflected the genuine aspirations of the people, as most of them tended to distrust the activities of the central government. In India, the notion of subsidiarity is largely made applicable with respect to the development functions of local government leaving out the regulatory functions. E.M. Sankaran Namboodiripad, the former chief minister of Kerala, was an ardent advocate of a radical form of decentralization which brought within its ambit not only development functions, but also regulatory functions such as revenue and police, as can be seen in his dissenting note to the Asoka Mehta Committee Report, 1978.

DECENTRALIZATION AND ALLOCATIVE EFFICIENCY

Decentralization, despite the benefits claimed by its supporters, can lead to greater regional disparities, promote instability, and undermine overall efficiency by creating more rent-seeking opportunities at the local level (Prud'homme 1995). But there is no conclusive evidence about corruption in all settings. There are in fact conflicting claims about these. For example Fisman and Gatti (2002: 325) found that fiscal decentralization 'is strongly and significantly associated with lower corruption'. This contrasts with the study made by Fan, Lin and Treisman (2009: 32-3), which concluded: 'In countries with a larger number of administrative or governmental tiers, reported bribery was both more frequent and more costly to firms. . . . The more tiers of government and the more local personnel with pockets to fill, the greater the danger that the rent of office will be "overgrazed".'

The argument runs that if natural resources are managed at the local level, by communities or local government, then they will be looked after better, and more efficiently, resulting in improved opportunities for sustainable livelihoods. Systems of accountability are more effective and transparent as a result, and local leadership can make effective demands on the central state. Such decentralized arrangements thus allow more community participation and therefore the voices of the people are more likely to be heard in policy decisions.

Agrawal and Ribot's (1999) 'actors, powers, and accountability' approach to empirically characterize decentralization is common. In India, the categories are functions, functionaries and finance. In this approach, researchers first focus on which actors are receiving new powers, what those powers are, and the kinds of accountability relations in which those actors are located. The domain of local discretion is important since it is the domain of freedom around which democratic local government, citizenship, and civil society can form and develop. Even if elected, local authorities who do not hold discretionary powers are not worth the name. Elite capture and upward accountability can compromise the effectiveness of representation and service delivery. The failure of the central government to empower elected local authorities also undermines their effectiveness and legitimacy. Local authorities need discretion over meaningful matters in order to serve the population.

One area of concern for local governments that has come into being as a result of a robust legal framework is how to accommodate customary authorities where they continue to hold sway over the community. Under some conditions, customary authorities can pose a threat to the development of local democratic government and to effective decentralization by remaining as a parallel power centre. In other places, they often act as intermediaries between the local councillors and people. The challenge is to come up with schemes of decentralization that draw on the strengths and wisdom of traditional authorities while reinforcing and legitimating modern local government institutions and processes.

PARTICIPATORY DEVELOPMENT

Traditionally, periodic elections alone were seen as the means of ensuring citizen participation and accountability. Elected representatives took decisions behind closed doors. This has been found inadequate at a time when there is a wide recognition that local elections that are infrequent need to be supplemented by avenues for direct citizen engagement in decision-making, and this can help forge accountability. The presence of an effective mechanism of downward accountability presupposes the existence of a vibrant civil society. But if the participatory budgeting experience of Brazil is to be taken into consideration, conflict can emerge between the legitimacy of the elected members vis-à-vis the citizens who have elected them. This suggests that care has to be exercised to ensure that participatory processes do not undermine the representation of the elected representatives on whom alone responsibility can be pinned.

Participatory development received a boost with the publication of the works of Robert Chambers (1983; 1997), an expert on participatory methods based in the Institute of Development Studies, Sussex, who critiqued conventional development practice for their lack of participation and insisted on the ability of the local and illiterate people to gather data, analyse it and make observations about their life situation, which could serve as the basis for addressing their needs. Unlike the earlier methods like Rapid Rural Appraisal (RRA) where the researcher often collected information from the public for his/her own use, in Participatory Rural Appraisal (PRA), the information collection itself is a quick, cheap and participatory process involving the local people who also get empowered to act on the basis of the information. More recently, some have referred to these approaches as Participatory Learning and Action and Participatory Action Research.

In comparing RRA and PRA, Chambers (1997) noted that although RRA does draw on people's local knowledge, the collection of data is done by outsiders for the purpose of taking away this knowledge and applying it to plans, publications, and projects developed by people outside the local community. Although PRA also seeks to discover local knowledge by engaging with local people, its purpose is to draw on people's wisdom in ways that strengthen their capabilities and empower them to take local, self-willed, community-led action; to use their own skills to monitor and evaluate the action they take; and to build locally owned institutions that can become self-sustaining. Participatory methods also create the potential for developing new and lasting democratic institutions. The application of PRA requires a change of mindset. Community practitioners must renounce their 'expert' role to become co-learners with community members, believing in and developing the capacity of the ordinary people to take charge of their lives.

FROM PARTICIPATORY DEMOCRACY TO DELIBERATIVE DEMOCRACY

The most definitive account of participatory democracy in modern times from the angle of political science was provided by Carole Pateman (1970). Her account drew on the political thought of Mill, Rousseau and G.D.H. Cole. She concluded that active participation is a means of citizen's self-empowerment and makes them experience a sense of political potency. She, however, extended this notion beyond the governmental level so as to embrace other forums like work place democracy as in the former Yugoslavia. While Pateman spoke about extending participation from the governmental sector to other arenas, Macpherson (1977: 108) stated that even within the governmental sector itself, democracy needs to deepen in several sites. He called for a 'pyramidal system with direct democracy at the base and delegate democracy at every level above that'. According to him, as the base of the pyramid is direct democracy with a provision for recall of the delegates at the higher levels, it is possible to exercise control over the representatives by the citizenry, although he is fully aware of the debilitating effects of social and economic inequalities in achieving such a democracy.

Shifting the centre of the citizenship idea from one focused on state-citizen relations to a pluralist model (Young 1990) has led to new definitions of the concept such as participatory citizenship, inclusive citizenship (Gaventa 2002; Kabeer 2002), active citizenship (Lister 1997), and citizenship from below or 'insurgent citizenship' (Holston 1998). Seen in this way practices of citizenship extend beyond 'taking up invitations to participate' or 'invited' spaces of citizenship to creating 'own opportunities and terms of engagement' reflecting greater agency (Cornwall 2002: 50). Miraftab (2004) has referred to it as 'invented' spaces of citizenship, suggesting including both invited and invented spaces of citizenship. This idea has resemblances with the type of subjectivity with which people participate. One can distinguish between people's participation with a focus on formally ensuring that a certain number of people are present regardless of whether they have the right subjectivity informing their participation. The distinction between engineered participation and citizen participation (John and Chathukulam 2007) is useful here.

Participatory democracy declined due to its utopianism and its failure to confront the complexity, size and scale of advanced industrial societies. The assumption that people are enthusiastic and capable of participating in arenas of governance closest to them is quite naive and does not adequately take into consideration factors like the burden or cost of participation (Warren 1996). Dryzek (2000: 1) says:

> Deliberation as a social process is distinguished from other kinds of communication in that deliberators are amenable to changing their judgements, preferences, and views during the course of their interactions, which involve persuasion, rather than coercion, manipulation, or deception. The essence of democracy itself is now widely taken to be deliberation, as opposed to voting, interest aggregation, constitutional rights, or even self-government.

Although deliberation is a constitutive element of democracy, it is only recently that it has been brought to the centrestage of the democratic discourse. The ideas of Habermas (1989) on civil society and public sphere have contributed considerably to this new focus. More particularly, the value of deliberation has been underlined by his idea that individual preferences can be changed through active interaction including patient attention to the voices of others. This penchant for deliberative democracy reflects dissatisfaction with liberal political theory, particularly the interest aggregation model of politics.

The theme of decentralization through a network of communities was echoed by political philosophers like Charles Taylor. He thought that devolution based on the principle of subsidiarity can be good for democratic empowerment inasmuch as it will help citizens to identify with the political community. The creation of inclusive communities is the concern of a host of scholars (Tam 1998; Taylor 1990). Market individualism and authoritarianism are to be replaced by enlightened individualism and pluralism in such inclusive communities. In this way, active citizenship and democratic power relations can be made to thrive, and a sense of mutual responsibility can be developed. A participatory exercise should lead to dialogical action and in a dialogue, the participants see and act

> unencumbered by any corrective device, any conditioning, any pre-conceived image of one another, or any fear or design of any kind. Otherwise no one really relates to one another, and the dialogue is transformed either into a multi-monologue, a sheer waste of time and energy or into an opportunity for some to manipulate others with greater subtlety. (Rahnema 1990: 206)

Deliberative democracy is a form of participatory democracy formulated by a host of writers coming mainly from the Western countries. Shapiro (2003), in fact thinks that participatory democracy can be subsumed under deliberative democracy. Despite this, participatory democracy continues to have its sway globally, particularly in the non-Western world. Deliberative democracy represents a form of democracy where issues are discussed and consensus achieved through the 'force of the better argument', as Habermas says. Influenced by the post-modernist dislike for consensus, we now have agonistic forms of democracy which see agonism as opposed to antagonism as the very stuff of politics (Mouffe 2000). Deliberative democracy, although having several strands, has a number of common defining features. According to Jeffrey D. Hilmer (2010: 51):

> . . . deliberative democratic theorists emphasise rational public deliberation among free and equal citizens about matters of common concern. The goal of deliberation is to come to an understanding of what is in the best interest of those deliberating—the common good or in Rousseau's famous terminology the 'general will' of the community. Ideally, the process of deliberation transforms private preferences into public claims that pass or fail the test of public assessment. Of equal importance, the deliberative process is understood to legitimate subsequent policies. Thus much of deliberative democratic theory focuses on the mode of participation—that is deliberation among citizens.

The moot point as Pateman (1970: 136) says is 'how do we reconcile the demands of deliberative and participatory democracy?' Mutz (2006) states that participation may undermine deliberation and vice versa. Deliberation that requires expression of differing views with friends and associates in face to face settings would prevent many people from partaking in such forums, thereby undermining participation as such.

According to Stoker (2006: 150-1):

> Arguments for more participation too often reek of a sort of moral conviction about how citizens should conduct themselves and engage in the world. . . . Insisting that people are something they are not can also lead to desperately unrealistic expectations. There are practical arguments against participation, given the cognitive limitations and difficulties faced by citizens, and complexity

and dilemmas of the modern political process. More participation is not always the right or even the viable option.

Fung and Wright (2001: 7) spoke about 'Empowered Deliberative Democracy' that seeks to build democracy and participation in the capabilities of the ordinary people and enable them to translate what they deliberate into specific actions for their betterment. Cases of democratic decentralization that satisfy their criterion include the Kerala experiment in participatory planning, and participatory budgeting in Porto Alegre in Brazil. In other cases, marginalized groups were able to claim political space and achieve outcomes beneficial for them, contrary to the traditional appropriation of such decisions by landed interests. In such cases the manner of defining citizenship entails the ability to assert one's rights and expand the political space for such assertion. The transformation of individuals from subjects, clients and beneficiaries to citizens capable of engaging in decision-making is what is meant here (Stewart 1995).

A number of thinkers concerned with theories of political renewal and the invigoration of the public sphere have advocated a radical form of democracy. Commentators like Chantal Mouffe and William Connolly have highlighted the political and democratic implications of diversity and value pluralism in communities. Unlike mainstream notions of community built around a broad consensus, radical democracy does not see the need to forge consensus out of difference. Instead it argues that social diversity gives rise to incommensurable value pluralism, which in turn may generate conflict and dissent leading to the expansion of political debate reflective of the diverse interests that communities represent.

Decentralization in India has been guided by mixed motives. Apart from providing the local populace some control over local affairs by attempting to make the local bodies self-governing institutions, the 73rd Constitutional Amendment sought to achieve goals that local governments in other countries have not contemplated. Social justice has been one of the key goals of decentralization in India. Apart from providing representation to the excluded groups, it is seen as a key agency for local economic development through local planning. How these contradictory goals have brought ambiguity and a lack of direction in the decentralization process is a matter that needs investigation.

One development associated with decentralization is to go beyond the putting in place of elected representatives and take recourse to mini publics like the Gram Sabha and neighbourhood groups. In some countries like the UK, this has been known as 'double devolution'. This is aimed at democratic renewal suggesting 'a rethinking of the role of local authorities and particularly councillors, which has at its root consideration the interaction of representatives and more 'direct' democracy at local level. Here the representative is re-cast as facilitator, moving 'towards a job that is more proactive and community focused than the current role' (Barnett 2011: 279). While this sounds great as an idea, operationalizing this concept has been found wanting. Can the Gram Sabha be considered as a deliberative forum? Gram Sabhas in India are not spaces where reasoned debate takes place. Instead, the participants tend to adopt a beneficiary orientation, demanding public goods from the panchayat rather than partaking in the process of allocating them by asserting their citizenhood (Rao and Sanyal 2009; Moolakkattu 2005). What the people engage in is a type of 'discursive competition' comparable to a court room where the goal is to influence the judges rather than decide through deliberation (Rao and Sanyal 2009: 35). Gandhi also had reservations on the ability of an amorphous body like the Gram Sabha to perform a deliberative role in local governance. He continued to repose faith in the panchayat, which of course could be disbanded by the people when it fails to perform its mandated tasks (John 2007). Early commentators on panchayat raj in India also thought it unwise to strengthen the Gram Sabha at the expense of the Gram Panchayat. For example, Henry Maddick (1970: 79) stated:

> . . . the existing public attitude to the Gram Sabha hardly warrants extension of more statutory powers to it at the expense of the Gram Panchayat. The growth of Gram Sabha as an active, articulate body, with a further subdivision of responsibilities for executive functions at the lowest level would be detrimental to effective and efficient administration.

The same opinion was voiced by the Diwakar Committee which

made the first study on the status of the Gram Sabha (Government of India 1963). They all agree that a committee between the panchayat and the Gram Sabha is a more useful means to factor in deliberation.

NGOs, CBOs AND SHGs IN LOCAL GOVERNANCE

With the shift from the narrow notion of government to governance, several actors have been drawn into the process of governance. Along with this shift, it is widely recognized that civil society organizations can play an important role to make local governance more transparent, participatory and accountable. Non-governmental organizations (NGOs) that constitute an integral part of civil society have been actively engaged in working with local institutions to achieve useful synergies. Over the past two decades, the number and types of NGOs have expanded greatly, and they have played an ever-increasing role in grassroots mobilization, service delivery, and policy-making. The space of NGOs expanded as many governments are being restructured. The revival of democracy especially of the participatory kind has made it necessary for NGOs and local governments to redefine their roles and look for new forms of collaboration (Meyer 1999: 18). NGOs also act as intermediaries, providing links between governments, donors, other NGOs, and local communities. NGOs have an important role to play in strengthening the capacity of local bodies. Many NGOs have skilled personnel and wealth of experience which could be made available to the local governments. The NGO approach to capacity development and training will be different from the conventional governmental approach and is likely to go beyond the rigidities that characterize the latter. The NGOs as well as community-based organizations (CBOs) can play a mediating function to conscientise and empower citizenry and also engage in advocacy on their behalf. But in all these, one has to accord primacy to the local elected representatives even as pressures are brought to bear on them to take people-friendly decisions.

Another area of interest for decentralization watchers in some parts of the world, especially in places like Kerala, is the organization of a large number of self-help groups (SHGs) of relatively poor women, centred around each local body with support and partial funding by the state government. This is in contrast to most areas where the SHGs function independently. The working of the Kudumbasree Mission in the state in partnership with local bodies has been found to serve a number of functions. Not only do these women derive monetary assistance for their various income-generating projects, particularly under the Women Component Programme, the Panchayat linked SHG women have also been identified as a useful conduit for the effective implementation of centrally sponsored schemes like the National Rural Employment Guarantee Scheme and for ensuring a minimum level of participation in the Gram Sabha. The SHGs thus provide a support structure to the panchayat even as they derive economic benefits from it.

SECOND GENERATION GOVERNANCE

Local government is seen as the institutional reflection of webs of relations, the framework within which interaction can take place, and as a consensus builder, building links across disparate networks (Healey 1997). Ideas of 'metagovernance' and 'second generation' theorizing on governance draw on deliberative and inter-subjective approaches (Sorensen 2005). Here local politicians have a 'meta-governance' role in constructing and influencing local networks (Sorensen and Torfing 2009). 'Metagovernance' 'involves the organization of the conditions for governance in its broadest sense' (Jessop 2003: 107). For Jessop and others, it represents the ways in which the state has 'modified and reconfigured its presentation and operation to adapt to changes in the politico-social environment' (Kelly 2006: 607), and is essentially concerned with changing 'technologies' of state power. Others have seen it more in terms of the negotiation of a set of values, norms and principles designed to facilitate interactive governance and societal learning—'governing how to govern' (Kooiman and Jentoft 2009: 823), and fundamental values of respect, equity and inclusion are proposed. However, actors in the network are seldom accountable to elected local governments or represent the populace in the strict sense (Bogason 2004; Johanson 2006). In as much as it allows the possibility of non-elected actors entering the political sphere, it is a matter of concern as well (Andersen 2004).

CONCLUSION

Decentralization has become a new *mantra* not only in the public sector, but also in large organizations, including the corporate sector. This chapter has dealt with some of the theoretical aspects of this process. The manner and the goals of decentralization reforms in different parts of the world vary. This makes comparisons to measure the degree of decentralization difficult. Supporters of decentralization who tend to emphasize its political spinoffs are less concerned about questions of allocative efficiency. Those initiatives focused on allocation efficiency in turn are less concerned about whether decentralization leads to genuine democratization. The question of decentralization as a mechanism to dispense with social justice is an additional factor to be considered, particularly in contexts like India. This is one of the unique goals of decentralization unlike in the rest of the world due to historical and sociological reasons. Ultimately, the success of decentralization will depend on achieving a balance among these seemingly contradictory roles. The current trend is to make decentralization more participatory and deliberative by extending it beyond the realm of the level of representatives to an appropriate level so as to reflect some nascent form of direct democracy. While this is generally seen as a welcome development, its potential to undermine the legitimacy of elected representatives should also be taken seriously. What matters most is the degree of political commitment that the higher level political leadership, particularly the dominant parties, have towards effective devolution, given the lack of pressure from the grassroots for realizing it. CBOs and NGOs can play a role in generating such pressures from below as well as play an advocacy and capacity-building role in support of the structures that have been created in the wake of decentralization reforms.

Although decentralization in India is based on the framework provided by the 73rd and 74th amendments to the Constitution, the extent to which devolution has actually taken place varies depending on the willingness of the individual states to do so. The relative power of each tier in the three-tier panchayat system also varies from state to state, so also the relations among the three tiers. The centrally sponsored schemes and grants from the Central Finance Commissions constitute a significant source of income particularly in states that are wary of devolving more funds to the local bodies. The example of Kerala shows that, even states that have lagged behind in decentralization, can make rapid strides and emerge as frontrunners if the political will to decentralize powers is present.

REFERENCES

Agrawal, Arun and Jesse Ribot (1999): 'Accountability in Decentralization: A Framework with South Asian and West African Cases', *The Journal of Developing Areas*, 33(4): 473-502.

Andersen, Ole Johan (2004): 'Public–private Partnerships: Organisational Hybrids as Channels for Local Mobilisation and Participation?', *Scandinavian Political Studies*, 27(1): 1-21.

Avritzer, Leonardo (2002): *Democracy and the Public Space in Latin America*, Princeton: Princeton University Press.

Balogun, M. J. (2000): 'The Scope for Popular Participation in Decentralization, Community Governance, and Development: Towards a New Paradigm of Centre-Periphery Relations', *Regional Development Dialogue*, 21(1), Spring: 153-73.

Bardhan, Pranab (2002): 'Decentralization of Governance and Development', *Journal of Economic Perspectives*, 16(4): 185-205.

Barnett, Neil (2011): 'Local Government at the Nexus?', *Local Government Studies*, 37(3): 275-90.

Bogason, Peter (2004): 'Local Democratic Governance: Allocative, Integrative or Deliberative?', in Peter Bogason, Hugh T. Miller and Sandra Kensen (eds.), *Tampering with Tradition: The Unrealized Authority of Democratic Agency*, Lanham, MD: Lexington Books: 23-39.

Bray, Mark (1999): 'Control of Education: Issues and Tensions', in R.F. Arnove and C.A. Torres (eds.), *Comparative Education: The Dialectic of the Global and the Local*, Lanham, MD: Rowman and Littlefield.

Chambers, Robert (1983): *Rural Development: Putting the Last First*, London: Intermediate Technology Publications.

—— (1997): *Whose Reality Counts? Putting the First Last*, London: Intermediate Technology Publications.

Cohen, John M. and Stephen B. Peterson (1999): *Administrative Decentralization: Strategies for Developing Countries*, West Hartford: Kumarian Press.

Collins, Charles and Andrew Green (1994): 'Decentralization and Primary Health Care: Some Negative Implications in Developing Countries', *International Journal of Health Services*, 24: 459-75.

Conyers, Diana (1990): 'Centralization and Development Planning: A Comparative Perspective', in Peter de Valk and K.H. Wekwete (eds.), *Decentralization for Participatory Planning*, Aldershot: Avebury.

Cornwall, Andrea (2002): 'Locating Citizen Participation', *IDS Bulletin*, 33(2): 49-58.

Crook, Richard C. (1994): 'Four Years of the Ghana District Assemblies in Operation: Decentralization, Democratization and Administrative Performance', *Public Administration and Development*, 14(4): 339-64.

Crook, Richard C. and James Manor (1998): *Democracy and Decentralisation in South Asia and West Africa: Participation, Accountability and Performance*, Cambridge: Cambridge University Press.

Devas, Nick (1997): 'Indonesia: What do we mean by Decentralization?' *Public Administration and Development*, August, 17(3): 351-67.

Dryzek, John S. (2000): *Deliberative Democracy and Beyond*, Oxford: Oxford University Press.

Dubois, Hans F. W. and Giovanni Fattore (2009): 'Definitions and Typologies in Public Administration Research: The Case of Decentralization', *International Journal of Public Administration*, 32(8): 704-27.

Falleti, Tulia G. (2005): 'A Sequential Theory of Decentralization: Latin American Cases in Comparative Perspective', *American Political Science Review*, 99(3), August: 327-46.

Fan, C. Simon, Chen Lin and Daniel Treisman (2009): 'Political Decentralization and Corruption: Evidence from Around the World', *Journal of Public Economics*, 93: 14-34.

Fisman, Raymond and Roberta Gatti (2002): 'Decentralization and Corruption: Evidence across Countries', *Journal of Public Economics*, 83: 325-45.

Francis, Paul and Robert James (2003): 'Balancing Rural Poverty Reduction and Citizen Participation: The Contradictions of Uganda's Decentralization Program', *World Development*, 31(2): 325-37.

Fung, Archon and Erik Olin Wright (2001): 'Deepening Democracy:

Innovations in Empowered Participatory Governance', *Politics and Society*, 29(1): 5-41.

Furniss, Norman (1974): 'The Practical Significance of Decentralization', *The Journal of Politics*, 36(4): 958-82.

Gaventa, John (2002): 'Exploring Citizenship, Participation and Accountability', *IDS Bulletin*, 33(2): 1-11.

—— (2006): 'Triumph, Deficit or Contestation: Deepening the Deepening Democracy Debate', Working Paper No. 264, Sussex: IDS.

Government of India (1963): *Report of the Study Team on the Position of Gram Sabha in Panchayat Raj Movement*, New Delhi: Ministry of Community Development.

Habermas, Jürgen (1989): *On Society and Politics: A Reader*, Boston: Beacon Press.

Healey, Patsy (1997): *Collaborative Planning*, London: Macmillan.

Heller, Patrick (2001): 'Moving the State: The Politics of Democratic Decentralization in Kerala, South Africa, and Porto Alegre', *Politics and Society*, 29(1): 131-63.

Henkel, Christoph (2002): 'The Allocation of Powers in the European Union: A Closer Look at the Principle of Subsidiarity', *Berkeley Journal of International Law*, 20(2): 359-86.

Hilmer, Jeffrey D. (2010): 'The State of Participatory Democratic Theory', *New Political Science*, 32(1): 43-63.

Holston, James (1998): 'Spaces of Insurgent Citizenship', in Leonie Sandercock (ed.), *Making the Invisible Visible: A Multicultural Planning History*, Berkeley: University of California Press: 155-73.

Jessop, Bob (2003): 'Governance and Meta-governance: On Reflexivity, Requisite Variety and Requisite Irony', in Henrik P. Bang (ed.), *Governance as Social and Political Communication*, Manchester: Manchester University Press: 101-66.

Johanson, Jan-Erik (2006): 'Business in Metropolis: Local Governance of For-Profit Organisations in Finland', *Public Organizational Review*, 6: 57-77.

John, M.S. (2007) 'Gandhi and the Contemporary Discourse on Decentralization', in T.M. Joseph (ed.), *Local Governance in India: Ideas, Challenges and Strategies*, New Delhi: Concept: 20-31

John, M.S. and Jos Chathukulam (2003): 'Measuring Decentralization: The Case of Kerala (India)', *Public Administration and Development*, 23(4): 347-60.

—— (2007): 'Between Euphoria and Scepticism: Ten Years of Panchayati Raj in Kerala', in M.A. Oommen (ed.), *A Decade of Decentralisation in Kerala: Experience and Lessons*, New Delhi: Har Anand: 54-87.

Kabeer, Naila. (2002): 'Citizenship, Affiliation and Exclusion: Perspectives from the South', *IDS Bulletin*, 33(2): 12-23.

Kelly, Josie (2006): 'Central Regulation of Local Authorities: An Example of Meta-governance', *Public Administration*, 84(3): 603-21.

Kooiman, Jan and Svein Jentoft (2009): 'Meta-governance: Values, Norms and Principles, and the Making of Hard Choices', *Public Administration*, 87(4): 818-36.

Lister, Ruth (1997): *Citizenship: Feminist Perspectives*, New York: New York University Press.

Litvack, Jennie, Junaid Ahmad and Richard Bird (1998): *Rethinking Decentralization in Developing Countries*, Washington D.C.: The World Bank.

Litvack, Jennie and Jessica Seddon (eds.), (1999): *Decentralization Briefing Notes*, Washington D.C.: World Bank Institute.

Macpherson, C.B. (1977): *The Life and Times of Liberal Democracy*, Oxford: Oxford University Press.

Maddick, Henry (1970): *Panchayat Raj: A Study of Rural Local Government*, London: Allen and Unwin.

Manor, James (1999): *The Political Economy of Democratic Decentralisation*, Washington D.C.: The World Bank.

—— (2001): *Local Government in South Africa: Potential Disaster Despite Genuine Promise*, Brighton, Sussex: Institute of Development Studies.

—— (2006): 'Renewing the Debate on Decentralisation', *Commonwealth and Comparative Politics*, 44(3): 283-88.

Maoffe, Chantal (2000): *The Democratic Paradox*, London: Verso.

Mintzberg, Henry (1980): 'Structure in 5'S: A Synthesis of the Research on Organization Design', *Management Science*, 26(3), March: 322-41.

Miraftab, Faranak (2004): 'Invented and Invited Spaces of Participation: Neoliberal Citizenship and Feminists' Expanded Notion of Politics', *Wagadu: Journal of Transnational Women's and Gender Studies*, ww.web.cortland.edu.

Mohan, Giles and Kristian Stokke (2000): 'Participatory Development and Empowerment: The Dangers of Localism', *Third World Quarterly*, 21(2): 247-68.

Moolakkattu, John (2006): 'Musings on Deliberative Democracy and the Gram Sabha', *Gandhi Marg*, 27 (3&4): 349-64.

Musgrave, Robert A. (1959): *The Theory of Public Finance: A Study in Political Economy*, New York: McGraw-Hill.

Mutz, Diana C. (2006): *Hearing the Other Side: Deliberative versus Participatory Democracy*, Cambridge: Cambridge University Press.

Oates, Wallace E. (1972): *Fiscal Federalism*, New York: Harcourt Brace Jovanovich.

—— (2006): 'On the Theory and Practice of Fiscal Decentralization', *IFIR*

Working Paper Series, College Park: Institute for Federalism and Inter governmental Relations, University of Maryland.

Osborne, David and Ted Gaebler (1993): *Reinventing Government: How the Entrepreneurial Spirit is Transforming the Public Sector*, New York: Penguin.

Parker, Andrew N. (1995): 'Decentralization: The Way Forward for Rural Development', *Policy Research Working Paper 1475*, Washington D.C.: The World Bank.

Pateman, Carole (1970): *Participation and Democratic Theory*, New York: Cambridge University Press.

Pollitt, Christopher (2005): 'Decentralization: A Central Concept in Contemporary Public Management', in Ewan Ferlie, Lawrence E. Lynn and Christopher Pollitt (eds.), *The Oxford Handbook of Public Management*, Oxford: Oxford University Press: 371-97.

Porter, David O. and Eugene A. Olsen (1976): 'Some Critical Issues in Government Centralization and Decentralization', *Public Administration Review*, 36: 72-84.

Prud'homme, Rémy (1995): 'The Dangers of Decentralization', *The World Bank Research Observer*, 10(2): 201-20.

Rao, Vijayendra and Paromita Sanyal (2009): 'Dignity through Discourse: Poverty and the Culture of Deliberation in Indian Village Democracies', Policy Research Working Paper 4924, World Bank, May.

Rahnema, Majid (1990): 'Participatory Action Research: The Last Temptation of Saint Development', *Alternatives*, 15(2): 199-226.

Romeo, L.G. (2003): 'The Role of External Assistance in Supporting Decentralization Reform', *Public Administration and Development*, 23: 89-96.

Rondinelli, Dennis A., John R. Nellis and G. Shabbir Cheema (1983): 'Decentralization in Developing Countries: A Review of Recent Experience', *Working Paper 581*, Washington D.C.: The World Bank.

Rondinelli, Dennis A, and John R. Nellis (1986): 'Assessing Decentralization Policies in Developing Countries: The Case for Cautious Optimism', *Development Policy Review*, 4(3).

Rondinelli, Dennis A., James S. McCullough and Ronald W. Johnson (1989): 'Analysing Decentralization Policies in Developing Countries: A Political Economy Framework', *Development and Change*, 20(1): 57-87.

Rondinelli, Dennis A. (1990): 'Decentralization, Territorial Power and the State: A Critical Response', *Development and Change*, 21(3): 491-500.

—— (1999): 'What is Decentralization?', in Jennie Litvack and Jessica Seddon (eds.), *Decentralization Briefing Notes*, Washington D.C.: World Bank Institute.

Samoff, Joel (1990): 'Decentralization: The Politics of Interventionism', *Development and Change*, 21: 513-30.

Schroeder, Larry and Paul Smoke (2002): 'Intergovernmental Transfers: Concepts, International Practice and Policy Issues', in Yun-Hwan Kim and Paul Smoke (eds.), *Intergovernmental Fiscal Transfers in Asia: Current Practice and Challenges for the Future*, Manila: Asian Development Bank.

Shah, Anwar and Theresa M. Thompson (2004): 'Implementing Decentralized Global Governance: A Treacherous Road with Potholes, Detours and Road Closures', in James Alm, Jorge Martinez-Vazquez and Sri Mulyani Indrawati (eds.), *Reforming Intergovernmental Fiscal Relations and the Rebuilding of Indonesia*, Northampton, MA: Edward Elgar.

Shapiro, Ian (2003): *The State of Democratic Theory*, Princeton: Princeton University Press.

Smith, Brian C. (1985): *Decentralisation: The Territorial Dimension of the State*, London: Allen and Unwin.

Smoke, Paul and Blane D. Lewis (1996): 'Fiscal Decentralization in Indonesia: A New Approach to an Old Idea', *World Development*, 24(8): 1281-99.

Smoke, Paul (2003): 'Decentralization in Africa: Goals, Dimensions, Myths and Challenges', *Public Administration and Development*, 23: 7-16.

Sorensen, Eva (2005): 'Network Governance and Post-liberal Democracy', *Administrative Theory and Practice*, 27(2): 197-237.

Sorensen, Eva and Jacob Torfing (2009): 'Making Governance Networks Effective and Democratic through Metagovernance', *Public Administration*, 87(2): 234-58.

Stewart, Angus (1995): 'Two Conceptions of Citizenship', *British Journal of Sociology* 46(1): 63-78.

Stoker, Gerry (2006): *Why Politics Matters*, Basingstoke: Palgrave Macmillan.

Tam, Henry B. (1998): *Communitarianism: A New Agenda for Politics and Citizenship*, New York: New York University Press.

Taylor, Charles (1990): 'Modes of Civil Society', *Public Culture*, 3(1): 95-118.

The Federalist (1937): New York: The Modern Library.

Treisman, Daniel S. (2000): 'Decentralization and the Quality of Government', www.imf.org.

—— (2002): 'Defining and Measuring Decentralization: A Global Perspective', *UCLA Working Paper*, Los Angeles: University of California.

Turner, Mark, and David Hulme (1997): *Governance, Administration and Development: Making the State Work*, Houndmills: Macmillan.

Warren, Mark E. (1996): 'What Should We Expect From More Democracy? Radically Democratic Responses to Politics?' *Political Theory*, 24(2): 241-70.

Wolman, Harold (1990): 'Decentralization: What it is and Why We Should Care', in Robert J. Bennett (ed.), *Decentralization, Local Governments, and Markets: Towards a Post-welfare Agenda*, Oxford: Clarendon Press.

Young, Iris (1990): *Justice and the Politics of Difference,* Princeton: Princeton University Press.

CHAPTER 7

Gram Sabha and Deliberative Democracy

D. JEEVAN KUMAR

Deliberative democracy is a form of democracy in which deliberation is central to decision-making. It adopts elements of both consensus decision-making and majority rule. Deliberative democracy differs from traditional democracy in that authentic deliberation, not mere voting, is the primary source of legitimacy for the law. Deliberative democracy holds that, for a democratic decision to be legitimate, it must be preceded by authentic deliberation, and not merely the aggregation of preferences that occurs in voting.

Proposed as a reformist and sometimes even a radical political ideal, deliberative democracy begins with a critique of the standard practices of liberal democracy. Although the idea can be traced to Dewey and Arendt, and then further back to Rousseau and even Aristotle, in its recent incarnation, the term stems from Joseph Bessette, who explicitly coined it in 1980 to oppose the elitist or 'aristocratic' interpretation of the American Constitution (Bessette 1980).

The Deliberative Democracy school of thought in political theory claims that political decisions should be the product of fair and reasonable discussion and debate among citizens. In deliberation, citizens exchange arguments and consider different claims that are designed to secure the public good. Through this conversation, citizens can come to an agreement about what procedure, action or policy will best produce the public good. Deliberation is a necessary precondition for the legitimacy of democratic political decisions. Rather than thinking of political decisions as the aggregate of citizens' preferences, deliberative democracy claims that citizens should arrive at political decisions through reason and the collection of competing arguments and viewpoints. In other words, citizens' preferences should be shaped by deliberation *in advance of decision-making* (Eagan 2014).

Deliberation in democratic processes generates outcomes that secure the public or common good through *reason*, rather than through political power. Deliberative democracy is based not on a competition between conflicting interests but on an exchange of information and justifications supporting varying perspectives on the public good. Ultimately, citizens should be swayed by the force of better argument, rather than by private concerns, biases or views that are not publicly justifiable to their fellow deliberators (Eagan 2014).

James Fishkin, who has designed practical implementation of deliberative democracy describes five characteristics essential for legitimate deliberation: (1) *Information:* Accurate and relevant data is made available to all participants; (2) *Substantive Balance:* Different positions are compared, based on their supporting evidence; (3) *Diversity:* All major positions relevant to the matter at hand and held by the public are considered; (4) *Conscientiousness:* Participants sincerely weigh all arguments; (5) *Equal Consideration:* Views are weighed based on evidence, and not on who is advocating a particular view (Fishkin 2011). In Fishkin's definition of deliberative democracy, lay citizens must participate in the decision-making process, thus making it a subtype of direct democracy.

Cohen (1989) presents deliberative democracy as more than a theory of legitimacy, and forms a body of substantive rights around it, based on achieving 'ideal deliberation': (1) *It is free in two ways*: (a) the participants consider themselves bound solely by the results and preconditions of the deliberation. They are free from any authority of prior norms or requirements; (b) and the participants suppose that they can act on the decision made; the deliberative process is a sufficient reason to comply with the decision reached. (2) Parties to deliberation are required to state reasons for their proposals, and proposals are accepted or rejected based on the reasons given, as the content of the very deliberation taking place.

(3) Parties are equal in two ways: (a) *Formal*: Anyone can put forth proposals, criticize and support measures. There is no substantive hierarchy; (b) *Substantive*: The participants are not limited or bound by certain distributions of power, resources or pre-existing norms. (4) Deliberation aims at a rationally motivated consensus: It aims to find reasons acceptable to all who are committed to such a system of decision-making. When consensus or something near enough is not possible, majoritarian decision-making is used.

Studies by Fishkin and others have found that deliberative democracy tends to produce outcomes which are superior to those in other forms of democracy (Fishkin and Luskin 2005). Deliberative democracy produces less partisanship and more sympathy with opposing views; more respect for evidence-based reasoning rather than opinion; a greater commitment to the decisions taken by those involved; and a greater chance for widely shared consensus to emerge, thus promoting social cohesion between people from divergent backgrounds. Fishkin cites extensive empirical support for the increase in public spiritedness that is often caused by participation in deliberation, and says theoretical support can be traced to foundational democratic thinkers such as John Stuart Mill and Alexis de Tocqueville. Carne Ross (2011) writes that the debates arising from deliberative democracy are also much more civil, collaborative and evidence-based, when compared to the debates in traditional town hall meetings or in internet forums. For Ross, the key reason for this is that in deliberative democracy, citizens are empowered by the knowledge that their debates will have a measurable impact on society.

Charles Blattberg (2003) has criticized deliberative democracy on four grounds: (1) The rules for deliberation that deliberative theorists affirm interfere with, rather than facilitate, good practical reasoning; (2) Deliberative democracy is ideologically biased in favour of liberalism as well as republican over parliamentary democratic systems; (3) Deliberative democrats assert a too-sharp division between just and rational deliberation on the one hand, and self-centred and coercive bargaining or negotiation on the other; and (4) Deliberative democrats encourage an adversarial relationship between state and society, one that undermines solidarity between citizens. A major criticism of deliberation is that it potentially allows those most skilled in rhetoric to sway the decision in their favour. This criticism has been made since deliberative democracy first arose in ancient Athens.

In the following pages, an attempt will be made to locate the Gram Sabha as an institution of the Panchayati Raj system in India, in the discourse on deliberative democracy. What is the legal basis for the Gram Sabha? Is it functioning as an instrument of deliberative democracy? What is the experience of the various states in India in this regard? What are its strengths and weaknesses? If the Gram Sabha is not functioning in accordance with the law and as per the norms of deliberative democracy, what could be the reasons behind the divergence between theory and practice? What are the corrective steps that could be taken to remedy the situation? This paper seeks to find the answers to these questions.

PANCHAYATI RAJ AND DELIBERATIVE DEMOCRACY IN INDIA

Panchayati Raj in India has a chequered history. Scholars have traced the beginning of panchayats to ancient India. The reality is that rural India had systems of local governance, particularly for local dispute resolution, from ancient times. They did not look to provincial or central government for their day-to-day living (Buch 2012). However, the prevalence of local governance seems to have been severely compromised with the march of time, particularly when we come to medieval India and after. While several reasons can be attributed to the eclipse of local bodies, a discussion on them has not been attempted here.

Coming to the British period, it was the Royal Commission on Decentralization (1907) which said that 'it is most desirable, alike in the interests of decentralization and in order to associate the people with the local tasks of administration that an attempt should be made to constitute and develop Village Panchayats for the administration of local village affairs'. The Montague-Chelmsford reforms of 1919 brought local self-government as a provincial transferred subject, under the domain of Indian ministers in the British

Indian provinces. And provincial autonomy under the Government of India Act of 1935 introduced popularly elected governments in the provinces, and these governments enacted legislation to further democratize institutions of local self-government.

There have been two divergent views on the place of village panchayats in independent India and its new Constitution (Buch 2012). Mahatma Gandhi favoured *Gram Swaraj*, strengthening of village panchayats and giving them centrality in local governance, but B.R. Ambedkar believed that the village represented a regressive India, a source of oppression of the downtrodden communities. Hence the new state had to build safeguards against social oppression. Village panchayats and their organization were then placed as Article 40 under the Directive Principles of State Policy in the Indian Constitution in 1950, which were not justiciable.

The Panchayati Raj system was a subject of study by a number of committees and study teams, starting with the B.R. Mehta Committee recommending a three-tier structure. In 1986, the L.M. Singhvi Committee suggested that the Gram Sabha be the base of a decentralized democracy and Panchayati Raj institutions be viewed as institutions of self-governance which would actually facilitate participation of the people in the process of planning and development. It also recommended constitutional recognition of local self-government and inclusion of a new chapter in the Indian Constitution for this purpose.

The 73rd Constitutional Amendment of 1992 included the Gram Sabha as a deliberative body of decentralized governance, along with a three-tier system of panchayats, from the village to the district level. Article 243B defines the Gram Sabha as 'a body consisting of persons registered in the electoral rolls relating to a village comprised within the area of the Panchayat at the village level'.

The Gram Sabha is to enable each and every voter of the village to participate in decision-making at the local level. It is a constitutional body consisting of all persons registered in the electoral rolls of a Gram Panchayat. It provides a political forum to people in the village to meet and discuss their common problems and understand the needs and aspirations of the community. It also provides a forum to debate and analyse the development and administrative actions of elected representatives and thereby ensure transparency and accountability in the functioning of the Gram Panchayat. Thus, the Gram Panchayat is expected to be an epitome of deliberative democracy. Additionally, the Gram Sabha is expected to act as a watchdog in the interest of the village by monitoring the functioning of the Gram Panchayat (Buch 2012).

Article 243A of the Constitution states that 'a Gram Sabha may exercise such powers and perform such functions at the village level as the legislature of a state may, by law, provide'. In the exercise of this mandate, state legislatures in India did provide for an impressive list of duties and responsibilities for them. It would be useful to recount some of the common provisions in Panchayati Raj legislation of state governments relating to the Gram Sabha:

1. The Gram Sabha shall meet at least once in six months. Provided that a special meeting of the Gram Sabha shall be convened if a request is made by not less than 10 per cent of the members of the Sabha, with items of agenda specified in such request. There shall be a minimum three-month period between two special meetings of the Gram Sabha.
2. The quorum for a meeting of the Gram Sabha shall be not less than one-tenth of the total number of members of the Gram Sabha, or one hundred members, whichever is less. As far as may be, at least ten members from each Ward Sabha within the Panchayat area shall attend the meeting, and not less than 30 per cent of the members attending the Gram Sabha shall be women. As far as possible, persons belonging to the Scheduled Castes and Scheduled Tribes shall be represented in proportion to their population in the Gram Sabha.
3. Subject to such rules as may be prescribed, the Gram Sabha shall exercise powers and discharge functions as hereinafter provided, namely:
    (a) To consider and approve the Annual Plan prepared by the Gram Panchayat.
    (b) To generate proposals and determine the priority of all schemes and development programmes to be implemented

in the Panchayat area by the Zilla Panchayat or Taluk Panchayat, after considering the recommendations and suggestions of the Ward Sabhas through the Gram Panchayat.

(c) To identify and select the most eligible persons from the Panchayat area for beneficiary-oriented schemes on the basis of criteria fixed by the Gram Panchayat, Taluk Panchayat, Zilla Panchayat or the government, and to prepare lists of beneficiaries in the order of priority, after considering the priority lists of individual beneficiaries sent by the Ward Sabhas. Such lists shall be binding on the concerned Gram Panchayat, Taluk Panchayat, Zilla Panchayat or the Government, as the case may be.

(d) To disseminate information on development and welfare programmes and to render assistance in the effective implementation of development schemes by providing facilities locally available, and to provide feedback on the performance of the same.

(e) To render assistance to the Gram Panchayat in the collection and compilation of details required, in the formulation of development plans, in the collection of essential socio-economic data and in ensuring participation in health, literacy and other development campaigns.

(f) To get information from the officers of the Gram Panchayat as to the services they will render and the works they propose to do in the succeeding period of six months after the meeting of the Gram Sabha.

(g) To get information from the Gram Panchayat on the rationale of every decision of the Gram Panchayat concerning the Panchayat area.

(h) To get information from the Gram Panchayat on the follow-up action taken on the decisions of the Gram Sabha.

(i) To mobilize and provide voluntary labour and contributions in cash and kind for development works, and to supervise such work through volunteer teams.

(j) To resort to persuasion of Gram Sabha members to pay taxes and repay loans to the Gram Panchayat.

(k) To decide, after considering the suggestions of the Ward

Sabhas, the location of street lights, street or community water taps, public wells, public sanitation units, irrigation facilities and such other public amenity schemes; to identify deficiencies in them, and after considering the suggestions of the Ward Sabhas, to suggest remedial measures, and to report on the satisfactory completion of the works.

(l) To impart awareness on matters of public interest, such as cleanliness, preservation of the environment and prevention of pollution.

(m) To assist employees of the Gram Panchayat in sanitation arrangements in the Panchayat area, and to render voluntary assistance in the removal of garbage.

(n) To promote programmes of Adult Education within the Panchayat area.

(o) To assist the activities of School Betterment Sanghas, Anganwadis, Mahila Samajas, youth associations, self-help groups and women activities in the Panchayat area.

(p) To assist the activities of Public Health Centres in the Panchayat area, especially in disease prevention, family welfare, population control and control of cattle diseases, and create arrangements to quickly report the incidence of epidemics and natural calamities.

(q) To promote communal harmony and unity among various groups of people in the Panchayat area; to arrange cultural festivals, literary activities and sports meets, to give expression to the talents of the people of the locality.

(r) To conserve and maintain public properties such as 'gomalas', tanks, tank beds, ground water, grazing grounds of cattle and the village commons, within the limits of the Gram Panchayat.

(s) To take action to prevent discrimination on the basis of caste, religion, gender, etc., and to direct the Gram Panchayats not to grant licences to shops selling liquor or narcotic drugs or places of gambling, or any other activities prejudicial to public interest.

(t) To identify child labourers, if any, present within the limits of the Gram Panchayat, and to take action to rehabilitate them and to assist in the implementation of legal action specified by the union or state governments; and

(u) To exercise such other powers or discharge such other functions as may be prescribed.

4. The Gram Sabha shall, in its ordinary meeting or a special meeting convened for the purpose, discuss the budgetary provisions, details of the plan outlay and subject-wise allocation of funds, and also the details of estimates and cost of materials of the works executed or proposed to be executed in the Panchayat area.
5. The Annual Statement of Accounts of the preceding financial year, the last Audit Note and replies thereto, and the Panchayat Jamabandi report and action taken thereto—shall be placed by the Gram Panchayat for the consideration of the Gram Sabha in its meeting. The views, recommendations or suggestions of the Gram Sabha shall be communicated to the Gram Panchayat. The Gram Panchayat shall give due consideration to the views, recommendations and suggestions of the Gram Sabha.
6. The procedure for convening and conducting the meeting of the Gram Sabha shall be such as may be prescribed.
7. Every meeting of the Gram Sabha shall be presided over by the Adhyaksha of the concerned Gram Panchayat and, in his absence, by the Upadhyaksha, and in the absence of both, by any member of the Gram Panchayat nominated by it.
8. The officers of the Gram Panchayat shall attend the meetings of the Gram Sabha as may be required by the Adhyaksha, and an officer specially nominated by the Gram Panchayat as Convenor of the Gram Sabha meeting shall assist in convening and conducting its meetings and recording its decisions in a Minute Book, and also in taking follow-up action thereon.
9. The Gram Sabha may constitute sub-committees, consisting of not less than ten members of whom not less than half shall be women, for in-depth discussion on issues and programmes for effective implementation of the decisions of the Gram Sabha, and in furtherance of the exercise of powers and discharge of functions of the Gram Sabha.

10. All resolutions in respect of any issue in the meetings of the Gram Sabha shall be passed by a majority of the members present and voting.

EFFECTIVENESS OF THE GRAM SABHA

It is clear from the above section that the Gram Sabha is the cornerstone of the entire scheme of democratic decentralization in the country, thanks to the 73rd Amendment to the Constitution. It may not be an exaggeration to state that the success or failure of the Panchayati Raj system largely depends on the effectiveness of the Gram Sabha in performing its constitutional mandate and fulfilling the desires and aspirations of the people. Was it not Mahatma Gandhi who had said that 'true democracy cannot be worked by some persons sitting at the top: It had to be worked from below by the people of every village', in other words, by the members of the Gram Sabha? S. Narayanaswamy (1996) reflects the high expectations from the Gram Sabha when he writes:

> The Gram Sabha is one of the most important of the three basic institutions of the new direct democracy at the village level, the other two being the 'Gram Kosh', a village fund, and the 'Gram Shanti Sena', a village peace corps. This is a structure based entirely on people's power (Lokshakti), expressing itself in the form of village power (Gramshakti). *However, the idea of Gram Sabha, by and large, has not struck roots in the minds of the people.*

What do studies on the effectiveness of the Gram Sabha reveal? It would be useful to take a look at some of the efforts in this direction. One study conducted by the National Institute of Rural Development on the impact of state legislation on the empowerment of the Gram Sabha in Schedule V areas as well as to examine the levels of awareness of the people, observed that 'such empowerment is found to be limited' (NIRD 2005). The study on 'Gram Sabha and Social Audit' conducted in the states of Rajasthan, Maharashtra and Madhya Pradesh revealed that a large majority of the members of the Gram Sabha were *not aware* of the powers of the body in all the three states, and more so, in Madhya Pradesh.

A study conducted on transparency of Panchayats in West Bengal found very low attendance of the people in Gram Sansad meetings. According to Nirmala Buch (2012), 'the main reason for low attendance is that the Panchayats are not interested in making people interested in the activities of the Panchayats. Less involvement of the common masses in the functioning of local bodies certainly reduces the chances for being transparent in the eyes of the people. The public view is that these institutions are nothing but an extension of Block level government offices.'

Choudhury and Jain (nd) observe that the Gram Sabha meetings are generally held as prescribed, yet the purpose is hardly served in the absence of a well-defined and well-directed mandate. More often, there is a tendency to conduct the meetings in a formal manner and finalise the proceedings in haste. Field experiences from Madhya Pradesh and Rajasthan show that most people do not know the dates of the Gram Sabha meetings. Since Gram Sabha meetings are generally held at Panchayat headquarters, people from distant villages find it difficult to attend them (Mathew 2000). Cases were cited about the meetings that were conducted without any consideration to the requirement of quorum. The absence of womenfolk in the meetings was a common feature. The participation of people belonging to the weaker sections was also minimal. Only those people from these groups participated in the meetings who were to be identified as beneficiaries under a given scheme. The entire exercise thus becomes formal and incapable of yielding the expected results. It becomes more pathetic when the losers in the Panchayat elections mobilize support only to oppose the *Sarpanch* and frustrate his development plans in the Gram Sabha. All this highlights the lack of a culture of Gram Sabha, despite all the talk about India's legacy of participatory democracy (Reddy et al. 2010).

By and large, there is a consensus that rural people are generally apathetic towards the Gram Sabha. It has been widely noticed that meetings of the Gram Sabha are a mere formality. Decisions which are supposed to be taken by the Gram Sabha are actually taken by the local elite. Meetings are conducted, even without a quorum. The marked absence of women and the weaker sections of rural society is yet another glaring fact. People, particularly those below the poverty line, do not wish to lose their daily wage, by attending the Gram Sabha meeting, as this is generally held during the day.

Taking serious note of the shortcomings in the functioning of the Gram Sabha, the Ministry of Panchayati Raj and Rural Development of the Government of India declared the year 1999-2000 as the 'Year of the Gram Sabha'. This does not seem to have met with the desired result, warranting the ministry to declare, after a decade, the year 2009-10 as the 'Year of the Gram Sabha', once again. This time around, the ministry issued detailed guidelines for activating the Gram Sabha, the Ward Sabha and other People's Assemblies. Highlights of these guidelines are reproduced below:

- For rural local governance to be effective, energizing Gram Sabhas is the real challenge. There is a need to evolve mechanisms for regular and meaningful meetings of the Gram Sabha, active participation of its members and monitoring its functioning. Good practices that provide for People's Assemblies below the Gram Sabha such as Ward Sabha, Mahila Sabha and Bal Sabha should be promoted. Formation and federation of Self-Help Groups of women on the pattern of Kudumbshree of Kerala should be expedited.
- States should make appropriate provisions in their State Panchayat Raj Acts for the establishment of Gram/Ward development Sabhas, along the lines indicated in the draft 'Model Panchayat and Gram Swaraj Act' circulated by the ministry. These provisions include equipping the Gram Sabhas with monitoring powers; power of recalling the Chairpersons of Gram Panchayats; preparation of Citizen Report Cards; conducting Social Audit; and so on.
- Gram Sabhas should discuss issues such as (i) Quality of life and Millennium Development Goals; (ii) Social security, gender justice, female foeticide, substance abuse, hygiene and nutrition; (iii) Sustainable development, diversification of agriculture, better cropping practices, opportunities for increasing incomes, drought/flood management, soil and water conservation, and the like; and (iv) infrastructure development.

- The Gram Sabha should fully participate in planning, implementing and conducting performance reviews of schemes like BRGF, NREGA, NRHM, SSA, ICDS, IWMP, RKVY, etc.

  Notwithstanding all these efforts, recent studies reveal that the Gram Sabha continues to be a non-functional body in most states mainly because of lack of faith of the rural people in its effectiveness, resulting in their indifferent attitude towards this body.

THE GRAM SABHA AND DELIBERATIVE DEMOCRACY: NORMATIVE EXPECTATIONS *VS.* GROUND REALITY

It may be useful at this juncture to capture the essence of the normative expectations of deliberative democracy and the ground reality vis-à-vis Gram Sabhas in the country.

NORMATIVE EXPECTATIONS

- Political decisions should be the product of fair and reasonable discussion and debate among citizens.
- Deliberation is a necessary precondition for the legitimacy of democratic political decisions.
- Deliberative democracy claims that citizens should arrive at political decisions through reason and the collection of competing arguments and viewpoints.
- Deliberative democracy is based, not on a competition between conflicting interests, but on an exchange of information and justifications supporting varying perspectives on the public good.
- Five characteristics are essential for the success of deliberative democracy: information; substantive balance; diversity; conscientiousness; and equal consideration.
- Deliberative democracy produces outcomes which are superior to those in other forms of democracy.
- Deliberative democracy produces less partisanship and more sympathy with opposing views; more respect for evidence-based reasoning; a greater commitment to the decisions taken by those involved; and a greater chance for widely shared consensus to

emerge, thus promoting social cohesion between people from divergent backgrounds.
- In deliberative democracy, citizens are empowered by the knowledge that their debates will have a measurable impact on society.

Ground Reality

The ground reality regarding the actual working of the Gram Sabha across the country reveals a sharp contrast, when measured against the normative expectations of deliberative democracy:

- A large majority of the members of the Gram Sabha are not aware of the powers of the body.
- There is a very low attendance of people at Gram Sabha meetings.
- Since Gram Sabha meetings are held at Panchayat headquarters, people from distant villages find it difficult to attend them.
- Meetings are conducted without any consideration to the requirement of quorum.
- The absence of women at meetings is a common feature.
- The participation of people from the weaker sections is minimal.
- Only beneficiaries of schemes participate at meetings.
- Rural people are generally apathetic towards the Gram Sabha.
- Decisions of the Gram Sabha are actually taken by the local elite.
- Gram Panchayats are generally not concerned about making people interested in their activities. Less involvement of the common man in their functioning and decisions reduces their responsibility of transparency and accountability.
- Gram Sabha meetings are held mechanically, in the absence of a well-defined mandate, and the proceedings are finalised in haste.
- Notwithstanding the efforts of the government in issuing Guidelines for strengthening the Gram Sabha as instruments of deliberative democracy, it continues to be non-functional in the strict sense of the term.

THE CHALLENGE AND THE WAY FORWARD

According to Vaddiraju and Mehrotra (2004):

Panchayat Raj institutions operate in a complex social environment. Caste, class and gender hierarchies have a crucial bearing on institutional processes and democratic practices. Secondly, participation in the Gram Sabha is affected by the apathy of the villagers. This indifference has its roots in the long historical background of non-participation in governance, entrenched because of caste, class and gender hierarchies, which are quite un-participatory, to say the least. The political culture promoted since independence has also been one of patronage and this has certainly not encouraged the participation of people in institutional processes. Thirdly, where the Gram Sabha did take place, the issues discussed were important and participation was genuine.

According to Ajai Pal Sharma (2013), the following initiatives should be taken for empowering the Gram Sabha: *Creating Awareness:* Awareness needs to be created at the village level about the rights and responsibilities of Gram Sabha members; *Education:* The generally low level of learning in rural areas needs to be strengthened through transformation in education policies, keeping the rural areas in focus; *Regular Meetings:* Meetings of the Gram Sabha should be held regularly, in a cordial atmosphere; *Training of Panchayat Members:* Elected Members of the Gram and Taluk Panchayats should be trained and educated about their roles and responsibilities towards the Gram Sabha. Further, they should be motivated to rise above petty politics; *Capacity-Building of Villagers:* This should be done through education, awareness, training, increased participation in development works, etc.; *Display of Information on the Notice Board:* Information about meetings, works being carried out and future plans should be posted on the Notice Boards of Gram Panchayats; *Social Audit:* Social Audits are mandatory as per the 73rd Constitutional Amendment, through which village communities audit all the developmental work being carried out in their respective villages.

The Gram Sabha can be empowered only when there are institutional mechanisms to make people aware of the importance of participation, through government campaigns, actively supported by civil society. Other measures include the division of larger Gram Sabhas into more manageable and functional units like Ward Sabhas, and the establishment of functional relationships between the Gram Sabha and other bodies like the Gram Panchayats, Project-specific Committees and Civil Society Organizations (Buch 2012). A strengthened Gram Sabha is more effective, both in the short run for immediate accountability and in the long run for building a healthy decentralized democracy (Vaddiraju and Mehrotra 2004).

Jean Dreze and Amartya Sen (2002), however, are not unduly disturbed by the poor track record of the functioning of the Gram Sabha. In their words:

> The practice of local democracy is also a form of wider political education. In the context of village politics, people are learning (if only at varying speed) to organise, to question established patterns of authority, to demand their rights, to resist corruption, and so on. This learning process enhances their preparedness not only for local democracy alone, but for political participation in general.

Vaddiraju and Mehrotra are convinced that a decentralized democracy has more possibilities of being participatory than any other. According to them, participation is not only the means to an end, but an end in itself. While there is no doubt that the performance of Gram Sabhas is less than satisfactory, 'the limitations are best addressed through democratic practice itself, and as far as the potential for the latter is concerned, there is much ground for hope' (Dreze and Sen 2002).

CONCLUSION

To revert to the title of this paper and the broad theme of the book, a pertinent question that needs to be posed, at the end of a discussion on the Gram Sabha, is its effectiveness as an institution of deliberative democracy. Whatever might be the verdict at the end of the day, scholars like James Bohman (1998) see certain maturation in discussions on deliberative democracy. Tempered with considerations of feasibility, disagreement and empirical limits, deliberative democracy has now 'come of age' as a practical ideal.

Bohman (1998) argues that a feasible theory of deliberative democracy has three components: it must have complex, moral and epistemic procedures of justifications; it must understand the importance of historical and social constraints on democracy, such as ongoing collective practices within a constitutional framework; and it must consider the opportunities and constraints of larger social conditions and deliberative settings. Such an adequate theory is realistic, without being sceptical. Bohman states:

> It emphasises the core ideal of public justification that makes deliberative democracy so attractive, without demanding too much social consensus or epistemic virtue. . . . It recognises the tensions in the deliberative ideal and the many forms and avenues in which democratic deliberation can be exercised. In every case, deliberative democracy must vindicate its claim to improve democratic practice in the light of its morally inclusive, yet cognitively demanding, ideal. Above all, the coming of age of deliberative democracy means that it has now become a fully developed democratic theory, with an increasingly large space for politics within the normative constraints of public justification and the many empirically feasible variations of its ideal of public reason.

Should we be unduly worried about the limitations in the functioning and effectiveness of the Gram Sabha, or should the body be assessed from a larger perspective? At the end of the day, one tends to agree with Dreze and Sen, when they state that the limitations are best addressed through democratic practice itself and as far as the potential for the latter is concerned, there is much ground for hope.

REFERENCES

Bessette, Joseph (1980): 'Deliberative Democracy: The Majority Principle in Republican Government', in Robert A. Goldwin and William A. Schambra (eds.), *How Democratic is the Constitution?* Washington D.C.: AEI Press: 102-16.

Blattberg, Charles (2003): 'Patriotic, Not Deliberative Democracy', *Critical Review of International Social and Political Philosophy*, 6(1): 155-74.

Bohman, James (1998): 'The Coming of Age of Deliberative Democracy', *The Journal of Political Philosophy*, 6(4), Oxford: Blackwell: 422-3.

Buch, Nirmala (2012): 'Gram Sabha and Panchayati Raj', *Social Action*, 62, January-March.

Choudhury, R.C. and S.P. Jain (n.d.), 'Panchayati Raj in India: An Overview', in R.C. Choudhury and S.P. Jain (eds.), *Patterns of Decentralized Governance in Rural India*, vol. I, Hyderabad: National Institute of Rural Development: 1-24.

Cohen, Joshua (1989): 'Deliberative Democracy and Democratic Legitimacy', in Alan Hamlin and Philip Pettit (eds.), *The Good Polity*, Oxford: Blackwell: 17-34.

Dreze, Jean and Amartya Sen (2002): *India: Development and Participation*, New Delhi: Oxford University Press.

Eagan, Jennifer (2014): 'Deliberative Democracy', *Encyclopaedia Britannica Online*, www.britannica.com.

Fishkin, James and Robert Luskin (2005): 'Experimenting with a Democratic Ideal: Deliberative Polling and Public Opinion', *Acta Politica*, 40: 284-98.

Fishkin, James (2011): *When the People Speak*, Oxford: Oxford University Press.

Mathew, George (2000): 'Panchayati Raj in India: An Overview', in George Mathew (ed.), *Status of Panchayati Raj in the States and Union Territories in India*, New Delhi: Institute of Social Sciences and Concept Publishing Co.: 2-22.

Narayanaswamy, S. (1996): 'Gram Sabha in the New Panchayati Raj System', in G. Palanithurai (ed.), *Empowering People: Issues and Solutions*, New Delhi: Kanishka: 147-60.

NIRD (2005), S.K. Singh (ed.): *Empowering the Gram Sabha and Social Audit*, vol. IV of series on 'Self-Governance for Tribals', Hyderabad: NIRD.

Reddy, Gopinath, Madhusudan Bandi and S. Ramachandra Reddy (2010): 'Changing Role of Gram Sabha in Decentralized Governance: An Overview of Andhra Pradesh Experience', in *Gram Sabha*, Proceedings of a National Seminar, Mysore: Abdul Nazir Sab Institute of Rural Development.

Ross, Carne (2011): *The Leaderless Revolution: How Ordinary People Will Take Power and Change Politics in the 21st Century*, New York: Simon and Schuster.

Sharma, Ajai Pal (2013): 'Empowering Gram Sabha through Social Audit', *Kurukshetra*, May.

Singh, Rita (2003): 'Good Governance and Decentralization in India', in C.P. Barthwal (ed.), *Good Governance in India*, New Delhi: Deep and Deep.

Vaddiraju, Anil Kumar and Shagun Mehrotra (2004): 'Making Panchayats Accountable', *Economic and Political Weekly*, 39(37), 11 September.

CHAPTER 8

Democratic Deficits and Digital Compensation: The Digital Promises Revisited

SABU THOMAS

> As the internet becomes mobile and ubiquitous, it will bring about changes of its own. Precisely what these will be is not yet clear, but the earliest claims of cyber dreamers—that the internet will produce a shift of power away from political élites to ordinary citizens—may well become reality.
>
> *THE ECONOMIST*, 23 JANUARY 2003

A democratic society rests upon the foundation of freedom. A true democracy is possible only when all people in the system have a voice and participate in the governing of the society, for which citizens are to be kept informed and enlightened. Tuzzi et al. (2007) view democracy as a political concept, concerning the collectively binding decisions about the rules and policies of a group, association or society. Such decision-making can be said to be democratic to the extent that it is subject to the controlling influence of all members of the collectivity considered as equals. The starting point of democracy thus, is in effect 'popular control' and 'political equality'.[1] Consequently, it becomes evident that effective participation and ability for citizens to make their views known is a major criterion for the success of any democratic system. Citizens should have the ability and opportunity to control the political agenda.

Coleman (1999: 67) identifies three levels of relations in modern democratic politics. It includes the relation between the represented, representatives and the ruling elites. The success rate of the system is in proportion to the quality and quantity of communication between these three layers. It follows that the concept of representative democracy, relies on the view that informed citizens make informed decisions to influence and control those people who are elected to make decisions on their behalf.

The development of new citizen values made serious dents on the 'Government' claim to give way to 'Governance' (Crozier 2010: 505). People demanded new avenues of participation and new platforms of interaction. The traditional constituency representative mode of representative democracy was further subjected to sudden stress with the emergence of the 'informed citizen'. Castells (2004) states, 'Never in history has democracy been more pervasive throughout the world. Yet, available evidence points to a growing, widespread crisis of legitimacy of governments, parliaments, political parties, and politicians in most countries, including the United States and Western Europe.' This situation is well evidenced with Norris (1999: 264-9) when she speaks about 'critical citizens'. She observes, 'There are now globally, more critical citizens, who value democracy as an ideal yet who remain dissatisfied with the performance of their political system and particularly the core institutions of representative government.' Political scientists who were engaged in studying who gets what, when and how were forced to reflect upon new themes. This included *Why Americans Hate Politics* (Dionne 1991), *The Vanishing Voter* (Patterson 2002) and *Disaffected Democracies* (Pharr and Putnam 2000).

Castells (2007: 239) observes that the state, traditionally the main site of power, is being challenged all over the world by the postulates of modernity. Globalization comes in the first place. It limits the sovereign decision-making powers of the state, leading to a crisis of equity.

> The process of globalization led by market forces in the framework of deregulation often increases inequality between countries and between social groups within countries. In the absence of a global regulatory environment it compensates for growing inequality, the demands of economic competition undermine existing welfare states. The shrinking of welfare states makes it increasingly difficult for national governments to compensate for structurally induced inequality because of the decreased capacity of national institutions to act as corrective mechanisms. (Castells 2008: 82-3)

Furthermore, market pressures toward deregulation diminish state capacity as it is followed by a crisis of political legitimacy that weakens state influence over its citizens. This legitimacy crisis is a serious threat to the existence and sustainability of democracies (Castells 2007: 239).

Critics of modern democracy envisage a paradigm shift from a democratic state to a democratic society. The focus is shifted from the government to the larger society and its members. The concept of democracy as society, an idea that is closely associated with the idiom of the 'commonwealth', had broad appeal across ideo-logies during the 1940s. Alexis de Tocqueville's classic, *Democracy in America,* used such a definition as the lens through which citizen agency, not government, was the focus. His views had many twentieth-century counterparts. People like Jane Addams, John Dewey, Liberty Hyde Bailey, and Langston Hughes view democracy as far more than elections (see Boyte 2005: 538). Here the individual acquires clear democratic entitlements. Boyte observes:

> The shift can be conceived of as a move from seeing citizens as voters, volunteers, clients, or consumers to viewing citizens as problem solvers and co-creators of public goods. It involves a shift in the role of public professionals such as civil servants, non-profit managers, and office holders from providers of services and solutions to partners, educators, and organisers of citizen action. Overall, it entails a shift in the meaning of democracy, from elections to democratic society. In the paradigm of democratic society, government is a crucial instrument of the citizenry, providing leadership, resources, tools, and rules. Yet officials are not the centre of the civic universe, nor is government the only location for democracy's work.

Here the poignant question is how the individual can become an active participant of the new democratic society. For this he needs more capacities and entitlements. The information level of the citizen is to be furthered to meet the demands of new society. The communication gap between the people and their governing structures needs to be bridged. Information and Communication Technologies (ICT) offer alternatives both to the government and the people.

ICT AND DEMOCRACY

Democracy is described as a communicative brand of politics. In democracy communication necessarily occurs between governments and the people; between the people and governments; between governmental structures and among the people. These layers of communication comprise the soul of any democratic society. Any democratic deficit is the outcome of the communication gap in any of these layers. It is in this background that ICT is discussed as a robust ally of democracy. ICT has radically revolutionized the patterns of communication and information exchange in modern society. According to the International Telecommunication Union (ITU) two-thirds of the world's Internet users are from the Third World. New information and communication technologies have narrowed the gap between individuals across the globe. At the same time the psychological and sociological gap between individuals and their governing systems have also narrowed down. With the advent of the Internet, and the extraordinary growth in ICT, more information than ever before has become freely available and easy to share. Information is now available in a plethora of digital formats and can be exchanged across time zones, countries and groups in seconds, and this makes communicating and connecting easier and more efficient. The Internet and new technologies assist the citizen in gathering information at a never before volume and speed. This information helps the citizen to make informed decisions.

> More voices, on more alternative platforms, allow citizens to criticize government, leaders, policies, and even the system of government itself, whether the target of the criticism is the rule of the clerics in Iran or the Communist Party in China. In fact, the Internet may be the only avenue left for citizens in authoritarian regimes to influence government, fight corruption, or defend their rights, since local and national officials are often appointed by the central government and are more concerned with pleasing Moscow or Beijing than occupying themselves with the demands of citizens. (Etling, Faris and Palfrey 2010)

Inter-citizen communication has also improved with the formation of networks and new connectivity. With the advances in technology, where information can be transmitted quickly, the notion of global network and global democracy has been envisioned. The result is the widening of citizen capabilities. The Internet is creating a new environment of deliberation. The Internet delivers political information without any constraints of time and space, and enables people to engage in easy and free communication at an affordable cost. In addition, the Internet has the potential to liberate people from social hierarchies and power relations that exist in the 'off line' life. Porta (2011: 805) observes: 'As for representative democracy, the use of the Internet has been seen as improving communication between citizens and elected politicians, with increasing accessibility to information, occasions for feedbacks and transparency. The e-governance is supposed to reduce the discretionality of public administrators by improving public access.'

ICT interventions have made modern democracy more deliberative and fluid, and thus accommodate hitherto sidelined actors in the process. This commitment emanates from technology mediated empowerments and entitlements. As Starr (2010: 4) points out, 'Digital media have unquestionably expanded the democratic repertoire. Political campaigns and social movements now have cheap, instant means of communication that circumvent the established mass media, and these resources can be used to mobilize followers, coordinate their activities, and aggregate contributions of money, labour, and knowledge.' There is also a visible network pressure on policy mechanisms all over the political system. Here citizen groups and networks operate fervently to make new claims and demands for public goods The networks also pressurize for effective service delivery in government and public institutions.

In a democracy, the government is best placed to respond to citizen needs meaningfully and appropriately. This requires new patterns and structures to cope with the change. Many governments have developed tools and solutions to meet the exigencies. There are online platforms for community interactions, active web solutions for constituency-representative mediations, transparency portals and the like. The debate that emerges, when considering the impact of the digital age in democracy, is far beyond these technical solutions. It is about the democratic transformations and creation of new democratic spaces. The Internet represents a new public sphere for public interaction where democracy can be revitalized. It potentially allows people participating in an interactive discussion group to share a basis of understanding as a common ground from which to mediate consensus.

NEW DEMOCRATIC SPACES

The link between technology and democracy is very evident. The Industrial Revolution and allied technologies led to participatory democracy and democratic institutions. The Utilitarian movement which ignited many new political experimentations including adult franchise was the result of the Industrial Revolution which created a new middle class. This technological impact on political processes became more evident with the advent of the Information Society. In modern times the proliferation of ICT has resulted in an unprecedented and unpredicted change in the nature and course of human society. The scenario is well articulated by Matthews (2003: 204):

> Widely accessible and affordable technology has broken government's monopoly on the collection and management of large amount of information and deprived government of the deference they enjoyed because of it. In every sphere of activity, instantaneous access to information and the ability to put it to use multiplies the number of players who matter and reduces the number who command great authority. The effect on the loudest voice—which has been governments—has been the greatest.

Evidently the information society, which is a product of the digital society heavily influences the nature of power relations in modern society. In the digital society the theme of authority is information and information structures are decentralized. This has created new power centres and effective power delegations. 'The internet completely redefines the meaning of democracy. The many can now simultaneously "speak" to the few in power, and derive the required response' (Bedi et al. 2001: 21). The governmental monopoly of power itself is questioned. With adequate information resources at hand the individual can take more learned decisions on politics and positively transmit his ideas to society. In this context an interesting development also takes place. The society and political audience, with respect to an individual grows beyond traditional expectations. Social or new media has evolved as a genre with a history of its own, carrying within it immeasurable social, political and economic implications, which seem to crystallise into a new category of global citizenry. The 'citizen journalist' who through near obsessive blogging, tweeting, photographing and texting, networks with individuals, collectives, political parties and movements alike, may be the first and the most basic manifestation of a digitalized democracy, the first step towards stripping the definition of citizenship from its conventional markers (Gupta 2011: 11). A Facebook comment or a blog post may fetch millions of responses, likes and comments which may solidify into direct actions.

The technical rationality of new governance is further supported by the governance 'gap' arguments. Coleman (2007) identifies the absence of open space and venues of critical discussion in current democracies. With ever-increasing channels of engagement and ever-growing space for deliberation, technological innovations compensate the gaps and deficits and provide for smooth interaction between the governors and the governed. To Manuel Castells (2008), there is a shift from a public sphere anchored around national institutions of territorially bound societies to a public sphere constituted around the media system including the Internet. It is in this context that Castells identifies the multi-modal functionality of the new medium as expanding the horizons of the public sphere. The resultant political structure highly demands articulation and social solidarity. Pippa Norris (2002) clarifies the situation:

> The Internet is a medium where users have almost unlimited choices and minimal constraints about where to go and what to do. Commitments to any particular online group can often be shallow and transient when another is but a mouse click away. Most online communities without any physical basis are usually low-cost, 'easy-entry, easy-exit' groups. Like adherents to particular left-wing or right-wing radio talk shows, or readers of highly partisan newspapers, the result of participating in online communities could be expected to reinforce like-minded beliefs, similar interests, and therefore *ideological* homogeneity among members.

With the reign of information, the organization and strategies of the political system are becoming obsolete, their autonomy being denied by the flow of information. The argument is: 'Politics is fundamentally framed in its substance, organization, process and leadership by the inherent logic of media system, particularly by the new electronic media' (Castells 2004). Consequently there is strong evidence for the development of a new pattern of sociability based on networked individualism.

> Interactive electronic communication and particularly wireless communication, provides a powerful platform for political autonomy on the basis of independent channels of autonomous communication, from person to person and from group to group. . . . The network logic of the communication process makes it a high volume communication channel, but with a high degree of personalisation and interactivity. (Castells et al. 2006)

THE DIGITAL PUBLIC SPHERE

From the above-mentioned arguments it is clear that new technologies create new spaces. The Internet reshapes the information environment within which citizens operate and make decisions about whether to participate or not in politics. It facilitates online communication networks, which allow the rapid spread of information. It reduces the costs of interacting and finding information. Thus a new public sphere and new patterns of digital social capital is created. The individual becomes the central theme of the governance debate. Kalam (2005: 37) notes:

> The Internet revolution has proved to be a powerful tool for good governance initiatives. An important dimension of the Internet potential is the possibility of providing anytime—anywhere services. Along with this, there is a conscious effort to place the citizen at the centre of focus of governance where citizens are being perceived as customers and clients.

This public sphere opens up new possibilities for democratic deliberations. It is universal in nature and unrestricted in operation. It is observed that this sphere is occupied by groups ranging from Gandhians to Al-Qaeda. The debates are open, free, cheap and interactive. A recent example in this context is the debate on the book *The Hindus: An Alternative History* by Wendy Doniger. The book was withdrawn from the Indian market by the publishers in the face of stiff objection from several quarters. But when the controversy broke out the book became popular among the Internet community. As of now free copies of the book are widely circulating over the digital space. This shows how a government ban or trial can no longer be a deterring element for public deliberations. If this deliberation is also banned they will have to pay a heavy political and economic price.

The provision of technological means enable new participants to derive new ways of existence and institutionalization, possibly free from larger state intervention.[2] This new public sphere is ultimately a strong socialization tool and agency that promotes freedom and democracy. The system itself is undergoing a transformation from a democratic state to a democratic society. In the post-industrial society the scenario is characterized by the evolution of multiple channels of civic engagements and new patterns of mobilization. This civic dimension of public culture is weaved and strengthened by the new social networks and their instantaneous interactions.

The democratic potentials of the digital space were well evidenced with the Arab Spring. There was a heavy exchange of information in the social media, which helped protesters to organize the people and transmit their messages. The information flow in social media enabled the people to make an accurate and learned judgement of the scenario. A clear deliberative sphere was constructed. This also contributed to the progress of the revolution. Iskander (2011) observes:

> In this way, information was relayed back and forth and across various networks inside and outside Egypt. This enabled Egyptians watching from outside to participate and ensure that all concerned parties were well informed and supported so that a community physically fragmented by location was able to connect around a common concern. This was important especially on the first Friday of the protests, 28 January, when the state media inside Egypt, such as satellite channels, Nile News TV and al-Masreya, were focusing their broadcasts on the rumours of looting and violence. This spread panic and fear among people because alternative sources of information were limited and some were convinced that the protests should end. By keeping the information flowing,

people were able to judge the situation more clearly, and this helped to maintain the momentum of the protests.

In India, the IAC (India Against Corruption) movement and the later establishment of a new political party, namely the Aam Aadmi Party (AAP) evidenced the use of online technologies for democratic deliberations. The IAC movement gained momentum and vibrancy through its effective use of new technologies ranging from SMS to new Apps. They used the social media effectively throughout the campaign. This tempo was later carried over to the establishment of AAP, which utilizes online platforms like Facebook and Twitter to develop and disseminate their policies. The AAP and its leaders regularly update their status online. Major policies are posted in online forums for public discussion. They also collect funds through online channels. This results in greater transparency and enlarged public trust.

STATE INTERVENTIONS

> Government power is also increasing on the Internet. Long gone are the days of an Internet without borders; and governments are better able to use the four technologies of social control: surveillance, censorship, propaganda, and use control. There's a growing 'cyber sovereignty' movement that totalitarian governments are embracing to give them more control. (Gasser and Zittrain 2013: 11)

It is a reality that ICTs promote democracy in society. Many states accommodate the use of ICT in their legal systems. In the United States, in the 2011 case of *Glik* vs. *Cunniffe* the federal appeals court recognized the constitutional right of citizens to engage in direct documentation including YouTube and mobile photography, at least when directed at the actions of the government. In *ACLU* vs. *Alvarez* the court linked the individual right of recording police or government actions with the First Amendment right. Some of the European states incorporated the right to broadband in their constitutional system. In countries such as Estonia, France, Finland, Greece and Spain, Internet access has already been made a human right. The demand for the right to broadband emanated from Article 19 of the UN Declaration of Human Rights (UDHR). The article states, 'Everyone has the right to freedom of opinion and expression; this right includes freedom to hold opinions without interference and to seek, receive and impart information and ideas through any media and regardless of frontiers' (www.un.org). Governments have been enablers: investing in infrastructure, encouraging private sector action, conducting training and education and setting up legal regimes to support market environments that are ripe for ICT innovation. The multifaceted governmental acknowledgement of ICT potentials in democratizing governance and society is a pointer to a bright future. International agencies including the World Bank also promote ICT for the development of democracy. Between 2006 and 2011, the World Bank provided more than $3 billion of funding for ICT projects in over 80 countries.[3] On the other hand, Internet and new technologies can pose serious threats to democracy. Bertrand Russell (1952: 62) observes: 'A totalitarian government with a scientific bent might do things that to us would seem horrifying. The Nazis were more scientific than the present rulers of Russia, and were more inclined towards the sort of atrocities that I have in mind.'

Governments have acted as constrainers: reining in illegal activity, filtering speech, and inhibiting behaviour online. Government monitoring and regulation of online life is a cause of constant friction between the state and the people. During public uprisings, government monitoring and regulation of the Internet becomes strong and wide. On the other side, the state can effectively use ICT to invade into private lives of individuals. However, these policies are accompanied with heavy economic and political penalties. On the economic side, the penalty is in terms of trade and money. During the 2011 revolution in Egypt, the government shut down the Internet to cut off social media campaigns, and the Organisation for Economic Cooperation and Development (OECD) estimates that the network shutdown cost Egypt 90 million dollars.[4] On the political side the immediate suffering is on the legitimacy of the government. There will be new citizen consolidations and protests.[5] In times of technology tensions, trade-offs often accompany government interventions. For example, cracking down on cybercrime may help stimulate online business, but it may also hurt innovation. Laws and mechanisms for combating harmful speech often come at the cost of legitimate speech. Thus the scope of governmental restriction in citizen involvements is also limited by the reign of ICT. The state can no more hide its hideouts. Any restraint is met with heavy political and economic costs.

CONCLUSION

In a democratic society, the evolution of digital technologies enables more effective and efficient discussion and participation. The traditional barriers of place, time and economy are effectively mitigated with the support of technology. Many of the new social movements are supported and supplemented by social media and technology tools. However, the democratic potential of e-Governance is conditional and depends on many factors. It is evident that technologies are neither democratic nor autocratic. In a democratic society it can be a potential aid for democratic movements whereas autocratic regimes use technologies to become more autocratic. But still ICT offers a potential for more effective communication and deliberation even in closed societies. The best example is provided with the Sichuan earthquake in China in May 2008. Before the earthquake, corruption in the country's construction industry was an open secret. During the earthquake most of the schools collapsed whereas private buildings were less damaged. When the schools collapsed, citizens began sharing documentations of the damages and their protests through social media tools. The consequence of government corruption was made broadly visible, and it went from being an open secret to public truth. The provincial government was forced to take action against the corrupt elements.

Digital spaces are a potential venue for political deliberations. They offer better possibilities to ordinary citizens to interact with their government. Positively the gap between citizens and the government is reduced to bits and bytes. The demystification of the structures of authority brings down new identifications. In this context the space provided by new social media deserves special mention. It offers an ever continuing platform of discourse which is essentially interactive and evidently constructive. A political stratum of society acquires new political identification in the digital spaces. This may be because of two reasons. The first is easy and instantaneous access. In the new digital space, deliberations are spontaneous and the targeted authority structures are only at the distance of a mouse click. The second advantage relates to the public sphere and the social capital aspect of digital spaces. The digital media construct strong psychological bonds among the participants. The likemindedness as observed by Castells, is clearly operating in this platform. Digital groupings are more solid than physical groupings as they share the freedom to freely express and at the same time the freedom to freely sign out of a debate. Thus, this public sphere is more participative and wide.

Digital platforms also raise many issues which need to be sorted out urgently. They narrow down the deliberative space to the techno-elitists. The agenda of new deliberations are centred around the peripheral issues of their politics and do not offer a clear probe into the underlying problems of society. Kampen and Snijkers (2003: 494) argue that e-democracy itself is a myth. It is based on four premises: the idea that convenience will lead to participation, that the public needs more information, that the Internet is a 'massive town meeting,' and that in the absence of so-called power brokers, democracy will flourish. The authors are of the opinion that none of these premises seem to be ultimately defensible.

> The safest characterization of recent quantitative attempts to answer the question, 'Do digital tools enhance democracy?' is that these tools probably do not hurt in the short run and might help in the long run, and that they have the most dramatic effects in states where a public sphere already constraints the actions of the government. (Shirky 2011: 30)

Identifying the Internet as a massive town meeting stands invalid in the context of the digital divide and underdevelopment. The proportionality between information and participation is yet to be established. The very concept of broker-elimination is also questioned. In the place of traditional power brokers new techno-brokers may come and reign. In the face of criticism, it is admitted that ICT cannot create democratic paradises. But it can change the modules and modalities of present-day democracy. At least it can be an amplifying agent of politics. This amplification theory suggests that ICT can act as an effective lubricant to the established systems. Best and Wade (2009: 256-7) comment:

> What this means is that the Internet acts as a politically neutral 'constant,' whose main effect is to amplify political situations to new heights. For instance, the Internet in an authoritarian political environment would tend to exacerbate the brutality of the regime, while the Internet in a democratic political environment would tend to improve civil rights and political liberties. As such, we can determine how much of an effect the Internet has on democracy merely by evaluating a given political situation and multiplying by some Internet factor.

The digital society and online spaces can ignite revolutions. A growing community of digital political activists can structure democratic deliberations and democratic processes on the right path.[6] As of democracy, the evils of the digital space can be well rectified with wider digital space. There is a clear linkage between digital tools and the democratization process of society. This link will be durable only if it has a parallel companion in democracy—the public sphere. With the development of a public sphere, ICT can enhance democratic capabilities and democratization processes.

NOTES

1. Tuzzi et al. (2007) further suggest certain 'evaluation' aspects that define democracy. (a) Rule of law, that the decisional output and implementation of the law are supreme, with an independent judiciary and fair resolution of lawsuits required; (b) Accountability, that the elected political leaders are obligated to answer for their political decisions when queried by citizens, opponents or constitutional bodies; this implies an informed public that actively participates in the political process; (c) Respect for rights and achievement for freedoms, that implementation of social, political and economic equality is progressive; and (d) Responsiveness, that those that are governed are able to be satisfied that their demands are met through policies, services and distribution; also requires an informed and engaged public/ society and e-Democracy.

2. Wael Ghonim, Google's Middle East marketing director, and a participant of the Arab revolution observes how technologies fortify individuals against the fear of authority. The individual is allied with a network. He says, 'Yet, nothing was happening. . . . The reason why everyone was silent was . . . the psychological barrier of fear. . . . And that psychological barrier of fear has worked for so many years. And here comes the Internet Technology Blackberry, SMS. It's helping all of us to connect. Platforms like YouTube, Twitter, Facebook were helping us a lot, because they basically gave us the impression that, 'Wow—I'm not alone!' (for a detailed discussion see Hofheinz, 2011).
3. See World Bank, 'About the ICT Sector Unit', Information and Communication Technologies, cited in Prasad and Ray (2012: 18).
4. See, 'Reaching the Kill Switch', *The Economist*, 12-18 February 2011, 398 (8720): 68.
5. The United States government initiated a bill to regulate Internet namely, Stop Online Piracy Act, in 2011. The Act was supposed to bring strong regulations on Internet copyright and allied fields. The bill was met with heavy opposition from the public and civil society. Wikipedia organized an online campaign against the Act and 162 million individuals signed the online petition (See Balaraman, *US Parliament Nettil Kurungunnu*, (Malayalam), *Mathrubhumi*, 25 January 2012, www.mathrubhumi.com.).
6. It is observed that the absence of political professionalism often makes many of these online initiated revolutions unsustainable. For example, during the Arab revolution there was no strong political agenda particularly with regard to the post revolutionary scenario.

REFERENCES

Allagui, Ilhem and Johanne Kuebler (2011): 'The Arab Spring and the Role of ICTs', *International Journal of Communication*, 5: 1435-42.

Bedi, Kiran, Paraminder Jeet Singh and Sandeep Srivastava (2001): *Government@net: New Governance Opportunities for India*, New Delhi: Sage.

Best, Michael L. and Keegan W. Wade (2009): 'The Internet and Democracy: Global Catalyst or Democratic Dud?', *Bulletin of Science, Technology and Society*, 29(4), August: 255-71.

Boyte, Harry (2005): 'Reframing Democracy: Governance, Civic Agency and Politics', *Public Administration Review*, 65(5): 536-46.

Castells, Manuel (2000): 'Global Information Capitalism', in David Held and

Anthony McGrew (eds.), *The Global Transformations Reader*, Cambridge: Polity.

—— (2004): *The Power of Identity*, Oxford: Blackwell.

Castells, Manuel, Mireia Fernandez-Ardevol, Jack Linchuan Qiu and Araba Sey (2006): 'Electronic Communication and Socio Political Mobilisation: A New Form of Civil Society', in Marlies Glasius, Mary Kaldor and Helmut Anheier (eds.), *Global Civil Society 2005/2006*, New Delhi: Sage.

—— (2007): 'Communication, Power and Counter-power in the Network Society', *International Journal of Communication*, 1: 238-66.

—— (2008): 'The New Public Sphere: Global Civil Society, Communication Networks, and Global Governance', *The Annals of the American Academy of Political and Social Science*, 616: 78-93.

Coleman, Stephen (1999): 'The New Media and Democratic Politics', *New Media Society*, 1(1): 67-74.

—— (2007): 'E-Democracy: The History and Future of an Idea', in Robin Mansell, Chrisanthi Avgerou, Danny Quah and Roger Silverstone (eds.), *The Oxford Handbook of Information and Communication Technologies*, New York: Oxford University Press.

Crozier, Michael P. (2010): 'Rethinking Systems: Configurations of Politics and Policy in Contemporary Governance', *Administration and Society*, 42(5): 504-25.

Dionne Jr, E.J. (1991): *Why Americans Hate Politics*, New York: Simon and Schuster.

Etling, Bruce, Robert Faris and John Palfrey (2010): 'Political Change in the Digital Age: The Fragility and Promise of Online Organizing', *SAIS Review, Summer-Fall 2010:* 1-13.

Gasser, Urs, and Jonathan Zittrain (2013): *Internet Monitor 2013*, Harvard: The Berkman Centre for Internet and Society.

Gupta, Monobina (2011): 'The Radia Tapes, WikiLeaks and Insurgent Media', *Economic and Political Weekly*, 46(4): 10-12.

Hofheinz, Albrecht (2011): 'Nextopia? Beyond Revolution 2.0', *International Journal of Communication*, 5: 1417-34.

Iskander, Elizabeth (2011): 'Connecting the National and the Virtual: Can Facebook Activism Remain Relevant After Egypt's January 25 Uprising?' *International Journal of Communication*, 5: 1225-37.

ITU and World Bank (2012): *The Little Data Book on Information and Communication Technology 2012*, Washington D.C.: The World Bank.

Kalam, A. P. J. Abdul (2002): *Ignited Minds*, New Delhi: Penguin.

—— (2005): 'A Vision of Citizen Centric E-Governance for India', in R.K.

Bagga, Kenneth Keniston and Rohit Raj Mathur (eds.), *The State, IT and Development*, New Delhi: Sage.

Kampen, Jarl K. and Kris Snijkers (2003): 'E-Democracy: A Critical Evaluation of the Ultimate E-Dream', *Social Science Computer Review*, 21(4): 491-6.

Matthews, Jessica T. (2003): 'Power Shift', in David Held and Anthony McGrew (eds.), *The Global Transformations Reader*, Cambridge: Polity Press.

Norris, Pippa (1999): 'The Growth of Critical Citizens and its Consequences', in Pippa Norris (ed.), *Critical Citizens*, Oxford: Oxford University Press.

—— (2001): *Digital Divide*, Cambridge: Cambridge University Press.

—— (2002): *Democratic Phoenix: Reinventing Political Activism*, Cambridge: Cambridge University Press.

Patterson, Thomas (2002): 'The Vanishing Voter: Why are the Voting Booths so Empty', *National Civic Review*, 91(4): 367-78.

Pharr, Susan J. and Robert D. Putnam (2000): *Disaffected Democracies: What's Troubling the Trilateral Countries*, Princeton: Princeton University Press.

Porta, Donatella Della (2011): 'Communication in Movement', *Information, Communication and Society*, 14(6): 800-19.

'Power to the People', *The Economist*, 23 January 2003.

Prasad, Rohit and Rupamanjari Sinha Ray (2012): 'Critique of the Common Service Centre Scheme', *Economic and Political Weekly*, 47(6): 18-23.

Russell, Bertrand (1952): *The Impact of Science on Society*, London: Routledge.

Shirky, Clay (2011): 'The Political Power of Social Media Technology: The Public Sphere and Political Change', *Foreign Affairs*, 90(1): 28-41.

Starr, Paul (2010): 'The Liberal State in a Digital World', *Governance*, 23(1): 1-6.

Tuzzi, Arjuna, Claudia Padovani, and Giorgia Nesti (2007): 'Communication and (e)democracy: Assessing European e-democracy Discourses', in Bart Cammaerts and Nico Carpentier (eds.), *Reclaiming the Media: Communication Rights and Democratic Media Roles*, Chicago: University of Chicago Press.

Walton, Douglas C. (2007): 'Is Modern Information Technology Enabling the Evolution of a More Direct Democracy?' *World Futures*, 63(5): 365-85.

Williamson, Andy (2011): 'Disruption and Empowerment: Embedding Citizens at the Heart of Democracy', *Journal of Democracy and Open Government*, 3(1): 22-32.

World Bank (2012): *Human Development Report 2012*, Washington D.C.: The World Bank.

CHAPTER 9

'Mediated' Public Sphere and Deliberative Democracy in India: A Critical Reflection

J. PRABHASH

The foundational feature of democracy, both in theory as well as in practice, is the idea of dialogue—dialogue between the state/ruling classes and the people, among the ruling classes themselves and among various social categories in society. The underlying assumption is that dialogue helps citizens in exchanging views and defending their supporting reasons concerning public political questions (Rawls 1999: 579-80). This, in turn, not only ensures administrative stability and system maintenance but also a degree of social peace and harmony, though it does not hold any promise of guaranteed social transformation.

The last point draws sustenance from the fact that dialogue *per se* could not usher in a restructuring of power and property relations which is basic to social transformation. Also dialogue participants are not equal partners in the process as they could hardly bracket their background inequalities and differential potential for reasoning.[1] Therefore, what dialogue could actually ensure is to create a feeling among various interests that they have a stake in the continuance of the system and further guarantee its legitimacy through their involvement in the deliberative process. This is a classic case of participation without empowerment. Be that as it may, dialogue still has relevance as a means for playing out differences among people in the best of parliamentary tradition and the spirit of democratic citizenship. At least, it enhances the potential of politics to moderate and contain conflicts and, in certain cases, even transform them from something base to something richer (Khilnani 2004: 26).

For the proponents of the above notion, this is the quintessence of deliberative democracy. Even this limited potential of dialogue/deliberation depends on the nature of public sphere and civil society of which it (public sphere) is a part. These two roughly constitute the space between the family (private sphere) and the state and is the place where individuals play out their self-interests. Though at the outset it may seem to be a bit paradoxical, this is a situation which Karl Marx had envisaged as the conflict between 'man as citizen and man as private individuals' (Femia 2001: 135). This would be clear if one understands the bourgeois origins of the two concepts.

CIVIL SOCIETY AND PUBLIC SPHERE: A THEORETICAL NOTE

Civil society, it may be noted, originated out of the need of the bourgeoisie to interrogate the power of the absolute state of the eighteenth century over which it did not have any control. This they expressed in the form of various open and underground movements and created various public spaces which took various forms such as clubs, coffee houses, salons, and library and literary societies (Koselleck 1988: 66). This way it was thought that they (bourgeoisie) could provide a critique of the absolutist order and thereby cut the sinews of its legitimacy *without posing any direct challenge to the existing power arrangement* (Singh 2008: 195).

The civil society was, therefore, viewed as an institutional arrangement with a clear objective of providing the bourgeois class access to political power and was hence democratic and even progressive. However, it is another thing that it conceded very little either by way of power or by way of rights to the mass of the people. It was 'democratization' without empowering the people. This exactly was the reason why Antonio Gramsci had identified the primary goal of civil society as one of offering justification to the exploitative class relations by making them appear right and normal. It has not changed much from this original objective though, of late, movements by marginalized sections like women, working class, Dalits and minorities have, on occasions, successfully challenged some of the exploitative ways, particularly of the market and the state. Hence, in this perception the capacity of civil society for empowerment is really limited. And public sphere which is supposed to be the medium through which civil society expresses itself cannot have a different intent and sense of purpose.

The public sphere which Jürgen Habermas has much eulogized as a dialogic space for rational debate (Alam 2005: 354) which determines agreements and actions in the place of inherited ideas or personal statuses (Calhoun 1993: 273) suffers from the same limitations which restrict the democratic potential of the civil society. Interestingly, Habermas himself acknowledges this when he accepts that deliberations in the general public sphere may reflect the influences of unequally distributed social power, violence and distorted communications, and again that communicative rationality presents difficulties in societies characterized by deep social and cultural divides (Habermas 1991: 25 and 1996: 63; Parkinson 2012: 63; Joseph 2004: 131-2; Pellizoni 2001: 66; and Henaff and Strong 2001). Thus the concept of public sphere and the discursive domain it creates, in Habermas' own terms, are contaminated by the difference in material conditions and the unevenness it produces in other areas of human life including intellectual life.

Added to this, is his view on the end result of discourse as generation of consensus on public good. Habermas believes that rational, critical and free debates can transcend power structures and consolidate the general interests of society by forging a consensus (Chandhoke 2005: 330) which is not true in actual practice. This is because, on the one side what often masquerades in the name of 'general interest' is the particular interests of the powerful and, on the other hand, the very notion of consensus could be misleading as it often progresses by neutralizing differences through a process of deliberate omission or even through appropriation. As the feminist and other minoritarian critiques of the civic republican ideal of 'common good' has shown us, the development of 'common good' as the so-called democratic ideal elbows out the politics of difference based on inferiorised identities (Pandiyan 2002: 1738) and all forms of consensus are by necessity based on acts of exclusion (Mouffe 1992: 379; Ferrara 1989: 317). Interestingly, Habermas' solutions to this lies in procedural safeguards which allow 'free and equal' participation in discourse, though one is at a loss to grasp as to how such safeguards could ensure this in a society characterized by unequal power and property relations.

GLOBALIZATION AND DEVELOPMENT IN ICT

Further, globalization and revolutionary changes in the field of ICT have affected the nature of public sphere in ways which were unimaginable a few decades ago. The combined impact of these two has not only made people individualistic in nature but, more than that, robbed them of their role in decision-making. At a different plane, it has also reduced the potential of the public sphere for critical debates on public issues.

The modern globalized world is noted for two contradictory trends: on the one side individuals are connected with each other by a maze of communication networks to such a degree that it robs everyone of even his/her privacy and, on the other side, each individual remains socially disconnected. Though ICT enables individuals to remain in constant touch with each other, they do not feel that they are part of a social whole. This is basically because individual concerns are put ahead of community interests. One is reminded of the statement made by the former British prime minister, Margaret Thatcher, that 'society has disappeared from the contemporary world and what remains is the individual, and at the most families'. It is only natural that in individualistic societies, the private sphere displaces the public (Paz 1998: 14). This is a sure recipe for depoliticization. As individuals show a gross disinclination to intervene in public issues, they are actually distancing themselves from politics leaving enough room for vested interests to manipulate the democratic processes. Robert Hassan (2008: 191) puts this situation thus:

'Power geometry' is no longer clustered around specific (and relatively stable) sites such as government and institutional politics as it was during much of the period of modernity, but linked to the commodity and to the market. Accordingly, in a context where the market and the commodity dominate our post-modernity, power is now a 'thing' that is contestable and flows through the structures of not only the state, but the corporation too.

The trend today, therefore, is to keep as much decision-making as possible outside the range of public and politics or at least to sidestep the process of representative governance which means both the ultimate electorate and the activities of assemblies and agencies elected by it (Hobsbawm 2007: 111). This is a classic case of 'privatization' of public policies and politics itself, i.e. statecraft slipping out of public control and available for manipulation by private interests who are accountable to none save themselves. In a situation like this, the high talk about deliberative democracy and public sphere becomes meaningless.

One is also witness to a parallel development here—the very forces which manipulate the state also control the public sphere through their ownership right over mass media including the new social media. Further, the ICT revolution which is at the root of the modern information society—the locomotive of public sphere today—is not an ideologically neutral one. Recall here Bill Gates' (1995: 168) widely debated statement about ICT's role in bringing about 'friction free capitalism' and the realization of Adam Smith's notion of the ideal market where would-be buyers and sellers share 'complete information through which they could make fully informed decisions'. No matter how we look at them, the information society and its chief engine, the ICT, have been originated and developed first for the interest of capital (Hassan 2008: 65). One could also imagine the prospect of rational and critical debates through new social media where people, as Jean Baudrillard (2009: 90) said, 'no longer speak though they chat'. Interestingly, they also chat alone, as isolated individuals. All the theoretical suppositions of the public sphere and deliberative democracy become redundant here, as there is little space for face to face communication and organic dialogue.

Related to the above is the 'digital divide' inherent in the modern information society and the growth of cartels and monopolies in the media industry. As in the case of many other things, information is also reduced to the status of a commodity in the neoliberal world. It has a price tag attached to it. Therefore, the individual has to be able to pay to take part in what the information society has to offer, and to be unable to pay is to become marginalized and gradually more invisible as a member of the society (Hassan 2008: 59). And in actual practice there is a large class of people who cannot afford to pay the price of admission to the information age (Mosco 1958: 10). Information thus becomes the monopoly of a few and 'expresses the characteristics and prevailing relations of power' (Robins and Webster 1999: 70) creating a Foucaultian situation of information (read knowledge) being used to extend the field of power (Foucault 1980: 109-33). The prospect for this has become still brighter with the emergence of media cartels. According to one estimate, 75 per cent of the global media space is controlled by just five multinational corporations which in their turn are the subsidies of huge business cartels and weapons manufacturing companies (Sainath 2010). Thus control over business, media, information and power converges to form a rare mix which is inimical to both deliberative democracy and public sphere. It is against this theoretical background that the problem of media and public sphere in India has to be discussed.

PUBLIC SPHERE IN INDIA

The aforesaid theoretical issues conjoined with certain contextual limitations have produced in India a public sphere which is hardly conducive for deliberative democracy to flourish. It needs to be reiterated that even at its inception the Indian public sphere was not democratic. Neither was it secular in nature. The reasons for this need not be located solely on colonial intervention though its role cannot be discounted in any manner. It may be recalled that the colonial state viewed the public sphere not as an arena for critical engagement with the socio-political order, but one through which the upper caste elite could present before the ruling dispensation their aspirations and concerns in a manner which could at best be described as passive and gentle. The intention was clear—to offer elite Indians a semblance of participation in governance without, at the same time, giving them a voice in its actual running. Much more important than this were the impact of the caste/class system and the role of religion on the growth and emergence of the sphere during its formative period and also for a long time thereafter.

Since all the forces mentioned above had a pernicious hold over the public sphere, both participation and transactions in it were highly restrictive. It worked on the basis of exclusion rather than inclusion, i.e. it excluded more people than it included. The result was the marginalization of the lower castes and class in general, Dalits and women in particular, making public sphere a preserve of the educated upper castes. It is true that the mobilizational politics of nationalism urged people to act in ways strikingly different from the segmentation and community orientation in their daily life (Panikkar 2009). But it never debated the question of caste and religion in their finer details since it considered the realm of culture as something non-negotiable and hence unworthy of contestation. M.S.S. Pandian (2002: 1737) puts the consequences of this historic omission of the national movement thus:

> The so-called sovereign domain of culture uncolonized by the West remained a domain to affirm elite upper caste culture/spirituality as *the* culture of the nation. . . . This act of mobilizing a part of the national to stand for the whole, not only inferiorised vast sections of the lower castes as inadequate citizens-in-the-making; but also significantly *delegitimized the language of caste in the domain of politics by annexing it as part of the cultural.* It is only by unsettling the boundaries between the spiritual and material, inner and outer, the lower castes (and women) could contest the logic of exclusion inherent in the so-called national culture and talk caste in the colonial public sphere.

It was not that no attempt was made to discuss the centrality of the caste system in the Indian social order during the pre-Independence days. In fact, although leaders and social reformers like B.R. Ambedkar, E.V. Ramasami Naicker, Jyotiba Phule and others tried to put in perspective the imperative for deliberating the caste question and the need for separating the spiritual and the material, the whole debate continued to be marginal as the pedagogic process of the national movement remained silent on the issue. However, this was not the case with regard to religion. Not only did different religious groups (especially Hindus and Muslims) play out their differences in the public sphere, the debates even on secular socio-political issues were carried out on religious lines. As a result, what has become prominent in the public sphere was not secular reason but religious celebration based on rituals and superstitions (Panikkar 2009). All these trends were, more or less, carried on to the post-Independence period as well, though since the seventies lower caste resurgence that has happened in Indian politics started challenging the upper caste dominated public sphere.

MEDIA[TED] PUBLIC SPHERE

Needless to say, these unhealthy trends in the public sphere have their influence in the media as well. Media, in fact, became the medium through which they were staged and passed on to the civil society. Indeed, during both the pre-Independence and post-Independence periods and until the spread of regional dailies and TV channels, English media became the chief vehicle for this purpose. The narrow circle of English-educated upper caste Indians and an even smaller group of their counterparts belonging to other castes and religions raised critical issues pertaining to their interests through it. Significantly, all these were presented as concerns affecting their respective communities or even the nation as a whole. Thus, exceptions apart, these concerns provided the sinews for the so-called 'rational debates' in India's deliberative democracy. The argument here is not that the issues affecting the large mass of marginalized humanity had been totally blotted out, but only that the life realities and struggles of the majority had only found a minor reflection in the media and hence in the deliberations in the public sphere.

It is true that the spread of the regional press and television network has tremendously changed the situation, at least at a surface scan.[2] The proportion of India's population whose experiences and views which are disseminated by being reported in the mass circulation newspapers and popular television channels has vastly increased with the media's geographical spread reaching the countryside and its social spread penetrating well below the level of English-speaking people (Friedlander et al. 2009: 199-200). However, this only meant that the class whose interests which provided the fodder for deliberation in the public sphere got widened with the inclusion of regional elites. Even this was transient in a sense as neoliberal economic policies resulted in concentration of media ownership and the emergence of a new found relationship between the media, business and the political class since the 1990s. Additionally, the sway of organized religions over the public sphere and, thereby, over the state enhanced tremendously.

'CORPORATIZATION' AND 'POLITICIZATION' OF MEDIA

An important development in the media landscape since the 1990s which has all the potential to dampen the public sphere has been the corporate takeover of the media and the resultant concentration in ownership. According to one estimate, a handful of corporations control as much as 90 per cent of information flows that are publicly and easily available and which constantly invade people's living spaces (Ahmed 2014). Further, around seven major companies account for the bulk of circulation in the powerful English language media (Swami 2007: 187). With the acquisition of Network 18—a consortium of 13 news channels, 22 Internet channels, 18 websites, in 11 languages including CNN-IBN, IBN7, CNBC, TV18, Lokmat and an entire clutch of ETV channels—by Reliance Industries Ltd., the magnitude of this concentration has increased manifold[3] (Baruah and Mishra 2014; Raman 2014: 33).

This means that every platform which distils public opinion is controlled by the corporate establishments who then use it for disseminating views in the form of news so that the entire deliberative process in the public sphere becomes stage managed and hence meaningless from the vantage point of deliberative democracy. Even the emergence of social media could offer little relief in this regard. This is mainly because it could only provide an opportunity to challenge suppression of facts and could not establish a powerful social organization to create an alternative public sphere to undermine corporate control of information as the discrepancy between corporate power and opposition media is still great as to be incalculable (Ahmad 2014). One should also understand that what social media, *per se*, could do is to help in enhancing the potential of democracy and not rewrite its content as this involves the larger question of power and property relations. Robert Hassan (2008: 119-20) describes this situation thus:

> Freedom to use communication system does not make a democracy; democracy is about power relations, and the democratic use of social power. Neither can ICTs bring freedom in any deterministic sense. Freedom needs to be fought for, and in a networked, but still class-based and ideologically structured global system, struggle continues in cyber space as well as on the streets. No matter how small the world has become, defeat and victory are part of the ongoing fight for freedom by peoples elsewhere. What is certain is that the fostering of world peace will only come through more equality and more democracy, and not through simply being able to communicate on YouTube or My Space. These can help, but they are easily closed-off vectors for democratic communication, and when they are closed off, then the struggle for democracy suddenly becomes old fashioned and sometimes painfully slow.

'Corporatization' of media has also another side to it—media houses also control a large number of business concerns. Media corporations are into hundreds of businesses, from real estate, hotels, mining, steel, chemicals, rubber and banks to power and sugar (Sainath 2010). For instance, *Times of India* has business interests in 175 firms and *Dainik Bhaskar*, the Hindi daily with a readership of over 17 million, in 69 companies ranging from mining, power generation and real estates to textiles (Bisht 2012: 34). Interestingly, this 'corporatization' of media ownership coexists with 'politicization' of media ownership, i.e. political parties/leadership owning media networks. According to *Business Standard*, a third of the news channels in the country are, for all intents and purposes, controlled by politicians (Parthasarathy 2013: 24). This is particularly found at the regional level with states like Punjab, Karnataka, Kerala, Tamil Nadu, and former Andhra Pradesh taking the lead.[4] Here, therefore, politics, media and capital merge to form a new form of capitalism—media/political capitalism[5]—with interest in everything from business, culture and public policies to state power, to mention just a few.

This has affected every aspect of journalism from media philosophy to media ethics. Today, it is not concerned with substantive issues crucial to a functional democracy, but with market, consumers, voters and politics (Rao 2005: 41-3). Stories can be planted, headlines can be discussed, story positions can be dictated, corporate journalists belong to particular corporate camps and are obviously paid retainer fees, stories are slanted to serve patron interests, and journalists can be moulded to bridge between corporates and politicians (Chaudhury 2010: 45). Needless to say, this has breached the separation between media, politics and business.

To put the above proposition in a much more nuanced manner, a certain adversarial relationship between the media on the one hand, and political parties and corporations on the other, which was seen by media practitioners as a basic rule of their turf is not the order of the day (Pande 2010). Instead, now all the three work in tandem for private aggrandisement and accumulation of wealth. Media carries out the public relations work for the state/political parties, and the latter manages public policies for the former and the corporates who own it. And with the introduction of neoliberal economic policies, the role of the media has gone beyond mere public relations exercise to one of providing ideological support for the state to pursue such policies, particularly privatization of all vital sectors of the economy. In two separate analyses, Arvind Rajagopal and Vinod K. Jose neatly summarize this development in the following words:

> After liberalization and the growth of privately owned media in its wake, the targets of criticism should logically have extended beyond the state to the business and the new forms of globalisation resulting from it. But such criticism has been scarce, indeed. The institutional space for criticism has shrunk, but this is not the only reason. The expansion of the private sector has presented itself, courtesy of the major media, as a desirable phenomenon, driven not by corporations so much as by popular demand. (Rajagopal 2009: 18)

> By the 1990s, when the idea of large government became unfashionable and the market opened up, the media moved *en masse* to build and serve the new big

thing—private power. From nation building, we went to work again as masons of India Inc. building. (Jose 2013: 20).

Interestingly the success of journalism as a profession now depends not on its performance in terms of investigative reporting, but on its performance for the sake of the investors and the politics they support and represent. Neoliberalism has substituted market-friendly media for people-friendly media of the yesteryears. What Jagadish Chandra, the CEO of ETV, Rajasthan, said in the 2013 annual getaway for the senior management staff of Network 18 is the reality. 'Our channel is profitable in Rajasthan. I keep Vasundhara Raje [the then leader of opposition of the Assembly and the present Chief Minister of the state] happy, and I also keep Ashok Gehlot [the then Chief Minister of the state] happy. (I keep) both parties happy' [Bhatia 2013: 51]. The reverse side of this is that both these two leaders, in turn, keep the management of the media concerned and the business interests it represents always in good humour. The contribution such a captive media can make for the cause of strengthening public sphere and deliberative democracy is imaginable.

RELIGION AND PUBLIC SPHERE

Added to this is the stranglehold religion has over India's public sphere. It was already seen that even at its inception, the public sphere in India was not secular in nature as critical engagement with religion was considered blasphemous and as debates even on secular issues were carried out through religious idioms. In other words, like culture, religion was also placed above the discursive domain of the public sphere. This trend, more or less, continues to this day. Even informed debates on religion, particularly on their deviant ways, are discouraged and resisted. Books are forced to be banned/censored and films withdrawn from theatres simply because of threats coming from organized gangs who have the blessings of the religious leaderships.

Bans on books like Salman Rushdie's *Satanic Verses* and Stanley Wolpert's *Nine Hours to Rama* to the more recent work by Wendy

Doniger, *Hinduism: An Alternative History* are examples of such intolerance towards alternative conceptions of religious reality. Even public policy matters on issues like school/university curriculum and textbooks, academic writing, inheritance and the like are looked at through the prism of religion. The slightest interrogation of established patterns of belief or deviations in the existing thinking on such issues would invite the wrath of the religious hierarchy and its adherents. All these need not be mistaken as examples of religious intolerance towards outside criticism, but are, in fact, instances of intolerance towards fresh, free and open discussions that emerge from within, a classic case of religious obscurantism. Significantly, in most of the cases the mainstream media either remained neutral or aligned with the very forces of obscurantism, directly or indirectly.

IN LIEU OF CONCLUSION

From the aforesaid discussion, it is clear that public sphere and deliberative democracy function in ways which are neither public nor democratic. While in terms of conception and constitution the public sphere has all the trappings of a secular-democratic order, it is not so in actual practice. So is the case with regard to deliberative democracy which suffers not from an overdose of deliberation but from a clear deficit of the same. The unequally distributed social power, violence, distorted communication, communalism and religious obscurantism, depoliticization, 'corporatization' and 'politicization' of the media, all have contaminated the public sphere and democracy in India.

Mass media, in its turn, has grossly failed to arrest this trend and, instead, it has only aided this process in its own way. That is to say, it has not created Habermas' 'idealised public sphere in which informed citizens debate issues of common national concerns'. If anything, it has become establishmentarian in its nature, outlook and functioning with its own agenda—always the interests of its management, often a corporate house—to pursue and promote. Its objective is neither to promote cool and dispassionate reasoning on socio-political affairs, nor to dig deep into events so that deviations in the exercise of state power is brought to the limelight. What Regis Debray (1996: 91) said about contemporary media in general is applicable in equal measure to its Indian counterpart. 'The media sphere privileges' he said, 'the letter against the spirit, extension in space against comprehension, space against content. The methodological sensibility is not given to going to the bottom of things, keeping instead to faces, surfaces and interfaces.'

The result is that the media has become not only less reflective, but also less critical. To put the record straight, it is reflective and critical only on behalf of the powerful forces who control the state and political processes, and not for the mass of the people on whose behalf it is supposed to act as the watch dog in a democracy. Deliberative democracy, to repeat, is all about deliberation and conversation. This, therefore, begs two fundamental questions: Who hosts the conversation/deliberation? Who are its participants? If the answers are corporate media and corporate houses/powerful interests, respectively, then deliberative democracy and its vehicle, the public sphere, will have very little of democracy in them. This, in short, is the case in contemporary India.

NOTES

1. Habermas himself concedes that what carries weight in decision-making is the 'force of the better argument'.
2. There is a tremendous growth in the regional media in the country since the 1970s. For instance, for the first time, the sales of Hindi dailies outnumbered those in the English language. By 2001, nine out of ten were language dailies, whereas in 1954 only one out of ten was in an Indian language. Added to this, by 2006 television coverage expanded to 40 million households (Rajagopal 2009: 17).
3. *Forbes India* and news websites such as firstpost.com and IBNlive.com and the Colours entertainment channel also form part of this cartel.
4. For instance in Punjab, Chief Minister Prakash Singh Badal's family controls Fastway, a leading cable company; in Karnataka former chief minister and JD(S) leader, H.D. Kumaraswamy, controls Kasturi Channel; and in Tamil Nadu each of the five major political parties own at least one TV channel

each. While in Kerala both CPI(M) and Congress (I) have their newspapers and TV channels, in Andhra Pradesh each of the state's 15 news channels was politically affiliated, in one way or the other (Parthasarathy 2013: 24-6).

5. Recall the famous phrase of Max Weber on 'Political Capitalism', which he used to describe the phenomenon of making money by using state power.

REFERENCES

Ahmad, Aijaz (2014): 'Facts as Democratic Value', *Inaugural Address*, Asian School of Journalism, 7 July.

Alam, Javed (2005): 'A Look at Theory: Civil Society, Democracy and Public Sphere in India', in Rajeev Bhargava and Helmut Reifeld (eds.), *Civil Society, Public Sphere and Citizenship: Dialogues and Perceptions*, New Delhi: Sage.

Baruah, Amit and Lalatendu Mishra (2014): 'Reliance to take over Network 18', *The Hindu*, 30 May.

Baudrillard, Jean (2009): *The Transparency of Evil: Essays on Extreme Phenomena*, London: Verso.

Bhatia, Rahul (2013): 'The Network Effect', *The Caravan*, 5(12), December.

Bisht, Narendra (2012): 'Interview with Arundhati Roy', *Outlook*, 52(47), 26 November.

Calhoun, Craig (1993): 'Civil Society and the Public Sphere', *Public Culture*, Winter, 5(2).

Chandhoke, Neera (2005): 'Explaining the Mythology of Public Sphere', in Rajeev Bhargava and Helmut Reifeld (eds.), *Civil Society, Public Sphere and Citizenship: Dialogues and Perceptions*, New Delhi: Sage.

Chaudhury, Shoma (2010): 'Media Ethics, Why We Need Both Panic and a Pinch of Salt?', *Tehelka*, 7(48), 4 December.

Debray, Regis (1996): *Media Manifestos: On the Technological Transmission of Cultural Forms*, Eric Rauth (Translator), London: Verso.

Femia, Joseph (2001): 'Civil Society and the Marxist Tradition', in Sudipta Kaviraj and Sunil Khilnani (eds.), *Civil Society: History and Possibilities*, Cambridge: Cambridge University Press.

Ferrara, Allesandro (1989): 'Critical Theory and its Discontents: On Wellmer's Critique of Habermas', *Praxis International*, 9(3).

Foucault, Michel (1980): 'Truth and Power', in Colin Gorden (ed.), *Power/Knowledge: Selected Interviews and Other Writings 1972-1977*, New York: Pantheon Books.

Friedlander, Peter, Robin Jeffrey and Sanjay Seth (2009): 'Subliminal Change: How Hindi-Language Newspaper Expansion Affects India', in Arvind Rajagopal (ed.), *The Indian Public Sphere: Readings in Media History*, New Delhi: Oxford University Press.

Gates, Bill (1995): *The Road Ahead,* New York: Penguin.

Habermas, Jürgen (1991): *The Structural Transformation of the Public Sphere: An Enquiry into a Category of Bourgeois Society,* Cambridge: Polity Press.

—— (1996): *Between Facts and Norms: Contributions to a Discourse Theory of Law and Democracy,* Cambridge: Polity Press.

Hassan, Robert (2008): *The Information Society,* Malden, MA: Polity Press.

Henaff, C. Marcel and Tracy B. Strong (eds.) (2001): *Public Sphere and Democracy,* Minneapolis: University of Minnesota Press.

Hobsbawm, Eric (2007): *Globalization, Democracy and Terrorism,* London: Abacus.

Jose, Vinod K. (2013): 'Habits of Mind', *The Caravan,* 5(12), December.

Joseph, Sarah (2004): *Political Theory and Power,* New Delhi: Foundation Books.

Khilnani, Sunil (2004): 'Branding India', *Seminar,* 533, January.

Koselleck, Reinhart (1988): *Critique and Crisis: Enlightenment and Pathogenesis of Modern Society,* Cambridge, MA.: The MIT Press.

Mosco, Vincent (1988): 'Information in the Pay-per Society', in Vincent Mosco and Janet Wasko (eds.), *The Political Economy of Information,* Madison: University of Wisconsin Press.

Mouffe, Chantal (1992): 'Feminism, Citizenship and Radical Democratic Politics' in Judith Butler and Joan W. Scott (eds.), *Feminists Theorize the Political,* London: Routledge.

Pande, Mrinal (2010): 'Operating Above the Faulty Lines', *The Hindu,* 17 March.

Pandian, M.S.S. (2002): 'One Step Outside Modernity: Caste, Identity Politics and Public Sphere', *Economic and Political Weekly,* 37(18), 4 May.

Panikkar, K.N (2009): 'Religion in the Public Sphere', *The Hindu,* 8 September.

Parkinson, John R. (2012): *Democracy and Public Space: The Physical Site of Democratic Performance,* Oxford: Oxford University Press.

Parthasarathy, Suhrith (2013): 'The Broken Estate', *The Caravan,* 5(12), December.

Paz, Octavio (1998): *In the Light of India,* New York: Harcourt Brace and Company.

Pellizoni, Luigi (2001): 'The Myth of the Best Argument: Deliberation and Reason', *British Journal of Society,* 52(1), March.

Rajagopal, Arvind (2009): 'Introduction: The Public Sphere in India's Structure and Transformation', in Arvind Rajagopal, *The Indian Public Sphere: Readings in Media History,* New Delhi: Oxford University Press.

Raman, Anuradha (2014): 'Big Ed in the Chair', *Outlook*, 54(27), 14 July.

Rao, N. Bhaskara (2005): 'A Critical Review of Indian Television News Series', in South Asia Free Media Association (ed.), *Media Monitor South Asia 2005*, London: South Asian Free Media Association.

Rawls, John (1999): *Collected Papers*, Cambridge, MA.: Harvard University Press.

Robins, Kevin and Frank Webster (1999): *Times of the Technoculture: From the Information Society to the Virtual Life*, London: Routledge.

Sainath, P. (2010): Talk on 'Media Criticism: Peoples' Right', T.K. Ramakrishnan Centre, Cochin, 27 March.

—— (2010): 'The Republic on a Banana Peel', *The Hindu*, 3 December.

Singh, Mohinder (2008): 'Civil Society', in Rajeev Bhargava and Ashok Acharya (eds.), *Political Theory: An Introduction*, New Delhi: Pearson.

Swami, Praveen (2007): 'Breaking News: The Media Revolution', in Sumit Ganguly, Larry Diamond and Marc F. Plattner (eds.), *The State of Indian Democracy*, Baltimore: The Johns Hopkins University Press.

CHAPTER 10

Development, State and Mobilization: Reflections from the Margins

SHEEBA K.M.

European enlightenment that posited the ideas of democracy and liberty as ideals was the backdrop for the emergence of modern disciplines. Knowledge construction through these disciplines implied the simultaneous establishment of colonial power as well as the logic of capitalism over the non-Western world. This Janus-faced relationship of knowledge and power had implications for the ways in which the colonized Asian and African countries situated their development agenda.

Liberal neo-classical economics, as a product of Western modernity, with emphasis on rational and scientific objective thinking largely set the agenda for development. Economic growth epitomized the primary goal and meaning of development (Kabeer 1994: 13). These market oriented models, based on assumptions of rational behaviour, assumed the ability of human beings to allocate scarce resources between competing ends to maximize utility/satisfaction. This led to economic growth being equated to individual rational choices supported by the institutions of private property and free markets where private property posed as the critical institutional support for ensuring rational competitive behaviour. The magic of the market supposedly lay in its potential for promoting choice with efficiency (ibid.: 14-15).

Modernization theories on development depicted it as an evolutionary, unilinear process taking societies from pre-modern status to modernity; pushing the 'barbarians' to 'civilised' avenues of social living. Claimed to be a value-free social process, modernization was a desirable end, marking a cumulative improvement in living standards. It entailed a total transformation of pre-modern societies, institutions, cultures and behaviours. With the emergence of specialized institutions, a corresponding expansion and differentiation of roles of individuals in society would follow. Family and kinship would lose their central place; their functions transferred to the distinct public spheres of economy and state.

Individualism was institutionalized and individuals (white, heterosexual, male) were involved in impersonal and specialized interactions. Rational self-interest was a crucial component that would lead to the exclusion of personal, emotional, community based social transactions. Proclaimed as the positive implications of modern development, theorists were optimistic that socially marginalized groups (women, Afro-Americans and others) would benefit from the erosion of 'primordial' relationships (of race, ethnicity, gender, etc.) that would in turn be taken over by markets and the pursuits in science and technology. Markets were arenas that would reward impersonally according to achievement rather than through patronage or on the basis of characteristics of sex, caste or race. Achievements would become more important than ascribed status, offering attractive prospects for enterprizing individuals, whatever their affiliations may be.

Neoliberal policies employed as strategies in the operation of capitalism, especially since the 1980s, increased the pace of development but eroded the conditions in which development could occur long term; it depleted resources/nature on which it survived. (Hence the argument for sustainable development, which became a necessary plea for the continuation of capitalist production). Neoliberalism offers 'development' as a new source of political legitimacy with its emphasis on markets and the transmission of modern technology. Such development was to be channellized solely through the private sector accompanied by the state's withdrawal from questions of social welfare—employment and poverty reduction, healthcare, education, drinking water, housing and sanitation—with escalated inequality and exploitation as consequences. As for the 'Third World', the notion of its existence as an inferior 'other' was gradually positioned in the development discourses. The 'Third

World' was perceived as lacking in rational individualism and corresponding socio-economic institutions and hence termed as backward.

THE STATE AND NON-GOVERNMENTAL ORGANIZATIONS (NGOs)

Thomas Hobbes had long back opined that 'in a stateless world, people were required to pursue their individual interests in a context of social anarchy'. The primary goal of modern nation-states was, therefore, to pursue as well as create conditions for economic development. These states became increasingly competitive with their evolution into neo-capitalist economies. Under neo-liberalism, states no longer seemed accountable to its citizens with a shift from good government to 'good governance'. International discourses of bilateral aid donors or the World Bank, have been adopting the framework of according new ideological legitimacy to the market at a time when production was no longer definitive of national identity. With the new ideology of export led growth, production today becomes meaningful only when it is directed at destinations beyond national boundaries (Deshpande 1993: 5-36). In these contexts the informal sector, where high productivity was possible with low capital costs, got placed at the heart of the market economy. The arguments that proceeded are no longer that of *exploitation* but that of the poor, especially women, being much more *efficient* in managing poverty (John 1999: 112). Rather than assisting the poor in improving their access to society's productive resources, such as land (natural resources), finance capital (credit), or physical capital (technology), the poor were expected to build on their own social capital—to enhance their own capacities vis-à-vis their livelihood security, achieving the sustainability of their livelihoods (UNRISD 2000). Micro finance and credit projects were well suited to the neoliberal agenda in which risks were shifted to the individual entrepreneurs, often poor women, who were forced to compete for limited resources and opportunities in a very restricted market environment (Petras and Veltmeyer 2009: 24).

By the late 1980s, in India, there was increased 'NGO-ification of civil society' with these organizations working as service providers and sub-contractors to the state, providing cost-efficient, innovative and targeted services that withdrawing states cannot, or refuse to, provide (Kudva 2005: 234).

> The state's role as funder dates back to the grants-in-aid programme started in 1956 to disburse funds through the Central Social Welfare Board. . . . The active role as funder of NGOs began with the Sixth Plan (1980-85) formulated by the Janata Party which came to power after the Emergency. This funding has continued to expand as the state attempted to withdraw and increasingly rely on market based mechanisms to provide development. (ibid.: 237)

The NGOs attempted to build on the 'social capital' at the margins with an agenda of shifting away from confrontational politics. They were channels of managing discontent—of ostensibly moving up from exploitation to empowerment. Largely, the NGOs have presented a pro-liberalization and pro-technology perspective in tune with the logic of neoliberal capital initiatives. As in the Shetkari Sanghatana, an organization of farmers, farmer poverty was seen by many NGOs as caused by urban elites as well as by the state that holds on to technology and the surplus. 'In a remarkable reversal of social movement analysis in the past, the market became the solution and the state the problem' (Ray and Katzenstein 2005: 22). The NGOs were slowly but surely getting transformed from organizations set up to serve the poor into what the World Bank describes as 'operational NGOs' or private contractors.

IDENTITY POLITICS AND NEW SOCIAL MOVEMENTS

The neoliberal world is also characterized by the emergence of movements affirming identities. Identity politics indicates the 'new' identities of race, caste, sexualities, ethnicity, region, ecology, etc., in play that pushes back the identity of class that had emerged with industrial capitalism. In the European context, it locates itself within the domain of culture and is placed at a distance from material production relations. Identity politics as a mode of organizing is intimately connected to the idea that some social groups are oppressed—that is, that one's identity makes one peculiarly vulnerable to cultural imperialism (manifested in stereotyping, erasure or appropriation of one's group identity), violence, exploitation, marginalization or powerlessness (Young 1990). Rather than accepting the negative scripts offered by the dominant culture about one's inferiority, one transforms one's own sense of self and community often through consciousness raising. As with the Black movement, 'in the process of consciousness raising we (they) began to recognize the commonality of our (their) experiences and, from sharing and growing consciousness, to build politics that will change our (their) lives and inevitably end our (their) oppression' (Hull, Scott and Smith 1982). Political struggles that are classified as identity politics are undertaken by representatives of a collective with a distinctly different social location that has hitherto been neglected, erased or suppressed. It rests on unifying claims about the meaning of politically laden experiences.

Contemporary identity politics have been made possible with institutionalized liberal democracy (Brown 1995). Appeals have not been largely to the state but to the society for recognition and access to social and cultural capital. The leadership has emerged from among the educated middle classes while participation was not homogeneous or on the basis of formal membership but out of shared experiences of oppression. These movements have sought self-affirmation and control over personal dominion and aimed at securing post-material goods and celebration of life spaces. Identity politics have often been criticized for creating 'identity prisons' (Petras 1998) that would end up isolating exploited groups, one from the other, without confronting the social system in which the points of oppression are embedded. At present, identity politics faces the charge of not challenging the operation of neoliberal development agendas or of not calling for state provision of resources. Herein appears the need to recreate the nation.

The new social movements referred to as 'new democratic struggles' (Mouffe 1988) were movements that emerged in the face of attacks on the 'organic foundations of the life-world' (Habermas 1981: 33-7). Triggering new forms of protest and action, they were expressions of unsatisfied social needs that took new forms: feminist, ecological, ethnic, etc. that worked against a system that failed to transcend the limits of the actually existing capitalism as a world system (Amin 1995: 96). The state and its institutions, political processes and political parties have now left people at the mercy of forces to which they have to respond by other means—through their own social movements. The perceived failure of much of revolutionary and reformist movements have contributed to the rise of these social movements. These movements, then, are defensive and protective movements as most of them organize themselves independently of the state. However, in most cases the grievances are directed towards the state and its institutions seeking to influence state action (Frank and Fuentes 1990: 164). Whether social movements are anti-systemic is a matter of debate. They are so in the sense that they challenge the system or some aspects thereof. However, they are often not capable of destroying the system or replacing it with an alternative and may tend to end up being coopted by the system.

FROM MARGINALIZATION TO MOBILIZATION: THE INDIAN EXPERIENCE

Marginalization is essentially linked to the absence of democratic practices in development processes. Identities of Dalits, Adivasis, women, queer LGBT, displaced, ecological refugees and others emerge as valid and political, characterized by exclusion from the material benefits of development as well as social and cultural connections while also being pushed away from political decision-making. The counter-narrative that the new social movements give rise to is that of inclusion of the marginalized sections—Dalits, Adivasis, sexual minorities, ecological refugees, women and others—both in the processes and outcomes of development. These mobilizations that contest development are articulations of interests that resonate with the democratic ethos of inclusion and equality. Their goal is not the capture of state power, but curbing of that power to make the state respond to its neglected citizenry.

With the Indian state linking itself to the vertical hierarchies of global economic and political power, strong counter movements both social and political have emerged at the local and regional levels. These movements have begun to raise a new discourse on democracy and invent political practices, expanding the arena of politics much beyond the representational institutions of elections and political parties (Sheth 2004). They have been variously described in literature as 'grassroots movements', social movements, non-party political formations or processes, community based or mass-based organizations and see as their long-term goal the democratization of development and transformation of society. After the initial attempts by the Nehruvian state to include ever new groups into the fold of electoral and party politics, by the mid-1970s large sections of ex-untouchables, Adivasis, occupationally marginalized and minorities were left out in the margins of the mainstream of Indian politics (ibid.). The people who were drawn into this process of political alienation were dispersed and fragmented on many dimensions besides that of class. Nevertheless, these multiple forms of 'subaltern politics' eventually took the form of resistance to the established order. Initiated by those who have been objects of oppression, they envisaged both *empowerment from without* expressed in demands for constitutional provisions for jobs, etc., as well as *empowerment from within* like that which has emerged from among marginalized communities (Corbridge and Harriss 2000: xix).

It was the eruption of the Naxalite movement in Bengal in 1967 that put an end to 'subaltern' acquiescence to the Nehruvian order and led to the emergence of new social movements that subjected the exclusionary and exploitative dimensions of state-led capitalist development to substantial critique (Vanaik 1990). During the 1970s there occurred a substantial radicalization of the youth outside the circles of the traditional left (ibid.: 195) which resulted in their mobilization around issues that had been hitherto neglected by the mainstream left. Significant movements that were launched in the 1970s and immediately after were, to name a few, the Chipko (1973) and Appiko (1983) movements for ecological redress and livelihood issues, movements by the Fishworkers' Forum (1984) in Kerala, organization of Bhil Adivasis through the Shramik Sanghatana of Maharashtra (1972), women's movements against dowry, price rise and mounting violence against women. These struggles witnessed mobilizations around issues of wages, rural poverty and ecological destruction but at the same time successfully infused dimensions of gender, Dalit and Adivasi identities into these agitations. The Gram Swarajya Samiti of the 1970s in Maharashtra, for instance, advanced the problems of unemployment and wages for the Bhils but the Shramik Sanghatana that grew out of it witnessed women raising issues of domestic violence and alchoholism among the men. Advancing the idea of empowerment from within, women had started beating men who beat their wives (Savara and Gothoskar 1984).

Towards the end of the 1980s, with the onset of neoliberal restructuring and Hindutva mobilization, these movements could not decisively advance their agenda for a while. The large presence of NGOs, by this time, with funds that were siphoned in from international agencies created a lull in the flow of protests. The Structural Adjustment Programmes (SAP) had led to the middle classes moving up at least marginally while at the same time systematically pushing the lower middle classes to circumstances of abject poverty. Caste and social hierarchies were sought out to maintain the exploitation of the primary producers (largely Dalits, Adivasis and women) by the urban industrial elite. In India the market-economy, instead of making a dent on the iniquitous social structure was being absorbed by it (Sheth 2004).

Globalization discourses shifted attention from issues of social and political transformations to those of 'governance'. This was in tune with the instrumental role the state was to bear in furthering the ideas of the globalized market forces. By the mid-1990s the negative impact of globalization became too hard to ignore even for the middle classes. Agitations soon gained momentum with the formation of the National Alliance for People's Movements (NAPM) and the Narmada Bachao Andolan waged against displacement and irrational dam building that began in the mid-1980s, in the struggles for repeal of Article 377 of the Indian Constitution that criminalizes male homosexuality, against dispossession as in Adivasi and Dalit movements, etc. With the identities of caste, gender, Adivasi life, displacement, ecological refuge, dispossession and sexualities in play, mobilizational strategies focus on new social-political formations which conflate the category of class with those of caste, ethnicity and gender (ibid.). The paradigm of 'Third World' mobilizations stand different from those of the West in the sense that it reflects both the 'material with cultural' as James Petras (1998) has rightly called for.

These movements were led by young men and women, with quite a few of them leaving their professions and careers to join in. Issues and constituencies that were abandoned by political parties and trade unions were taken up within the organizational form of civil-associational groups (Petras 1998). Most of these groups have articulated basic issues of development within the framework of rights. Poverty was no longer a purely economic problem but a result of the social locations of the poor which left them excluded from the world of development. Being not merely an issue of a class conflict between the haves and the have-nots they therefore demanded mobilization strategies that conflated the category of class with those of caste, gender, sexualities, ethnicity and ecological locations. The politics of these movements

> lies not merely in fighting particular infringements of legal rights of citizens, but in creating and expanding new political and civic spaces for them. . . . In the process, the activists of the movement link rights of access to and benefits from the development process with the issues of ethnic identity and human dignity, and view the satisfaction of material needs as a pursuit not detached from the spiritual and cultural aspects of human existence (Petras 1998).

In the same vein, ecology movements do not view ecology merely as a cost factor in development but as a basic principle of human existence which if better organized can transform the economy in a humane way with a focus on human well being (Sheth 2004). The activists of the women's movement articulate their issues not only in terms of claims to equality but as a breaking down of power relations not merely between the sexes but in other hierarchical relations as well.

In the Plachimada struggle in Kerala against the Coca Cola Company, rather than posing a purely environmental problem, the question of transnational corporations and globalization got linked to people's livelihood issues (Aiyer 2007). In Dalit-Adivasi struggles in Kerala at Muthanga as well as in Chengara the demands were for land, recognition and social space. At Muthanga where the Adivasis constructed hutments on government land, the demand was for right to livelihood and land for the landless (Raman 2004). Unlike struggles opposing forcible displacement, the Chengara struggle was a direct claim on land by the landless (Sreerekha 2012). Laha Gopalan, the leader at Chengara stated that the struggle will not end with the mere grant of land. Critiques of the existing development patterns and State policies (land reforms) opened up spaces for assertions as in the case of the analysis of land ownership in Kerala that exposed Dalit absence from access to resources (Kapikkad 2011). The land reforms that were implemented after Independence basically conferred ownership rights to the tenants practically deserting the actual tillers (Dalits) and leaving them untouched by development initiatives (Kunhaman 2011). It is pertinent to note that all the significant struggles of Dalits after the 1990s have been around the right to resources. The agitation at the Nitta Gelatin Company, Kathikkudam, was headed by women who campaigned against the carcinogenic wastes that flowed from the factory. The 'Ice Cream Parlour' case filed under the aegis of the women's organization Anweshi of Calicut grew into an agitation against a ruling minister involved in the sex racket. It effectively exposed the nexus between political power and crimes against women (*Sanghaditha* 2011). Apart from the few mentioned above, quite a large number of regional agitations have been witnessed in the last two decades in Kerala as well as outside.

These movements have gone ahead to establish strong ties with each other while fighting for issues at the 'grassroots'. A notable character of these movements is their ability to forge linkages between afflicted peoples and formulate campaigns that target multi-dimensional locations of oppression. The politics of these movements did not confine itself to individual incidents of loss of rights of citizens, but aimed at creating and expanding new political and civic spaces for them by linking the survival and development needs of the deprived into struggles for their economic, political, and cultural rights. The mobilizations in the new social movements have exposed the undemocratic nature of development projects and programmes with the market dictating the priorities of investments. It has underlined the exclusionary character of the nation state that has in turn responded through oppression making the collusion or apathy of conventional actors (political parties) even more open (Shah 2004). They have been movements arising out of everyday life targeting both the material and cultural forms of life and attempt to transcend NGO agendas in order to challenge the social system and forms of development. Their outcomes may not always be positive materially but they remain politically and ideologically relevant.

REFERENCES

Aiyer, Ananthakrishnan (2007): 'The Allure of the Transnational: Notes on Some Aspects of the Political Economy of Water in India', *Cultural Anthropology*, 22(4): 640-58.

Amin, Samir (1990): 'The Social Movements in the Periphery: An End to National Liberation?', in Samir Amin et al. (eds.), *Transforming the Revolution: Social Movements and the World System*, New York: Monthly Review Press: 96-138.

Brown, Wendy (1995): *States of Injury: Power and Freedom in Late Modernity*, Princeton: Princeton University Press.

Combahee River Collective (1982): 'A Black Feminist Statement', in Gloria T. Hull, Patricia Bell Scott and Barbara Smith (eds.), *All the Women are White, All the Blacks are Men, But Some of Us are Brave: Black Women's Studies*, New York: Feminist Press.

Corbridge, Stuart and John Harriss (2000): *Reinventing India: Liberalization, Hindu Nationalism and Popular Democracy*, Cambridge: Polity Press.

Deshpande, Satish (1993): 'Imagined Economies: Styles of Nation Building in Twentieth Century India', *Journal of Arts and Ideas*, 25-6 December: 5-36.

Frank, Andre Gunder and Marta Fuentes (1990): 'Civil Democracy: Social Movements in World History', in Samir Amin et al. (eds.), *Transforming the Revolution: Social Movements and the World System*, New York: Monthly Review Press: 139-80.

Habermas, Jürgen (1981): 'New Social Movements', *Telos*, 49, Fall: 33-7.

Hull, Gloria T., Patricia Bell Scott and Barbara Smith (eds.) (1982): *All the*

Women are White, All the Blacks are Men: But Some of Us are Brave: Black Women's Studies, New York: Feminist Press.

John, Mary E. (1999): 'Gender, Development and the Women's Movement', in Rajeswari Sunder Rajan (ed.), *Signposts: Gender Issues in Post-Independence India*, New Delhi: Kali for Women.

Kabeer, Naila (1994): *Reversed Realities*, New Delhi: Kali for Women.

Kapikkadu, Sunny (2011): 'Kerala Model: Dalit Critique', in K. Satyanarayana and Susie Tharu (eds.), *No Alphabet in Sight: New Dalit Writing from South India*, New Delhi: Penguin: 464-74.

Kudva, Neema (2005): 'Strong States, Strong NGOs', in Raka Ray and Mary Fainsod Katzenstein (eds.), *Social Movements in India*, New Delhi: Oxford University Press.

Kunhaman, M. (2011): 'Socio-Economic Development of the Dalits in India: A Macroeconomic Overview', in K. Satyanarayana and Susie Tharu (eds.), *No Alphabet in Sight: New Dalit Writing from South India*, New Delhi: Penguin: 516-24.

Mouffe, Chantal (1988): 'Hegemony and New Political Subjects: Towards a New Concept of Democracy', in Cary Nelson and Larry Grossberg (eds.), *Marxism and the Interpretation of Culture*, Chicago: University of Illinois Press: 89-101.

Omvedt, Gail (1993): *Reinventing Revolution: New Social Movements and the Socialist Tradition in India*, New York: East Gate.

Petras, James (1998): 'A Marxist Critique of Post-Marxism', *Links* 9, November 1997-February 1998.

Petras, James and Henry Veltmeyer (2009): *Social Movements and State Power: Argentina, Brazil, Bolivia, Ecuador*, Kolkata: Update Publications.

Raman, Ravi (2004): 'Muthanga: A Spark of Hope', *Social Analysis*, 8(1), Spring: 126-35.

Ray, Raka and Mary Fainsod Katzenstein (eds.) (2005): *Social Movements in India*, New Delhi: Oxford University Press.

Sanghaditha (2011): 'Ice Cream Parlour Case-nte Naal Vazhikal, Kallakkalikal', (Malayalam), February-March.

Santos, Boaventura de Sousa (2006): *Another Production is Possible: Beyond the Capitalist Canon*, London: Verso.

Savara, Mira and Sujatha Gothoskar (1984): 'An Assertion of Woman Power: Organising Landless Women in Maharashtra', in Madhu Kishwar and Ruth Vanita (eds.), *In Search of Answers: Indian Women's Voices*, London: Zed Books: 134-48.

Shah, Ghanshyam (2002): *Social Movements and the State*, New Delhi: Sage.

Sheth, D.L. (2004): 'Globalisation and New Politics of Micro-Movements', *Economic and Political Weekly*, 39(1), 3 January: 45-58.

Sreerekha, M.S. (2012): 'Illegal Land, Illegal People: The Chengara Land Struggle in Kerala', *Economic & Political Weekly*, 28 July, 47(30): 21-4.

UNRISD (2000): *Civil Society Strategies and Movements for Rural Asset Redistribution and Improved Livelihoods*, Geneva: UNRISD Civil Society and Social Movements Programme.

Vanaik, Achin (1990): *The Painful Transition: Bourgeois Democracy in India*, London: Verso.

Young, Iris Marion (1990): *Justice and the Politics of Difference*, Princeton: Princeton University Press.

CHAPTER 11

Dalit Counterpublics: Reading the New Political Language of Dalit Rights Organizations

ELIZABETH ABRAHAM

It is an undisputable fact that public spaces and discourses are gendered, casteist and are marked by many exclusive practices. The Habermasian notion of a single public sphere which was challenged by feminist theorists has brought the notion of coexisting subaltern 'counterpublics'. Most discussions on 'counterpublics' rely on group identity markers to differentiate these spheres. This paper argues that it is not merely the shared marginal identity that makes the existence of the space possible, but the discourse that they generate as well. The paper discusses how the universal norm of human rights adopted by Dalit human rights organizations has brought 'visibility' to Dalit counterpublics. By adopting the vocabulary of human rights, these organizations could effectively challenge the claims of democratic justice and secularism of the Indian state. The discourse of human rights that has been brought widely into the public sphere by these organizations has created a challenge to the Indian state in this regard. The new phase of civil activism which has adopted the vocabulary of human rights has opened up a new direction of Dalit discourse which holds the state accountable for the casteist practices still prevalent in the country. The discourse points to the inadequacy of modern democratic principles on which the so called secular spaces are built. The political language of challenging the state, i.e. the criminal justice system, the judiciary, and the Indian government is evident in almost all their dialogues and campaigns.

DALITS AND THE INDIAN PUBLIC SPHERE

The mid-1990s witnessed a new phase of transformation in Indian civil society. The end of the last century saw the rise of numerous Dalit human rights organizations in the public sphere that raised the issue of discrimination/exclusion at various forums. These organizations have played an important role in setting a new human rights discourse influencing the secular democratic space of the Indian public sphere. Over this period, these institutions, which are referred to as non-governmental organizations (NGOs) or civil society groups occupied a vital role in influencing political institutions and strengthening notions of good governance, human rights, etc.[1] The vocabulary of their discourse is an important matter to be analysed as it has set a new dialogue with the Indian state and has also played an important role in shaping a new Dalit 'self' in the public sphere.

Though the Indian state adopted a constitution abolishing untouchability, and subsequently put through certain statutes to address the issue, casteism has prevailed as the *de facto* system in the country. While the uninterrupted existence of Brahminical ideology in post-Independence Indian society was a challenge to the fabric of the Indian democratic structure, debates on casteism did not surface in the public sphere. In contrast, issues such as communalism vs. secularism were well discussed. Post-colonial Indian politics was shaped and mainly guided by principles of universalism. These principles of universalism were incorporated into the national struggle and later into the Constitution, and resonated throughout the early phase of nation formation through phrases like 'unity in diversity' (see Nigam 2006; Aloysius 1997; and Sarkar 1997). This is visible throughout Indian socio-political writings where caste and its cultural attributes were treated as traditional institutions which would get eclipsed by the agencies of modernity. The language of universalism adopted by the state and civil society was thus able to successfully veil the hierarchies actually existing in society.

Issues of discrimination and deprivation, the primary concerns of Dalit communities, were neither of prime interest to civil society nor a prime focus of Indian politics. India was to witness long decades of civil society struggles to uphold the democratic character of the state. While looking at civil society initiatives, certain questions come to the fore: Why has there always been a primacy of secularism over the caste question? Notions of 'modernity' and principles of universalism shaped Indian civil society at the initial stages of its development, and taking up issues of caste did not become its primary objective. The question of 'atrocities' and raising anti-caste issues always remained within the domain of Dalit groups themselves. These dissenting voices challenged the nation-building project, which the Dalits describe as the project of Brahminism/Hindu nationalism, meant to silence the Dalit 'self' (Ilaiah 1999). Nigam (2006) notes: 'Dalit politics embodies a dogged resistance to the binaries set up by modern politics in the era of national struggle and subsequently in the contemporary moment. It refuses to get incorporated into either term of the binary of nationalism/colonialism and secularism/communalism.'

DALIT COUNTERPUBLICS

In colonial India, both colonial modernity and the national movement facilitated the growth of a public sphere and at the same time also enabled the rise of multiple counterpublics. New concepts of public access and civil inclusion animated the action of Dalit counterpublics. It resisted inclusion into the Hindu fold and conceived the untouchable as a political subject which was constantly in dialogue with the state.

In post-Independence India, the Dalit identity was institutionalized within the state and the Constitution, and in the process they were marked with an identity of vulnerable subjects encoded with state protection. The earliest visible Dalit resistance came in the form of the Dalit Panthers who based their principles on Ambedkarism and Marxism. The Dalit Panthers proclaimed in their manifesto (1986: 146) that 'we don't want a little place in Brahmin galli [lane], we want the rule of the whole land . . . our revolution will flash like lightning'. Though the movement was based on Ambedkarite and Marxist philosophies, it identified casteism as the major challenge: 'We should uproot the varna system, caste system that enslaves us in its snares. The soil in which they survive and grow must be made infertile' (Dalit Panthers 1986: 146). Similarly, the Dalit Sangarsha Samiti, students of Karnataka who agitated on the streets, echoed this strain: '(T)hrow Brahmins in the Gutters along with the Gita.'[2] Ideologies akin to this were also expressed by Bahujan Samaj Party (BSP) and Bahujan Republic Party (BRP). The BRP refused to merge with any other political party and proclaimed the slogan of 'Every Caste a Nation'.[3] The BSP publicly announced in its campaigns that the upper castes would not be in power but for Dalit votes (Ram 1982). The Dalit Maha Sabha, a movement that originated in response to two major massacres, Karamchedu and Chundur, played an important role in shaping Dalit consciousness in coastal Andhra Pradesh. While the Marxist-Leninist parties which supported the movement depicted the incident as an attack by landlords against labourers, this was categorically rejected by the Dalit leadership. Instead, they represented it as an attack by 'Kamma Landlords' on 'madiga coolies' (Ilaiah 1995). Contrary to the class analysis, caste emerged as an important factor in pinpointing the causes of the attacks. In these struggles it was also decided that 'only Dalits' would occupy the dais and address others, and that no upper caste, however, radical and sympathetic to the Dalit cause, would be allowed to share this space (Gudavarthy 2005). The Brahminical philosophy of casteism was portrayed as the major challenge in all these outward assertions in the public sphere. During the post-Independence phase, Dalits stood on their own, away from mainstream society, resembling what Prakash Ambedkar has termed, 'every caste a nation' (cited in Omvedt 2001). Although a trajectory of this cannot be traced in its entirety, it can be outlined from Dalit literature, from the politics of the Dalit Panthers and similar resistance groups, writings of political leaders, the work of small Dalit organizations, etc. It is within this context that the growth of Dalit human rights organizations that became active from the early 1990s is delineated.

The National Campaign of Dalit Human Rights (NCDHR) is taken as a case to study Dalit human rights organizations, and the role they played in shaping Dalit discourse during the last decade.

This organization is singled out for study as it has played a significant role in shaping Dalit discourse in the public sphere.[4] This organization acted as a coalition of various Dalit human rights groups/ organizations, and plays a vital role in bringing the issue of Dalit human rights violations into the public sphere. Their major activities, actions in the public sphere, and the new vocabulary that they have adopted are outlined in brief here to give a sense of the role that they play in the public space.

The National Campaign of Dalit Human Rights was established on 10 December 1998 with the stated aim of ensuring that India and the international community recognize 'Dalit rights as human rights'.[5] The organization started as a campaign,[6] and was a coalition of numerous organizations spread over fourteen states, working primarily to bring visibility to the issue of Dalit rights. One of the first campaign memoranda published by the organization states:

> This organization felt that considering the fact that we are in the fiftieth anniversary of the Universal Declaration of Human Rights and we, having just completed the fiftieth year of our completion of independence, the continued prevalence of untouchability in many parts of our country in spite of our constitutional and international commitment to the contrary called for an urgent national campaign highlighting Dalit human rights and upholding that 'Dalit rights are human rights. (NCDHR 1999a)

The main strategy of the campaign was to 'put an end to the silence that surrounds India's hidden apartheid' (NCDHR 1999a). This new discourse of human rights was carried out through organizing their actions around issues of human rights violations of Dalits, opening up issues of social exclusion and the denial of human dignity.

CENTRALITY OF 'VIOLENCE' IN DALIT LIVES

One of the main strategies of the campaigns that were taken up by Dalit organizations was to bring forth issues of violence that dominate Dalit lives. Campaign documents term this as bringing 'visiblity' to the issue. Till the groups took up the campaign there was silence on the issue of caste aggression that Dalits face every day in their lives. Through constant monitoring of violations, holding public hearings, mock courts, press conferences, legal interventions, etc., issues of Dalit human rights attained visibility in the Indian public sphere for the first time. These narratives from the Dalit lifeworld challenged the whole concept of democracy upon which the Indian state's claims to principles of justice and equality are built.

The public hearings, of which published reports are available (see Jayshree et al. 2000; and Irudayam 2006), brought out testimonies of victims who have been facing silent discrimination. The individual narratives brought into the public domain the lifeworlds of the Dalits, problematizing the narratives of a 'beautiful rural India'. It was a phase where it was important to acquire visibility for these issues which were always silenced or merged with larger issues. The campaign also brought out fact-finding reports highlighting the caste factor involved in the crimes happening in the country. Public humiliations, rape, violent assaults, murder and similar violent measures adopted by the dominant caste to keep the caste structure intact were exposed through these efforts. The rules that govern the Indian villages, and the violence through which they are imposed on certain sections of the population in order to keep the hierarchies intact, were discussed in the public domain through numerous strategies adopted by the Dalit organizations. For instance, in the Kumher massacre in Rajasthan in 1992, 33 Dalits were killed but this was reported by the media and even authorities like the Scheduled Caste Commission as peasant killings and as riots.[7] There is a marked change from the earlier situation, and after many years, caste crimes and violence have come to occupy the discursive space of human rights.

Monitoring reports and public hearings speak a new language, of the failure of the Indian criminal justice system and Indian democracy to address the issue of casteism and untouchability.[8] Each monitoring report follows a similar blueprint, clearly stating the nature of the crime, the caste of the victim and the perpetrator, the status of the case, including whether the case managed to reach the police station, the relevant sections of the Indian Penal Code and of the Atrocities and the Protection of Civil Rights (PCR) Act under which the crime falls. These reports are often electronically circulated to a large audience and on various occasions are submitted to government bodies. During this phase, the campaign also trained numerous Dalit rights activists on the provisions of the Prevention of the Atrocities (Scheduled Caste/Scheduled Tribe) Act 1989; the Protection of Civil Rights Act 1975; and the international legal norms under which caste crimes may fall. This saw a new phase of Dalit activism, where numerous activists were trained to translate cases in accordance with national and international legal standards. The campaign could bring out the limitations of the law in sharp contrast to the rule of caste.

REDEFINING UNTOUCHABILITY

The discourse of 'purity and pollution' could ontologically link untouchability with Hindu religious practices, rituals, cleanliness, body, etc. In the process it came to be closely associated with religious rituals, places of worship, physical touch, water, defilement, etc. This concept had strongly influenced the earlier anti-caste movements that espoused temple entry, common dining, accessing common water sources and similar approaches, at the same time calling to give up 'polluting occupations' as that was always a prevailing norm to justify caste rank.

Campaign documents and international advocacy materials brought to the open the prevailing practice of untouchability that daunts the Indian social system. The new dialogue conveyed the reality that untouchability is a dominant factor that still continues in the matter of social relationships, and discrimination still takes the form of barriers against bathing, eating, drinking, worshipping, and having access to common properties. It also forbids all common interaction in the use of public facilities, the spirit of discrimination manifesting itself in the exclusion of Dalits from schools, common water resources, means of conveyance and access to land, water and other livelihood resources (NCDHR 2007). Untouchability also became an all encompassing term to refer to residential segregation, denial of access to basic public services, restrictions in the cultural sphere, economic and market discrimination, labour market discrimination, discrimination in accessing common property resources, discrimination in educational institutions, discrimination in government supported programmes, etc. (NCDHR 2006). Furthermore, the fact that untouchability is not a rural phenomenon, but is prevalent in urban settings was brought out through cases of discrimination in institutions of higher education (Thorat Committee Report).

Similarly, words like 'segregation' and 'discrimination' which were used earlier were termed as untouchability in the new context. For instance, when the new SC/ST Reservation Bill (2009) which sought to remove reservation from higher education institutes was introduced in the parliament, it was termed as academic untouchability. Also in the numerous campaigns at the national and international level, the Indian caste system was described as the 'Hidden Apartheid' drawing parallels with the South African system. These campaigns were supported by empirical research studies of untouchability prevailing in Indian villages. The studies could highlight persistent patterns of untouchability in Dalit lives. The widespread prevalence of untouchability, spreading from private domains to government services, and also dealing with government officials, was marked in these studies (Shah 2001). They provided empirical support for campaigns that untouchability is the norm of rural India and also with evidence to 'refute the belief that untouchability is limited to remote and economically underdeveloped corners of India' (www.navsarjan.org). Through these efforts a new ideological lexicon of untouchability emerged that featured it as a dominant factor in social relationships.

INTERNATIONALIZING THE DALIT ISSUE: 'RACE' AND 'DESCENT-BASED DISCRIMINATION' AS AN ANALOGUE TO EXPLAIN CASTE

Internationalization of the Dalit issue is yet another major step taken up by human rights groups. This was made possible by successfully translating the Dalit issue into a new language that was more acceptable to the international human rights community.

Concepts such as 'race' and 'descent-based discrimination' which are more cognizable in the international legal terrain were adopted to explain the experience of the Dalit community. From the last decade of the twentieth century these organizations took up intensive campaigns at international forums, particularly the United Nations bodies and other groupings like the World Social Forum.

The international discourse was built within the framework of International Covenants on Human Rights and similar human rights standards. 'Discrimination Based on Work and Descent', which falls within Article 1 of the Convention on Elimination of Racial Discrimination, was taken up to redefine caste as 'descent and work'. These campaigns achieved part of their objective by being referred to in the concluding observations of the Committee on the Rights of the Child (2004), Convention on the Elimination of All Forms of Discrimination Against Women (2007) and Committee on the Elimination of Racial Discrimination (2007).[9]

The breakthrough in this trans-border campaign was that the issue attained a different dimension at the national level during the World Conference Against Racism, Racial Discrimination, Xenophobia and Related Intolerance (WACR) that took place in 2001 in Durban. The Indian Dalit rights groups adopted race as an analogue to explain caste-based discrimination. However, the official position taken by the Indian government—that race has no place in the World Conference—sparked off a debate within the country. The government, along with some sections of the academia, argued that the move by Dalit voluntary organizations to bring caste-based discrimination within the purview of the International Convention on Elimination of Racial Discrimination, Xenophobia and Related Intolerance would demystify the issue. Interestingly, the major sociological argument raised was that race is a biological category having distinctive physical markers whereas caste is a social marker. The prominent sociologist Andre Beteille argued that treating caste as a form of race is 'politically mischievous and scientifically nonsensical' (Beteille 2001).

This race/caste debate garnered attention for Dalit issues for the first time in general discussions within the public sphere. The whole rationale of taking the issue outside national borders was also raised (Sarcar 2001). The Dalit reply was that 'caste may not be race' (Macwan 2001), and questioned who can set 'boundaries for the solution to the problem of caste' (Divakar and Mathew 2001). Thus, issues of funding, and the question of the right political context for raising the issue, emerged during these debates. For the Dalit activist, however, internationalization of the Dalit issue was a means of emphasizing the need for accountability, and a campaign for challenging the secular democratic self-image of the 'world's largest democracy'. The new dialect of Dalit discourse, asserting that 'Dalit rights are human rights', spoken through international campaigns shook the Indian state. It emerged as a major challenge to India's past history of leading anti-apartheid and anti-racist campaigns at international forums.

The sociological argument—that to acknowledge the reality of caste would only serve to perpetuate the situation—has been proposed at every stage when a debate on caste assertion was raised in the public sphere. This same argument was advanced during the Mandal and the post-Mandal days when issues of caste identity and caste-based reservations burst into the national imagination.

Indian Dalit activists, with the support of the international community, were able to gather considerable media and public attention during the Durban Conference. Despite all these efforts, caste-based discrimination was not mentioned in the WACR's final document. This occurred despite the fact that it was recommended by various UN bodies like the Committee on the Elimination of Racial Discrimination, the Special Rapporteur on Racism, and the Sub-commission on the Promotion and Protection of Human Rights. It was noted by these committees that international prohibitions on racial discrimination include caste-based discrimination,[10] and the conference was mandated to include not just racism but also racial discrimination, xenophobia, and related intolerance.

Though caste was not included in the final Durban Declaration, the debate opened up a new discourse of Dalit human rights. Interestingly, numerous public meetings were called in different parts of the country, post-Durban, to celebrate the triumph over the Indian state in Durban. These public meetings were vociferous in communicating yet another narrative to the Dalits in the country:

The manner in which the Indian state had been successful all this time in concealing from the larger world the inhuman treatment meted out to the Dalit masses. The Durban conference was thus one of the major breakthroughs in transnational Dalit activism. Numerous human rights groups came out in support of Dalits in the country, and they were successful in creating an international solidarity group voicing Dalit concerns at international platforms.[11]

CASTE INFESTED STATE MACHINERY

The apathy of the state in addressing the development issues of Dalits is also another important issue. The 'Black Paper' published in December 1999 and submitted to the Government of India by the Campaign in the 50th year of Indian Independence points out the failure of the state in implementing the policies that it had designed for Dalits. The document talks of security, land rights, education, livelihood issues, reservations, and the need for treating Dalit women as a special category. The document notes that '(s)tates do not have even the basic data to show as to how effective the implementation of land reforms has been'. It points out that

> the data pertaining to representation in services also indicates that while Scheduled Castes/Scheduled Tribes (SCs/STs) are engaged in lower category jobs such as sweepers, peons, clerks, no sincere efforts have been made by the government to ensure full quota for SCs/STs in top posts even after fifty years of independence. Near 'Nil' representation in Universities and the teaching profession exhibits the apathy towards these classes. (NCDHR 1999b)

It communicated that fifty years of targeted development programmes towards the Dalits has failed to give them any kind of dignified existence.

A major campaign exposing the indifference of the government was by bringing to the fore the neglect of the Special Component Plan. As per the Special Component Plan (SCP), the amount of planned expenditure of both the central and state governments should be according to their population. The plan designed in 1978 remained more or less unimplemented. Although the Planning Commission recommended to implement SCP from 1979-

80, it was only in 2005-6 that a separate allocation for Scheduled Castes (statement no. 21) appears in the budget (Mahaprashasta 2009). The Campaign refers to this 'trail of betrayal', and has raised demands to 'stop stealing the Dalit's share in the union and state budget' (www.ncdhr.org.in). The campaign to implement the Special Component Plan is simultaneously going on in different states and at the national level by numerous Dalit organizations.

Tsunami and floods were other occasions where discrimination against Dalits was exposed by human rights organizations. The fact that the government machinery is beset with caste-based discrimination is evident from the fact that even when disasters occur, caste identity matters. 'While the tsunami knew only geographical boundaries, NCDHR found the deep entrenched boundaries of caste and discrimination dividing affected people even in the deep hours of grief and helplessness'.

REPRESENTING 'THE DIFFERENCE' OF DALIT IDENTITY

The 'difference' of Dalit experience and the assertion of identity was always an important aspect of Dalit human rights organizations. The NCDHR Manifesto (www.ncdhr.org.in) substantiates this separation:

> The very desire to establish a nation on the values of equality, freedom and fraternity, is an anathema to the ruling caste, which has dogmatically fragmented the society into different castes and legitimises the same. . . . The State and the civil society in India are both violators of human rights, the State on the one hand abets violations of human rights by dominant caste civil society, and the caste society justifies the State violations of human rights.

This can be corroborated by the Dalit interaction with a larger civil society event, the World Social Forum (WSF). The Dalit presence in the WSF was centred on two concepts. Three coalitions —NCDHR, National Federation of Dalit Women (NFDW), and National Dalit Forum (NDF) took up the issue of identity and brought the issue of caste-basted discrimination to the fore, while a group under the leadership of the National Confederation of Dalit Organisations (NACDOR) joined with other marginalized groups and discussed the concept of 'dignity'.[12] Though marginalization of the Dalit community was discussed by both groups, the reason for this variation was that NACDOR believed that the WSF being a global forum and dignity being a global concern, it would be appropriate to join other marginalized groups to highlight 'dignity' as integral to human existence and a universal concern. The other three organizations, on the other hand, took the position that caste-based discrimination needs to be taken up separately as it is different from discrimination based on gender, class, disability, ethnicity, etc., and merging caste-based discrimination with other forms of discrimination would not be doing justice to their long efforts to bring the issue of caste into Indian social movements and civil society.

The 'Concept Note on Dignity' circulated at the WSF presented an all-encompassing concept. It notes: 'Dignity is a universal concern. In terms of the individual or the collective it assigns equal worth to all, without any distinction of colour, race, caste, gender, ethnicity or language' (Bharati and Sharma 2005: 203). Dignity seems to be built upon binaries and has a critical relationship with caste, class, race, disability, religious, and gender divisions. Women are objectified in order to maintain the 'dignity' of a patriarchal society. In India, the definition of the 'dignity' of a Brahmin depends on constructing the 'polluting' Dalit. The white identity gets actualized only in relation to the negative image of the African-American. The face of a communal Hindu is incomplete without reference to a stereotype of the Muslim 'other', and so on (Bharati and Sharma 2005: 204).

Despite the concept of dignity seeming to be an acceptable concept and the initiative of the Dignity Forum, the three Dalit coalitions worked on highlighting caste-based discriminations. The disagreement over the two concepts is an important issue to be noted. The concept of dignity expresses a universal concern, and though the discourse of caste and marginalization is founded on the concept of dignity, the majority of Dalit groups feared and read it as yet another move to obscure caste-based discrimination in a larger, universal discourse. Dalit groups from India were apprehensive that a merger with other issues may obstruct their agenda of highlighting caste-based discrimination and that caste may be subsumed in the larger 'dignity' concerns.[13] From the beginning, organic leadership and lived experiences have been major concerns for Dalit movements and Dalit writings.

At the Mumbai WSF, the organizing committee recognized the limitations of the Charter of Principles to address regional diversities and realities. Dalit groups insisted on amending the Charter of Principles to include casteism along with patriarchy and communalism. As noted by Anand Bolimera, a representative of NCDHR in the India Working Committee, a majority of the members of the committee saw the WSF as an international forum where caste could be part of larger issues like exclusion, race, etc., and also that it is country-specific. But this was strongly opposed by Dalit representatives, and it was through their insistence that caste emerged as a particular issue within the Forum and in the Charter of Principles.[14]

The groups which adopted race as an analogue to explain caste-based discrimination in the international discursive space refused to join with larger issues/groups that spoke of marginality, exclusion and dignity, or to be clubbed with issues like racism or ethnicity. Caste along with race came out as one of the seven core themes on which the main conferences were designed. The centrality of caste in shaping Dalit lives was always a focal point of discussion of Dalit groups and this was the significant communication at the Mumbai WSF. A factsheet published by NCDHR during the Asia Social Forum 2003 highlighted the centrality of the caste issue by itself:

> Caste has been the single factor in Indian society for the past three thousand years which has created and sustained a graded inequality in all aspects of life. . . . It underpins and operates the religious, cultural, social, economic and political systems in Indian society. Historically, each political system that evolved from the Princely states, to Muslim rule, to Western colonial rule to the present democratic system has based itself on the caste system, accommodated itself to the caste hierarchy and finally ended up strengthening

the political power of the dominant individuals and communities. (NCDHR 2003)

The Forum was seen as an important terrain for announcing to the world this 'graded inequality' of Indian society. However, given the anti-globalization conception of the Forum, the renderings on caste were coloured by an appropriately modified language. NDF clearly states that the popular analysis of the Dalit situation is inadequate: (I)n the context of the widespread resistance to globalization with promising concepts like 'Another World is Possible', in the Indian context generalized concepts, analyses and alternatives for globalization from the capitalist vs. labour/workers' perspective are insufficient to understand and fight the globalization process. As Dr. B.R. Ambedkar stated, in India the class of an individual is determined by the caste in which one is born, without addressing the caste question and its root, one cannot analyse the impact of anything on the masses (National Dalit Forum 2004). NCDHR (2003) described the challenge of globalization in a different language:

> As part of the process of entering the world market and ushering globalization into the Indian economy . . . policies built for last 55 years are dismantled. . . . Dalits and other marginalized communities are forced to buy all services through the market. . . . However, the market is not neutral. It works in a discriminatory manner. . . . Dalits thus face economic discrimination in various markets; that is, in the labour, land, output and input markets, and in social services such as education and health.

NDF describes globalization as 'casteisation' in its strengthening of the upper caste in India.[15] It is interesting that while the documents spoke about the impact of globalization, the vocal communications were focused more on the caste reality. Though Dalit lives are placed in interlocking and multiple layers of oppression, caste oppression remains the primary reality.[16] While caste remained the primary issue of concern, globalization and issues surrounding it were included to fit into the global mosaic of protest. However, much of the Dalit poetry that was translated and published in posters spoke a more direct language than other published documents. To quote a poem from one of the posters:

How did we ever get to this place
In this land which was never mother to us
Which never gave us even
The life of cats and dogs
I hold their unpardonable sins as witness
And turn, here and now
A rebel

(*Jyoti Lanjewar*, 'Caves')

THE 'DIFFERENCE' OF DALIT WOMEN

Dalit women's issues have received ample scholarly attention, but it is still important to mention it here, as one of the first attempts to disassociate from the feminist movement and the Dalit movement and to set up an organization was through the formation of the National Dalit Federation. The organization, engaged in a discourse on Dalit human rights, was the first attempt to bring the gendered caste relationship into the public sphere through various strategies. The last few decades have seen notable phenomena, such as the emergence of autonomous Dalit women's organizations that have disassociated themselves from mainstream feminism as well from the Dalit movement by pointing out the inadequacy of articulating a monolithic account of either patriarchy or casteism. The demands of these organizations were not merely for inclusion but for an analysis of gender relationships as they are inflected by the multiple and overlapping patriarchies of caste communities that produce multiple forms of vulnerability (Rao 2003: 5). The Dalit feminists raised issues of invisibility, distortion, and marginalization, criticisms that both the Dalit and feminist movements had earlier directed against mainstream social movements. By the 1990s, challenging the collapsing of identities, Dalit women's writings, public testimonies,[17] and certain NGO declarations[18] put forth Dalit feminist critiques. Two organizations, National Federation of Dalit Women (formed in 1993 in Bangalore) and Dalit Mahila Sanghatana (formed in 1995 in Maharashtra), were the early voices of Dalit women raising these issues.

Challenging the monolithic account of patriarchy given by mainstream feminism, they set about establishing the 'difference' in

Dalit women's lives. This difference is the two distinct patriarchal structures that Dalit women have to deal with—a Brahminical form of patriarchy that clearly stigmatises Dalit women, and another that they face within their own domestic spheres. The movement distanced itself equally from the mainstream feminist movement controlled by upper caste women and from the Dalit movement dominated by men: 'A look at the Dalit movement shows that the men are almost exclusively in leadership positions, though women participate actively. The agenda of the movement, like the fight for land (but not for entitlement for women), for minimum wages (but not equal wages), expose the male biases' (Bandhu 2003: 111).

A decade-long effort to voice their concerns, like distinct forms of sexual violence that Dalit women face, forms of occupational hazards, the multi-faceted nature of economic deprivation, has been able to articulate the 'difference' that constitutes Dalit womens' lives. Dalit feminist symbols, icons, and special occasions are celebrated to assert this identity. For instance, 25 December is remembered by Dalit women's organizations as Bharathiya Stree Mukti Diwas (Indian Women's Liberation Day), to commemorate the burning of the *Manusmruti* by Ambedkar during the Mahad Satyagraha. Dalit feminists have also been able to clearly express distinctions in their positions on many issues from the mainstream feminist positions. For instance, the term 'commercial sex worker' is rejected by Dalit feminists as it implies a freedom of choice. On the contrary, most Dalit women who are in this profession have been denied a choice and are forced into the situation, on many occasions out of adherence to religious and traditional caste practices. In international Dalit activism as well, the 'difference' that constitutes Dalit women has been expressed. These efforts have been able to open up certain invisible terrains, and allow a rereading of Dalit women to a certain extent.

CONCLUSION

The discourse of human rights that has been brought into the public sphere by the above organizations has created a challenge to the Indian state and the principles of secularism and democratic justice on which its claims are based. What was noticeable in the new phase of civil activism was that they had opened up a new direction of Dalit discourse which held the state accountable for the casteist practices still prevalent in the country. The discourse pointed to the inadequacy of modern democratic principles on which India's secular spaces are built. The political language of challenging the state (the criminal justice system, judiciary, and the Indian government) was evident in almost all their dialogues and campaigns. In contrast to the earlier Dalit discourse challenging Brahminism, this discourse of human rights has enabled a wider discursive space, and has facilitated the carrying of the issue to a wider public through transgressing national boundaries.

Yet, even while adopting a universal human rights discourse, a separation from the mainstream and assertion of identity is imminent in all actions of the organizations. All these organizations uphold the principle that only Dalits should hold important offices. For instance, at the WSF, a majority of Dalit organizations decided to voice their own concerns rather than join other marginalized groups. They refused to join the idea of the World Dignity Forum fearing that in the discourse of 'dignity', the issue of casteism may be subsumed. The activities of Dalit groups in the WSF have been characterized as a celebration and consolidation of caste identity. This trend has been strongly criticized by scholars as an ideology of 'confrontation and hatred' (Deliege 1999). The argument against identity assertion raised by scholars is that this rearticulates and consolidates caste identity. But these critiques often forget that even the new politics of Dalit assertion has to operate in a domain where graded spaces are allocated to each community and caste. And a new strength or rebirth for Dalits can come only from a language of assertion and celebration. Besides, the sense of assertion is generated not only by challenging the democratic principles of the state or highlighting human rights violations, but also through other cultural expressions.

These changes opened up a new discourse where Dalit rights are spoken of in the new language of 'Dalit rights are human rights', thus challenging the concepts of Indian democracy. This discourse treats Dalit rights violations in terms of national legislations, national human rights, and international human rights standards and mechanisms. There is a shift from radical Dalit challenges to Brahminism, to challenges to Indian democracy and its secularist principles. The new discourse holds the Indian state accountable for the caste crimes taking place in the country.

NOTES

1. Civil Society, as discussed in this paper, will focus on this particular attribute only, though the discussion at times may focus on other civil actors also.
2. The agitation erupted in the context of a Dalit minister dubbing upper caste Kannada literature as cattle-feed, for which Dalits were attacked (see Omvedt 2006).
3. Statement by Prakash Ambedkar (cited in Omvedt 2006).
4. The strategic presence of the organization's national secretariat in New Delhi and the political strategy of their actions have gained visibility for the organization to a level that has not been attained by other coalitions. Also, the diversity of their actions from the local to the international level is an interesting matter for academic reading. Above all, my own close acquaintance with many of the members of the organization has made it an easy choice for investigation.
5. The campaign documents say that NCDHR was born out of an initiative of concerned human rights activists in India working among Dalits engaged in the study of the effectiveness of the implementation of the SC/ST Atrocities Act (see NCDHR 1999a).
6. Though NCDHR still claims that it is a campaign, i.e. a loose network of organizations that came together to advocate a cause, it maintained this character only during the initial phase of its formation. Later it acquired the characteristics of any institutionalized organization.
7. On 6 June 1992, in the village of Kumher in the state of Rajasthan, 33 people were killed, 400 cattle were burnt alive, 500 houses were set on fire, and more than 50 women were raped. This was a pre-planned and organized crime, where the decision to attack the village was taken two days earlier in a public meeting of dominant castes from 46 villages; and the massacre took place in connivance with the state police. The massacre was in response to the action of a Dalit person who went to a local cinema and in the dark unintentionally sat next to a Brahmin priest of his village. No action was taken against the perpetrators.

8. A published volume of the monitored atrocities by NCDHR is available *Atrocities on Dalits: A Comprehensive Monitoring Report* (January 2006-September 2007).
9. Concluding Observations of the Committee on the Rights of the Child (CRC/C/15/Add.228, dated February 2004), Convention on the Elimination of All forms of Discrimination Against Women (CEDAW/C/IND/CO/3, dated 5 May 2007), Concluding Observations of the Committee on the Elimination of Racial Discrimination (CERD/C/IND/CO/19, dated 5 May 2007).
10. In 1996, in its concluding observations CERD noted that 'the situation of the Scheduled Caste and Scheduled Tribe' is covered under the treaty's 'descent' term which 'does not solely refer to race' (Concluding Observations of the Committee on the Elimination of Racial Discrimination: India, dated 17 September 1996, CERD, 49th Session, UN Doc CERD/C/304/Add.13. (Concluding Observations/Comments), Para 14 (1996), www.unhchr.ch.
11. NCDHR played a significant role in the establishment of the International Dalit Solidarity Network based in Copenhagen, Denmark.
12. NACDOR is a coalition of numerous grassroots organizations working in different sectors, primarily Dalit organizations focused on employment, education, poverty, women empowerment, etc., with a national office in New Delhi. Its major activities include campaign and advocacy on Dalit issues, for which strategies like mass meetings, street plays, *yatras*, press meetings, *dharnas*, etc., are used. Also, at some level the organization works with similarly marginalized communities like Muslim Dalits, minority Muslims, and denotified tribes. It was formed in 2001.

    NDF, established in 2000, acts as a platform for human rights organizations working for Dalits, Adivasis, and other marginalized communities. The organization has established a network in nearly 15 states and primarily stands for promoting Dalit assertion in social, political, cultural, and economic spheres. The organization has the stated objectives of providing a platform for Dalit activists, organisations and movements; supporting the Dalit advancement process; supporting emerging Dalit leadership; facilitating Dalit professional forums; developing alliances with other marginalized sections; and lobbying for Dalit-friendly policies (www.ndf.com).

    NFDW, a Bangalore-based organization, was established in 1995 as a platform for Dalit women to organize autonomously and independently. It works with the objective of enabling Dalit women to articulate social ostracism and exclusion, powerlessness and poverty, and violence and discrimination that they have to face. It supports Dalit women leadership in working independently and building a national Dalit women's perspective.

13. Interview with Anand Bolimera (April 2009).
14. Ibid.
15. 'Casteization' is the term used in the report to describe how the new phenomenon of globalization has strengthened the upper caste.
16. Interview with S.D.J.M. Prasad (April 2009). He pointed out that for the majority of Dalits caste remains the crucial challenge when compared with other oppressions. Similarly, while the primary focus in the Asia Social Forum was on education, the Dalit groups (NCDHR) presented the 'voices of the victims', which narrated the real life situations of Dalits in between major programmes.
17. One of the first public hearings on Atrocities against Dalit Women was organized in 1994 in Bangalore by Women's Voice, Bangalore and the Asian Women's Human Rights Council, Manila (see Bandhu 2003).
18. See the Dalit Women's Declaration in the Fourth World Conference of Women held in Beijing in 1995 (www.aworc.org), and the Declaration on Gender and Racism issued at the World Conference Against Racism, 28 August-7 September 2001, Durban (see Appendix in Rao 2003). The International Conference on Dalit Women in The Hague in November 2006 is another face of the internationalism of Dalit women.

REFERENCES

Aloysius, G. (2000): *Nationalism without a Nation in India,* New Delhi: Oxford University Press.

Bandhu, Panchali (2003): 'Dalit Women's Cry for Liberation', in Anupama Rao, *Gender and Caste,* New Delhi: Kali for Women and Women Unlimited.

Berg, Dag Erik (2007): 'Sovereignties, the World Conference Against Racism 2001 and the formation of a Dalit Human Rights Campaign', www.ceri-sciences-po.org

Beteille, Andre (2001): 'Race and Caste', *The Hindu,* 10 March.

Bharati, Ashok and Mukul Sharma (eds.) (2005): *Defining Dignity: An Anthology of Dreams, Hopes and Struggles,* New Delhi: World Dignity Forum and Heinrich Ball Foundation.

Clifford, Bob (2007): 'Dalit Rights are Human Rights: Caste Discrimination, International Activism, and the Construction of a New Human Rights Issue', *Human Rights Quarterly,* 29.

Concluding Observations of the Committee on the Elimination of Racial Discrimination (CERD/C/IND/CO/19 dated 5 May 2007).

Concluding Observations of the Committee on the Elimination of Racial Discrimination: India, 17/09/96, CERD, 49th Sess, UN Doc CERD/C/304/Add 13, Para 14, www.unhchr.ch

Concluding Observations of the Committee on the Rights of the Child (CRC/C/15/Add 228, dated February 2004), Convention on the Elimination of All forms of Discrimination Against Women (CEDAW/C/IND/CO/3 dated 5 May 2007).

Dalit Panthers (1986): 'Dalit Panthers' Manifesto', in Barbara R. Joshi (ed.), *Untouchable!: Voices of the Dalit Liberation Movement*, London: Zed Books and Minority Rights Group.

Das, Sona (ed.) (2004): *The Making of World Dignity Forum*, Delhi: World Dignity Forum, Heinrich Boll Foundation, National Conference of Dalit Organisation.

Deliege, Robert (1999): *The Untouchables of India*, Oxford: Berg Publishers.

Divakar, Paul and Ajai Mathew (2001): 'A Historical Overview of Achievements and Future Action Agenda', presented at the Global Conference against Racism and Caste-based Discrimination, National Seminar Cum Public Consultation on *Racism, Racial Discrimination, Xenophobia, and Related Intolerance*, National Human Rights Commission, New Delhi, 11 August.

Divakar, Paul (2004): 'Road to Freedom', *Communalism Combat*, 95, January.

Ghanta, Chakrapati (2004): 'National Campaign for Dalit Human Rights: Activities and Achievements in WSF IV', unpublished NCDHR in-house document.

Ghosh, Ashish (ed.) (1999): *Dalits and Peasants: The Emerging Caste-Class Dynamics*, New Delhi: Gyan Sagar Publications.

Gudavarthy, Ajay (2005): 'Dalit and Naxalite Movement in AP: Solidarity or Hegemony?', *Economic and Political Weekly*, 40(51), 17 December.

Guru, Gopal (1995): 'Dalit Women Talk Differently', *Economic and Political Weekly*, 30(41-2), 14-21 October.

—— (2000): 'Dalits in Pursuit of Modernity', in Romila Thapar (ed.), *India: Another Millennium*, New Delhi: Viking: 123-37.

—— (ed.) (2005): *Atrophy in Dalit Politics*, Mumbai: Vikas Adhyayan Kendra.

Ilaiah, Kancha (1995): *Caste or Class or Caste-Class: A Study in Dalit Bahujan Consciousness and Struggles in Andhra Pradesh in 1980s*, New Delhi: Centre for Contemporary Studies, Nehru Memorial Museum & Library.

—— (1998): 'Towards the Dalitization of the Nation', in Partha Chatterjee (ed.), *Wages of Freedom: Fifty Years of the Nation State*, New Delhi: Oxford University Press.

—— (1999): 'Dalits vs Brahminism: The Epistemological Conflict in History', in Ashish Ghosh (ed.), *Dalits and Peasants: The Emergence of Caste-Class Dynamics*, New Delhi: Gyan Sagar Publications.

Irudayam, Aloysius (ed.) (2006): *Dalit Women Speak Out: Violence Against Dalit Women in India*, vols. 1 & 2, New Delhi, Bangalore, and Madurai: National Campaign on Dalit Human Rights, National Federation of Dalit Women, and Institute of Development, Action and Studies.

Jayshree, P.M. et al. (eds.) (2000): *Dalit Human Rights Violations: Atrocities against Dalits in India*, vols. 1 & 2. Case Papers: Summary and Jury's Interim Observations and Recommendations, Madurai: National Campaign on Dalit Human Rights.

Joshi, Barbara R. (ed.) (1986): *Untouchable!: Voices of the Dalit Liberation Movement*, London: Zed Books and The Minority Rights Group.

Kannabiran, Kalpana (2006): 'A Cartography of Resistance: The National Federation of Dalit Women', in Nira Yuval-Davis et al. (eds.), *The Situated Politics of Belonging*, London: Sage.

Mahaprashasta, Ajoy Ashirwad, 'Neglected Component', *Frontline*, 26(15), 18-31 July 2009.

Macwan, Martin (2001): 'Caste May not be Race', paper presented at the National Seminar-cum-public consultation on *Racism, Racial Discrimination, Xenophobia, and Related Intolerance*, National Human Rights Commission, New Delhi, 11 August.

Michael, S.M. (ed.) (1999): *Dalits in Modern India: Vision and Values*, New Delhi: Vistar.

Mohanty, Manoranjan, Partha Nath Mukherji and Olle Tornquist (eds.) (1998): *Peoples Rights, Social Movements and the State in the Third World*, New Delhi: Sage.

National Campaign on Dalit Human Rights (1999): 'Memorandum to the Prime Minister', in *Dalit Rights: Advocacy Materials and Documents*, NCDHR Compact Disc.

—— (1999): 'Black Paper: Broken Promises and Dalits Betrayed', Folder of Fact Sheets, New Delhi: NCDHR. Also available in the Compact Disc, *Dalit Rights Advocacy Materials and Documents*.

—— (2002): *Manifesto*, www.ncdhr.org

—— (2003): *Dalits on Globalisation: Making Another World Possible*, New Delhi: NCDHR

—— (2006): *Dismantling Caste Based Discrimination: Report on Descent Based Discrimination and Access to Rights*, New Delhi: NCDHR

—— (2007): *Shadow Report to the UN*, CERD.

National Dalit Forum (2004): *A Report on WSF-2004*, Secunderabad: National Dalit Forum.

Nigam, Aditya (2000): 'Secularism, Modernity, Nation: Epistemology of the Dalit Critique', *Economic and Political Weekly*, 35(48), 25 November.

—— (2006): *The Insurrection of Little Selves: The Crisis of Secular Nationalism in India*, New Delhi: Oxford University Press.

Omvedt, Gail (1994): *Dalits and the Democratic Revolution: Dr. Ambedkar and the Dalit Movement in Colonial India*, New Delhi: Sage.

—— (2001): 'Ambedkar and After: The Dalit Movement in India', in Ghanshyam Shah (ed.), *Dalit Identity and Politics*, New Delhi: Sage.

—— (2006): *Dalit Visions*, New Delhi: Orient Longman.

Ram, Kanshi (1982): *The Chamcha Age: An Era of the Stooges*, New Delhi: Published by the author.

Rao, Anupama (2003): *Gender and Caste*, New Delhi: Kali for Women and Women Unlimited.

Rege, Sharmila (2006): *Writing Caste/ Writing Gender: Narrating Dalit Women's Testimonies*, New Delhi: Zubaan.

Sarcar, Rajendra (2001): 'Fight Caste in Delhi and Not in Durban', in *PUCL Bulletin*, November.

Sarkar, Sumit (1997): *Writing Social History*, New Delhi: Oxford University Press.

Shah, Ghanashyam (ed.) (2001): *Dalit Identity and Politics*, New Delhi: Sage.

Thorat Committee Report: *Discrimination in AIIMS*, www.endcampuscasteism.wordpress.com

Thorat, Sukhadeo and Umakant (eds.) (2004): *Caste, Race and Discrimination: Discourses in International Context*, New Delhi: Rawat Publications.

CHAPTER 12

Ecological Movements and People's Power

GEORGE K. ALEX

Ecological deliberations form an alternative political platform in the midst of the left-right divide of class politics, and its various shades. The debate on ecology provides new avenues of discourses to challenge and recreate deliberative spaces and democratic dialogues. Ecological policies have a wide range of influence on people's lives, culture and patterns of production with the link between ecology and economy being a determinant in the democratization process of any society. The term 'ecological movements' gained wide currency with the 1972 Stockholm Conference on Human Environment. The primary objective of the conference was to 'inspire and guide peoples of the world in the preservation and enhancement of the human environment'. The conference proposed institutional and financial arrangements for the successful implementation of environment management (Sohn 1973: 423). However, the social history of ecological movements can be traced back to the history of human struggle for natural resources.

ECOLOGICAL MOVEMENTS

Ecological movements are economic and socio-political movements that mainly address the relationship between the natural environment and the human environment. Socio-political and economic relations came under the keen scrutiny of ecological concerns during the late 1960s. Reuther (www.spunk.org) observes, 'Thus ecology emerged as a combined socio-economic and biological study in the late sixties to examine how human use of nature is causing pollution of soil, air and water, and destruction of the natural systems of plants and animals, threatening the base of life on which the human community itself depends.' The school of social ecology provides a profound base to understanding the relationship between the human environment and the natural environment. The symbiotic relationship between nature and culture was undermined for a long time. Such a defective view caused a lacuna in the derivation of knowledge on environment management. Murray Bookchin's (1996: ix-xi) theoretical contributions in eco-philosophy, views culture as an extension of *primary nature*. He refers to *primary nature* as 'first nature' and *culture* as 'second nature'. His thesis mainly explores the dialectical relationship between 'first nature' and 'second nature'. In his words, 'The first nature exists in both continuity and discontinuity with "second nature", or the evolution of society.' He continues, 'second nature develops both in continuity with first nature'. This dialectical relation between first nature and second nature naturally leads to the constitution of 'free nature'. According to him 'free nature' is a manifestation of an ideal ecological society. The generation of social hierarchies is also viewed as a result of this dialectical relation between first and second nature. Bookchin's key point is that second nature is an 'unfinished nature'. A development towards 'free nature' is the *Utopia* of Bookchin.

Ecological movements were constituted within the framework illustrated by Bookchin. The evolution of second nature disturbed the first nature and the changes in first nature disturbed the second nature. Both developed in a dialectical relation. At the same time the transformations of first nature put forward a wide range of social issues, including the question of rights, equality, justice, etc. It is undoubtedly clear that movements that do not address deep rooted social questions are not ecological movements. Ecological movements like the Zapata movement, Chiapas, Narmada, etc. address questions of the rights of the people. People's rights on natural resources are their central focus. Bastiaan Wielenga (1991: 76) writes, 'control over resources becomes the crucial question in today's struggle against imperialism'. Generally, ecological movements address political struggles for rights, and economic and cultural struggles for equality, while also launching socio-political struggles for social justice. It is absurd to confine ecological movements as *conservation movements.* Ecological movements address the complex relationship between nature and culture.

This definition of ecological movements challenged the traditional notion of ecological movements. At the same time it opened up a new explorative space in the study of social movements. The traditional classifications of social movements are mainly based upon its class nature and target group identity. Oommen (1990) and Shah (1990) classified Indian social movements in this regard. Ecology movements are treated as one of the pioneering new social movements by Jürgen Habermas. He defined ecological movements as new social movements on the grounds that old movements are class movements (Gibbins and Reimer 1999). Ecological movements are a unity of different classes, identities and ideologies. There is no doubt that the primary objective of ecology movements is the conservation of ecology. But it could go beyond the protection of nature.

The politics of ecological movements demands a wide range of structural transformations of society. The potential of these social movements was realized by Sidney Tarrow and Charles Tilly (2006). According to them this is an age of contentious politics. Tarrow (1998: 2) explains the nature of contentious politics as follows:

> Contentious politics occurs when ordinary people, often in league with more influential citizens, join forces in confrontation with elites, authorities and opponents. Such confrontations go back to the dawn of history. But mounting, co-ordinating, and sustaining them against powerful opponents are the unique contribution of the social movement—an invention of modern age and an accompaniment to the rise of modern state.

Ecological movements joined hands with trade unions, women, Dalit and tribal movements on the one side and on the other; they extended a helping hand to alternative politics as well as parliamentary movements. The presence of ecological movements is very profound in world politics today. However, these movements are facing an ideological crisis in the midst of the unpredictable expansion of capitalist ideology. The real eco-political agenda has been muted under the yoke of neoliberal environmental governance.

POLITICIZING ECOLOGY

The challenge of an environmentalist is to address ecology politically. The political understanding of ecology is still at the margins and the number of environmental victims is increasing day by day. The profound reason for this might be that ecosophy shares the views of 'anarchism, feminism and German critical theory' (Dobson and Lucardie 1993: i), outfitted in the male dominant, exclusive, repressive authoritarian politics of the state. There are divergent positions in eco-philosophy encompassing two different streams of thought. They are the 'deep ecologist' and 'social ecologist' positions of nature. The deep ecologist position argues that the popular political, economic and ethical positions are shallow and incapable of addressing the deep rooted crisis of Nature. Anthropocentrism is the central character of shallow ecology. Deep ecologists point out that human hegemony expands the rest of nature with a moral claim which is the central ideology of shallow ecology. Arne Naess, a Norwegian philosopher coined the word *deep ecology* and is known as the intellectual founder of this school of thought. He conceived deep ecology as a spiritual movement with an ethical commitment to nature. Here, the role of humans in nature is nullified and he further argues that nature can survive without humans. This argument expands, and places a critical position on modernity and capitalism (Forsyth 2003: 3). Above all, as Andrew Dobson (2003: 193) commented, deep ecology is a 'mystical answer' to the problems of society.

The intellectual positions of the deep ecologist were challenged by Bookchin with the concept of social ecology. There are different shades in social ecology. Bookchin rejected the deep ecologist position that it rejected the subjective role of humans in nature. No other form of life except the human has the ability to consciously manipulate nature. This capacity of the human gives the potential to creatively change human environment. A faith in human agency in nature is the central pillar of social ecology. Such an argument was put forth by Marcel Wissenberg in the context of a debate on ecological justice. Wissenberg argued that: 'Justice can only be applied by moral subjects to other moral subjects. A moral subject has to be a sentient being which can suffer harm . . .' In his view, a human being has a moral right to act upon non-human life forms. He placed nature as an object, rather than a subject. However, this contradictory position within eco-philosophy and eco-politics raised a pertinent question on the 'role of *human agency* in nature'.

Politics plays a major role in human life. Aristotle's statement on 'humans' and 'politics' needs to be restated in this context. '*Man*, by nature is a political animal.' This statement shows the human's 'subjective role' in the making of history. The human is not a passive spectator, but an active agent in change. But non-human life forms are governed by the laws of nature. That nature itself is not a God-like/God-given nature but the result of constant struggle of non-human life-forms. 'Pollution', is a *natural* precondition for the evolution of life-forms. Nature is not God-given, but a network of life forms, an evolving phenomenon. The human imagination of nature is a constructed one.

Mick Smith (2001) presented a constructivist understanding of nature in his *An Ethics of Place: Radical Ecology, Postmodernity and Social Theory*. In his view, nature is an epistemological and ontological construction, not a given one. Smith's view on nature is not without criticism. Environmental ethicist Holmes Rolston placed his criticism against the constructivist approach to nature. An ethical understanding of nature is a process of valuing non-human life-forms and thereby an ethical understanding of nature is untenable. In the context of the eco-political debate, one's understanding of nature is closely related to the social structure. Environmental conservation is not at all the conservation of a whole nature but a selective conservation programme. The choice of the selection ought to be problematic in the discourse on the conservation of nature.

A fourth dimension eco-political debate sprang from the school of *Critical Ecology*. Critical ecology tried to develop the political philosophy of environmental science. This concept is an offshoot of the understanding that science and politics are inseparable. The theoretical foundations of this school of thought are based on the principle that the root cause of ecological problems is not technological but political (Dobson and Lucardie 1995: 190). Critical theorists stress the emancipation of the human and nature in their mutuality. The present-day relationship between nature and the human is considered as a product of specific historical and material conditions. Philosophical contributions of Theodor Adorno, Marx Horkheimer and Herbert Marcuse are treated as the foundation stones of critical ecology. The core argument of critical ecology lies in Marcuse's (1964: 60) reading of the liberation of nature. He states: '"liberation of nature" cannot mean returning to a pre-technological stage, but advancing to the use of the achievements of technological civilisation for freeing man and nature from the destructive abuse of science and technology in the service of exploitation'.

Ecology is a political matter. The rejection of science and technology, and treating the human as alien from nature are false conceptions. The only solution to the present-day ecological crisis is the correlation of technological and social relations with nature. A micro-level and macro-level policy management is possible. But it is essential to critically understand neoliberal ecological governance in the context of people's struggle for nature.

NEOLIBERAL ENVIRONMENTAL GOVERNANCE: A CRITICAL NOTE

Neoliberal environmental governance simply means market-initiated ecological policies. Ecological movements consider capitalism as an arch enemy of the environment. Joel Kovel (2003: 38-9) says, 'For Karl Marx, capital was a "werewolf" and a "vampire", ravenously consuming labour and mutilating the labourer. Both notions are true; and the second one, applied to nature as well as labour, accounts for the ecological crisis in all essential features.' He continues that capital is a 'cancer-causing virus that invades living human beings, and forces them to violate ecological integrity'. Mario Pianta (1989: 129) states that the 'capitalist mode of production is thwarting *general conditions of production*'. Thomas O'Connor and James O'Connor (1989: 1-12; and 1994: 11-38) illustrate two types of contradictions in a capitalist system. The primary contradiction is a contradiction between labour and capital, and the secondary contradiction is between environment and capital. The crisis of the general conditions of production also disturbed the capitalists.

During the 1970s, the World Bank called for a review of its policies which recommended Green Investments for the sustainability of industrial growth.

The World Bank has been involved in ecological protection since the 1970s. It is claimed by the Bank that the 1970s was a turning point in its history, because it was forced to critically scrutinize its efforts in development. The Bank put forward the idea of sustainable development and environmental reconstruction with an imperative to rebuild ecology for development. According to the World Bank Report, *Ecologically Sensitive Sites in Africa* (1993):

> During the last two decades, there has been growing evidence that environmental degradation in its many forms constitutes a threat of growing significance to economic development. In addition, the rapid evolution of the environmental agenda has led to an increased understanding of the interdependence among economic activities and their environmental consequences, both within and between countries. The economic and physical interdependence between nations is illustrated by the emergence of new kinds of environmental problems, such as the deterioration of the ozone layer, the greenhouse effect, tropical deforestation and the trans-boundary movement of hazardous wastes.

The Bank charted out its policies in an eco-friendly manner; however its key focus was on the economic sector. There is a need to critically encounter these two areas and its relation with private capital investment on environment. A Green economy is an ambitious task that the Bank wants to materialize. As a part of this initiative the Bank decided to mark Ecologically Sensitive Areas (ESA) in the world. The Bank's first focus was on the African countries and it instituted special funds for the conservation of ecology. The Bank founded the Global Environmental Facility (GEF) in 1991 to conserve bio-diversity and control climatic changes. The activities of GEF can be seen in 165 countries with the financing of 3,900 projects (www.thegef.org). In addition to GEF, the Bank facilitated the Critical Ecosystem Partnership Fund (CEPF) which pumped this fund all over the world. CEPF was founded in 2000 with a motive to invite civil society partnership in conserving the most critical ecosystems in the world (www.cepf.net).

A firm faith in capital-intensive market-oriented ecological conservation is the primary objective of neoliberal ecological policy. The link with ecological investment and capitalism needs to be critically analysed. Classical economists have treated natural resources as free goods. However, as Andre Gorz (1980) commented, the saga of rampant industrialization proved that natural resources are vital, and ecological cleaning and maintenance is essential for the sustenance of industry itself. Ecological policies in Asian-African countries are mainly charted out in accordance with the policies and projects of WB-GEF guidelines.

PEOPLE'S MOVEMENTS AND ECO-CAPITALISM

In the name of ecology, the states of the world have decided to declare certain regions as ecologically sensitive areas (ESAs). In such regions they have declared laws to define or nullify the rights of the people over natural resources. Two catchy words, 'the heritage of the world' and 'common resources' are tricky and give manipulative reflection of the rights over natural resources. The claiming of common heritage neatly avoids the rights of the native communities over natural resources. Native communities are dependent communities of particular natural endowments. The takeover of natural resources from the indigenous/marginalized/ethnic minorities have occurred in many ways.[1]

The case of the Chagossians battle for the Chagos Archipelago is one of the best examples of the struggle for the ecological rights of the people. Chagos Archipelago is a chain of islands lying in the Indian Ocean. It is an oil-rich region which is strategically important and a former colony of Britain. United States established a military base in the island in 1970 by the forced eviction of two thousand Chagossians with the consent of the British government. Chagos is considered the most important military base of the United States outside the country. It is a strategically important place which helped the US in the rapid deployment of forces in Afghanistan and West Asia. In April 2010, United Kingdom's Foreign and Commonwealth Secretary, David Miliband, announced the creation of a Marine Protected Area (MPA) in the British Indian Ocean

Territory of Chagos (Evers and Kooy 2011). Non-governmental organizations (NGOs) supported the MPA, which affected 60 islands across the Chagos Archipelago. The act prevented resettled islanders from utilizing their marine resources for subsistence or income generation. The islanders viewed the MPA as a bar on the natives from their homeland. Fernand Mandarin, President of the Chagossian Social Committee, called it a 'violation of the rights of Chagossian people'. The managers of the environment were not concerned about the people. In a response to the critical comments of the natives, Miliband said, 'nothing about the Chagos and its environment without the Chagossians'. Olivier Bancoult, leader of the Chagos Refugees group, wrote:

> [t]he Chagos Archipelago is our native homeland. It is our sacred duty, responsibility and right to protect and preserve it as a home for its native people and a nature reserve for the world. We lived in harmony with our natural environment until we were forcibly removed to make way for a nuclear military base. We contest the assertion that pollutant levels in the Chagos 'are exceptionally low' in spite of continued military activities. We will oppose all plans, like yours, that want the world to believe that preserving the pristine nature of the Chagos is compatible with the maintenance of a nuclear military base—where you yourself have admitted the existence of extraordinary rendition activities—but not with the peaceful presence and ordinary activities of the native people. (Evers and Kooy 2011: 7)

The Chagossian people's movements have been fighting for their rights for more than a decade. World governments outweighed the rights of the natives and used the land for their military expeditions. Ecological laws are not pristine interventions for the protection of the environment but a double-edged sword. The legal right is a blatant denial of natural rights and ecological rights of native communities are natural rights. The governmental declarations of ESAs are part of the process of the reconfiguration of natural rights into the category of legal rights. So-called development projects are the other way of uprooting the rights of the people. 'Green development' is a new device for the rejection of the rights of the people over natural resources under the principles of the ecological governance of the World Bank. The declarations of ESAs are not undefiled ventures for the protection of ecology, but are a clear, ruthless grabbing of the resources of the native communities in an authoritarian manner.

The case of Kenyan ecological conservation is another one of the innumerable stories of the invalidation of the rights of the commons on the environment. Kenya adopted its Pastoral Lands Conservation Policy in 1977. In 2007, the Kenyan government issued a draft bill for wildlife protection and identified three regions as critically important. A survey recorded that the government's policies for wildlife protection during 1977-2007 marked a steep decline of the pastoral communities in Kenya. The government's policies not only affected people but also led to the extinction of certain species. The government's policy of environmental conservation benefitted the land owning elite class. The properties of poor pastoral communities were transferred into the hands of the rich. In the context of the Kenyan ecological policy, Homewood (2009: 315) states, 'there is a gulf between theoretically predicted policy impacts, and the actual outcomes of those policies'. Homewood continues 'conservation priorities at the macro-level, and development priorities at the household level, are rarely well-aligned'.

The greening of the economy may be an ambitious project indeed. The point of departure lies in the core question of the 'equitable sharing of risks and benefits'. The ivory tower perspective in ecology widely undermines the issues of the poor and minorities in association with ecological management. The victimization of farm workers through the use of pesticides, that of tribal people through nuclear waste dumping and the sufferings of slum dwelling communities as a result of urban waste dumping are not brought under the purview of ecological costs today. American sociologist, Bob Bullard, points out that 80 per cent of ecological movements are community-based resistance groups which began as ecological movements (Frechett 2002: 21). Studies show that socio-economically deprived communities are vulnerable to consume contaminated food, water and other resources.

A fundamental feature of the post-independent development policies of African countries is the strong bond with ecological and economic theories developed in other contexts (Frechett 2002: 21). Africa is undoubtedly a laboratory of the economic theories of the

World Bank and other transnational agencies. The demarcation of ESAs was first proposed by the World Bank (1993) as part of its policy shift in the 1970s. The underpinning objective of the ecological policy of the World Bank was development. The governing philosophy of the development theories of the World Bank is neoliberalism, which fundamentally challenges the principles of equality.

The neoliberal concept of equality needs to be critically scrutinised. Hayek (2012: 76-7) writes, '. . . people are very different . . . if we treat them equally, the result must be inequality.' [2] Hayek rejects the concept of 'equality before law' and 'material equality.' He places his argument as follows:

> The equality before the law which freedom requires leads to material inequality. Our argument will be that, though where the state must use coercion for other reasons, it should treat all people alike, the desire of making people more alike in their condition cannot be accepted in a free society as a justification for further and discriminatory coercion. (Hayek 2012: 77)

Equality is treated by neoliberals as a threat to liberty. Robert Nozick (1974: 232-8), a libertarian philosopher, claims that economic inequality is justiciable, adding that, 'there are particular rights over particular things held by a particular person'. He rejects the idea of general rights. A critical position of the understanding of rights originates from Duncan Ivison's (2008: 26) definition of rights. Ivison understands rights as a 'complex social practice', not 'an abstract set of metaphysical claims', which are not self-evident and not self-validating. For him 'rights are a political value'.

WESTERN GHATS ECOLOGICAL CONSERVATION

One of the major initiatives to protect the environment initiated by the Government of India (GoI) is the protection of the Western Ghats.

> The term 'Western Ghats' refers to the practically unbroken hill chain (with the exception of the Palakkad Gap) or escarpment running roughly in a north-south direction, for about 1500 km parallel to the Arabian Sea coast, from the river Tapti (about 210 16′ N) down to just short of Kanyakumari

(about 80 19′ N) at the tip of the Indian peninsula. (Government of India 2011)

The Government of India launched the Western Ghats Development Programme during the Sixth Five Year Plan. According to the reports of the government, a separate Western Ghats Development Programme (WGDP) was launched in 1974-5 as a special component programme for the development of hilly regions. The first development programme was instituted as a one-man committee headed by the father of the Green Revolution, M.S. Swaminathan. This programme was implemented in 159 taluks in the Western Ghats. The objectives of the programme are: maintenance of ecological balance, preservation of genetic diversity, restoration of the ecological damage caused by human interactions, creation of awareness among the people and educating them about the far-reaching implications of ecological degradation and securing their active participation for eco-development schemes (www.planning-commission.gov.in).

In 1987-8 the first Western Ghats conservation programme was launched by NGOs and during the 1990s it developed as a project covering the peninsular regions. In 1992, a group of NGOs launched the Peninsular India Project to discuss the ecological crisis of the region in the backdrop of the Rio Summit. The Earth Summit of Rio de Janeiro, Brazil in June 1992 opened up a global market for eco-technology. The main objective of the conference was to install environmental protection through technologically driven economic-based solutions to environmental problems. A good number of multinational corporations participated and presented their plan of action at this conference. The greening of the market with eco-technology is a capitalist enterprise for environmental protection. In 2000 all the events culminated in a framework for the protection of the Western Ghats ecological systems.

In 2000-1 GoI switched over to a comprehensive development project for the Western Ghats. The Twelfth Five Year Plan of the GoI has charted out a detailed outline of the market-oriented ecological policy. The PPP (Public-Private Partnership) is the central focus of management in every sphere of economic activity. Pricing natural resources properly, supporting green technologies, and boosting green private investments are part of the strategy for ecological planning. As per the guidelines of international agencies, ecological planning also incorporated a subsidy elimination agenda. Conversion of Special Economic Zones into eco-industrial hubs, sustainable management of the Himalayan Ecosystem and Western Ghats, Coastal Zone Management, green city development initiatives, promotion of eco-labelling are the major areas of focus in the Twelfth Five Year Plan (GoI).

The policy changes in transnational institutions and central governments are reflected clearly in the implementation of the Western Ghats Development Programme. The Government of India adopted the liberalization policy in the economic sector in the 1990s which is clearly reflected in the ecological systems management. Chilika Lake was provided for lease to Enron in the late 1980s. In 1981 Chilika Lake captured international attention, because of its rich bio-diversity. UNESCO listed Chilika as a world heritage site and in 1992 the World Bank started funding for the protection of the lake. Simultaneously with the blessing of the World Bank, GoI launched eco-tourism projects. The declared objective of the project was the protection of the life and livelihood of the coastal communities, conservation of ecological resources, etc. The lake sustains 150,000 fishermen who live in and around the lagoon (www.iczmpodisha.org). The centralized ecosystems management of the World Bank and the GoI is a multimillion dollar investment project (www.worldbank.org). Ecological conservation is a capital intensive project all over the world. The capital-intensive ecological conservation is an underlying principle of GoI and transnational agencies. This nexus of capital-state and ecology is disempowering ecology dependent communities all over the world.

In the backdrop of continuous policy formations the GoI decided to constitute an ecological expert committee under the Chairmanship of Madhav Gadgil, a veteran environmental activist. The Report of the Western Ghats Ecology Expert Panel alias Gadgil Committee Report was drafted not on the basis of the principles of ecological justice, but proposals made by and for the fulfilment of the neoliberal perception of environment management. The committee recommended the constitution of a Western Ghats Ecology Authority. This Authority designed as an authoritarian body was constituted by the GoI and its decisions are unquestionable. The report expressed a firm belief in the knowledge of the nominated committee members. The declaration of the ESAs was a major recommendation of the committee. But the parameters of the selection of ESAs do not include any concern for the rights of the native communities over natural resources.

CONCLUSION

The equal distribution of ecological opportunities is an untenable claim in neoliberalism. Although industrial pollution has resulted from the greed of the industrial class, ecological cleaning through the sacrifice of the common man for common benefit is the reality today. Most of the world's industrial sites demand ecological maintenance at the cost of public fund. On the other hand, industry pays little attention to ecological maintenance at its own cost.

The question of ecology and people's power is related to a wide range of theoretical positions connected with perceptions of justice, equality, liberty and rights. The declaration of ESAs is not a pristine one but a masked exposition of the privatization and marketing of the environment at the cost of commons. ESAs are nothing more than Special Economic Zones (SEZs). SEZs and ESAs have operative differences, but the logical and philosophical politics of the demarcation of the regions are the same. SEZs provide special protective environment for the booming of industries. ESAs provide a protective environment for the reproduction of natural resources. The unfettered flow of natural resources to industry is a precondition for the booming of industry. Selective conservation of nature is a human practice from the beginning of human civilization. The cultural preferences and mechanisms are different. Selective catching of fish was the practice of traditional fishermen before the mechanization of the fishing sector. Preservation of seeds was a cultural practice. Human civilization itself developed a conservation mechanism which was thwarted by industrial giants with a motive to increase profit. Today, the technology of conservation is monopolized and marketed under the reign of capitalism. The management of ecology is also under the yoke of capitalism and neoliberal philosophy. The challenge of the people's movement is mounted under capitalist rule. The doublespeak of the governments is the claim that they are protecting the ecology, but in fact they are nullifying the rights of the people. Denial of rights is the denial of power. The centralized/authoritarian management of ecology is the denial of people's rights for self-determination. In essence, a movement for ecological justice is inevitable in deliberative democracy.

Ecological justice needs to be the central concern of ecological policy. Ecological justice demands an equal sharing of ecological risks and benefits. Ecological risks and benefits distributed by the destination of cultural predetermination is the harsh reality of Indian society. The Western notion of 'cross-cultural distribution of ecological risks' is totally different from the Indian understanding. The word 'cross-culture' denotes an intergenerational perspective in the West (Syme et al. 2000). The beneficiaries of ecological resources and the victims of ecological degradation are lined up in a cultural proposition of castes in India. The 'basic communities', including scheduled castes, scheduled tribes and fishing communities are dependent on first nature for their livelihood and very survival. However, the logic of over-exploitation of natural resources is operating from the level of second nature. The second nature, that is the cultural sphere governed by the upper caste communities, are the real operators of the economy and makers of ecological policies. Ecological policies are mainly treated as an appendage of economic policies. A sustainable economy is the central focus of environmental governance. Policies are designed by hegemonic communities for their own cultural and social reproduction. The basic communities are not the real beneficiaries but they are dependents of first nature and thereby ecological degradation directly affects their lives. This complex cultural knot of caste and ecology trapped, culturally deprived communities, are the victims of market-ridden ecological governance. This reality presents a picture that ecological policies are not for the empowerment of the people but for the empowerment of market capitalism.

This inextricable relationship between economy and ecology generates dialogues on political power. There are certain fundamental questions in this debate. Who are the real custodians of nature and who are the real beneficiaries of natural resources? Such a categorical divide operates on the basis of caste, class and gender. Thus the debate on ecology provides new avenues of discourses to challenge and recreate deliberative spaces and democratic dialogues. Debates on eco-politics go beyond the traditional paradigms of political discourses. Eco-political debates generate notions of plurality, presenting claims of people's power in a profound manner, in tune with democratic discourses on justice, equality and liberty. This is the space and subject matter of alternative politics and deliberative democracy.

NOTES

1. The plunder of the commons is the staple of twenty-first century capitalism. The increase in struggles of indigenous communities is the response to the privatization of natural resources (See South Asian Alliance for Poverty Eradication 2010).
2. This is the fundamental position of neoliberalism. Hayek subscribes to Plato's idea that 'To unequals equals become unequal' (see Hayek 2012: 76-7).

REFERENCES

Bookchin, Murray (1996): *The Philosophy of Social Ecology: Essays on Dialectical Naturalism*, New Delhi: Rawat Publications.

Dobson, Andrew and Paul Lucardie (eds.) (1993): *The Politics of Nature: Explorations in Green Political Theory*, London: Routledge.

Dobson, Andrew (2003): 'Critical Theory and Green Politics', in Andrew Dobson and Paul Lucardie (eds.), *Politics of Nature: Explorations in Green Political Theory*, London: Routledge.

Evers, Sandra J.T.M. and Mary Kooy (2011): 'Redundancy on the Instalment Plan: Chagossians and the Right to be Called a People', in Sandra J.T.M. Evers and Mary Kooy (eds.), *Eviction from the Chagos Islands: Displacement and Struggle for Identity Against Two World Powers*, Leiden: Brill.

Forsyth, Tim (2003): *Critical Political Ecology: The Politics of Environmental Science*, London: Routledge.

Frechett, Kristine Shrader (2002): *Environmental Justice: Creating Equality, Reclaiming Democracy*, Oxford: Oxford University Press.

Gibbins, John R. and Bo Reimer (1999): *The Politics of Postmodernity: An Introduction to Contemporary Politics and Culture*, New Delhi: Sage.

Gorz, Andre (1980): *Ecology as Politics*, Montreal: Black Rose Books.

Government of India (2011): *Report of the WGEEP*, New Delhi: Ministry of Environment and Forests.

—— (2013): *Twelfth Five Year Plan 2012-2017*, New Delhi: Planning Commission of India.

Hayek, F.A. (2012): *The Constitution of Liberty*, London: Routledge.

Homewood, Katherine (2009): 'Policy and Practice in Kenya Rangelands: Impacts on Livelihoods and Wildlife', in Katherine Homewood, Patti Kristjanson and Pippa Chenevix Trench (eds.), *Staying Maasai? Livelihoods, Conservation and Development in East African Rangelands*, New York: Springer.

Iviso, Duncan (2008): *Rights*, Stocksfield: Acumen.

Kovel, Joel (2003): *The Enemy of Nature*, New Delhi: Tulika Books.

Marcuse, Herbert (1964): *One-Dimensional Man*, Boston: Beacon Press.

Nozick, Robert (1974): *Anarchy, State, and Utopia*, Englewood Cliffs: Basic Books.

O'Connor, James (1988): 'Capitalism, Nature, Socialism: A Theoretical Introduction', *Capital, Nature, Socialism*, 1(1): 11-38.

—— (1989): 'Uneven and Combined Development an Ecological Crisis: A Theoretical Introduction', *Race and Class*, 30(3): 1-12.

Oommen, T.K. (1990): *Protest and Change: Studies in Social Movements*, New Delhi: Sage.

Pianta, Mario (1989): 'The Conditions of Production: A Note', *Capitalism, Nature, Socialism*, 1(3): 129-34.

Reuther, Rosemary Radford, 'Ecofeminism', www.spunk.org

Shah, Ghanshyam (1990): *Social Movements in India: A Review of Literature*, New Delhi: Sage.

Smith, Mick (2001): *An Ethics of Place: Radical Ecology, Post Modernity and Social Theory*, Albany: SUNY Press.

Sohn, Louis B. (1973): 'The Stockholm Declaration on the Human Environment', *Harvard International Law Journal*, 14(3), September.

South Asian Alliance for Poverty Eradication (2010): *Poverty and Vulnerability Cycles in South Asia: Narratives of Survival and Struggles*, www.saape.org.

Syme, Geoffrey J., Elisabeth Kals, Blair E. Nancarrow, and Leo Montada (2000):

'Ecological Risks and Community Perceptions of Fairness and Justice: A Cross-Cultural Model', *Risk Analysis*, 20(6).

Tarrow, Sidney (1998): *Power in Movement*, New York: Cambridge University Press.

Tilly, Charles and Sidney Tarrow (2006): *Contentious Politics,* Boulder: Paradigm Publishers.

VAK (1993): Report, *Save Western Ghats*, Mumbai: VAK.

Wielenga, Bastiaan (1991): 'Ecological Movements: Struggle for a Sustainable Society', in John Desrochers, Bastiaan Wielenga and Vibhuti Patel (eds.), *Social Movements: Towards a Perspective,* Bangalore: Centre for Social Action.

World Bank (1993): *Ecological Sensitive Sites in Africa*, vol. 1, Washington D.C.: The World Bank.

Contributors

ELIZABETH ABRAHAM is Research Fellow, Inter-University Centre for Social Science Research and Extension, Mahatma Gandhi University, Kottayam.

GEORGE K. ALEX is Assistant Professor, Department of Political Science, St. Thomas College, Kozhencherry.

M.V. BIJULAL is Assistant Professor, School of International Relations and Politics, Mahatma Gandhi University, Kottayam.

JOS CHATHUKULAM is Director, Centre for Rural Management, Kottayam and Shri Ramakrishna Hegde Chair Professor, Institute for Social and Economic Change, Bangalore.

K.M. SAJAD IBRAHIM is Associate Professor, Department of Political Science, University of Kerala, Thiruvananthapuram.

SIBY K. JOSEPH is Dean of Studies and Research, Institute of Gandhian Studies, Wardha.

TERESA JOSEPH is Assistant Professor in Political Science and Director, Centre for Gandhian Studies, Alphonsa College, Pala.

SHEEBA K.M. is Associate Professor, Department of History, Sree Sankaracharya University of Sanskrit, Kalady.

D. JEEVAN KUMAR is Professor, Department of Political Science, Bangalore University, Bangalore.

JOHN S. MOOLAKKATTU is Professor and Director, Department of International Relations, Central University of Kerala, Kasargod, and Editor, *Gandhi Marg*, New Delhi.

J. PRABHASH is Professor and Head, Department of Political Science, University of Kerala, Thiruvananthapuram.

A.M. THOMAS is Professor and Director, School of International Relations and Politics, and Dean, Faculty of Social Sciences, Mahatma Gandhi University, Kottayam.

SABU THOMAS is Assistant Professor, Department of Political Science, Government College, Madappally, Calicut.

Index